CONGRATULATIONS
YOU HAVE JUST MET THE I.C.F.

CONGRATULATIONS
You have just met the I.C.F.
(West Ham United)

CASS PENNANT

Published by John Blake Ltd, 3 Bramber Court,
2 Bramber Road, London W14 9PB, England

First published in paperback in 2003

ISBN 978 1 90403 485 8

British Library Cataloguing-in-Publication Data: A catalogue record for this book is available from the British Library.

Design by www.envydesign.co.uk

Printed in the UK by CPI Bookmarque, Croydon, CR0 4TD

17 19 20 18 16

Papers used by John Blake Publishing Ltd are natural, recyclable products made from wood grown in sustainable forests. The manufacturing processes conform to the environmental regulations of the country of origin.

Pictures reproduced by kind permission of Grant Fleming, MSI and News International.

Dedicated to my football-hating wife, Elaine, who has shown loyalty equal to that of any long-suffering Hammers fan. And to my children, Marcus and Georgie. Watching them grow up replaced the buzz I missed going to football.

acknowledgements

Blake Publishing for their patience and a special mention to Michelle.Thanks to Sue Preston and Melissa Mudge for their help with transcribing and editing. Julia Skeggs: amateur photographer whose pictures are worth a thousand memories. Also to Grant Fleming who spent a full day getting the superb cover pictures just right. Special thanks to all those who shared their experiences with me, particularly the ones I have been unable to mention. You know who you are.

Bill Gardner: paviour mason
Andy Swallow: record company director
Big Ted: foreman electrician
Bunter Marks: warehouse manager
John Simpson (Simo): warehouse manager
Bill Stokes (Mouthy Bill): market trader
Grant Fleming: photographer and filmmaker
Brett Tidman: father of three
Micky Morgan (Ramsgate): building firm boss
Andrew Bowers: unemployed
Olajide Ikoli (Animal): contract cleaner
Nat Leslie: market trader
Mark Phillips (Woolwich): taxi driver
Lol Prior: record company director
Jon O'Brien (Jono): nightclub promoter
Steve Vaughan (Vaughny): incapacity beneficiary
John Turner: clothing company executive
Garry Bushell: TV critic and journalist
Vince Riordan: ex-Cockney Reject
Ian Stuttard (Butch): film producer/director
Tim McCarthy (Macca): company director
Terry Sherrin: interior refurbishment executive
Jimmy Smith: programme dealer
Bubbles: songwriter

contents

prologue

The Swansea ground looks a dump. We all gather near the middle, with no one saying a word. In the away end we hear the rest of West Ham chanting. All around where we're standing is a chilling silence. We're all getting edgy; it's nearly 3 o'clock. All of a sudden the atmosphere changes. A few big fat Taffies are confronting the front row of us… they are now all around us. This really is it. One of the Stratford lads leans over the crowd barrier and smashes a steaming potato pie in a Taff's face. The Taff screams and as he lifts his head up, someone boots him straight in the face.

We charge down into the front of 'em. I see Shane's arms waving, I try and make my way to him but a big fat Taff grabs my coat, taking me off balance. He's now pulling me towards him. I'm struggling to get my balance back to break his hold. Next, I find myself on the floor, thinking that's it, but as I scramble up there's two chaps on top of the Taff. I'm in, kicking, punching anything that moves. The whole side of the ground is in uproar as our mob kicks it well off with all these Taffy lumps.

The Welsh Old Bill come running in. They don't touch the Taffs, only us, beating us back with their truncheons. Eventually, cornering us, they put us all back into the West Ham supporters' end.

Don't bother watching the game, everyone is so charged up. The Old Bill keep us locked in the ground for thirty minutes after the game has ended. They tightly march us back to our corners and then they don't leave us. Using police vehicles they escort us all the way to the motorway. They aren't going to get caught out again...

The service station is packed and it's gone midnight. My first reaction is, who is the firm? There must be at least 300 of 'em. It's definitely going to go off, right off, but who the fuck are they? The rest of our mob come in. This is it. Swallow and his firm are surrounded.

I steam straight over and smash one of 'em on the head with an ashtray. I immediately get hit with something. People are screaming, the whole place has gone wild, throwing anything they can get their hands on, cups, plates, trays, everything. People are flying everywhere. I'm proud of my mob, we're right in the thick of it with the Brit boys. I'm being hit, pulled and punched... but we seem to be pushing them back. I'm lashing out at anyone.

There's now a stand-off and both sides are throwing things at each other. I sense one more charge and they'll go.

We steam in again and, yeah, they turn, then run down

the stairs and out into the car park. I run back into the main hall. It's here I see some of them jump over the food counter, fleeing into the kitchens to escape. Then I come back on to the stairs, where Andy, Danny Tiderman and a few others are pushing a pinball machine towards the stairs. There's a mob still at the bottom looking up when this pinball machine finally gets pushed off the edge of the stairs, crashing bumpety-bump, smack bang into 'em. The other mob runs; that's enough for them.

Congratulations! You have just met the InterCity Firm.

introduction

At 6 o'clock on the morning of January 28, 2001, a fleet of eight coaches from the Swallow coach company left the Swallow hotel near the M25 with 400 of the once-notorious InterCity Firm on board. We were on our way to a nostalgic reunion organised by one Andy Swallow. The event was Manchester United v West Ham in the fourth round of the FA Cup in the Theatre of Dreams. The name of United's new stadium was an apt choice when we took a record 9,000 fans up there. After losing 7-1 and 4-1 in previous games, the Hammers had no chance against United on paper, but the East Enders all shared a dream of the country's biggest football stage.

The specially invited men on those coaches were among the 9,000 Hammers fans travelling to the game all hoping for glory. This was no reunion with the intent to make trouble. That was clear when I arrived and was met by double-chinned men in Stone Island coats, worn more for warmth than as any fashion statement. Bald, thinning hair had replaced the once-lengthy locks and the conversation was now along the lines of 'How's the kids?', 'Business tough?', 'Did you go to Ted's fiftieth?'

Even so, to any neutral they still looked formidable enough, they still had that inner menace, by their mere presence. In fact, as a firm, they were still pretty untouchable. For me, the I.C.F. was the only firm I would have at my back. Sticking together for your mates was something you never had to ask a West Ham fan to do.

Spurred on by the inaccuracies in accounts of the exploits of West Ham's InterCity Firm in various publications, I decided to use my unique position as a former member of the I.C.F. to set the record straight. So before the I.C.F. became a fast-fading memory, I seized the chance to write the first-ever book on the real I.C.F. Those men on the coach remembered exactly how it was back in the Seventies and Eighties, when the risk of getting your head kicked in at a football match was very real, and very much par for the course. Crazy days for sure, mad days that some said were the best-ever days.

There was something special about being around the I.C.F. Something more than being the best firm or mob. What was it that set us aside from our rivals when it came to our reputation as a firm? By the time I came to complete this remarkable story, I had found my answer – character. Character of the highest quality, old-fashioned values and a loyalty no longer prevalent in today's world. Bottled, it would be priceless. And the I.C.F. was full of characters.

This must have been what the filmmaker Ian 'Butch' Stuttard saw when he said we all had the ability to do almost anything. This was our strength and the very reason not one person should tell our story. In our gang we were all walking stories.

So that no one can dispute the authenticity of the events that the I.C.F. were involved in, those who were there have told their stories on the pages that follow...

Chapter 1

HOW IT ALL BEGAN

I.C.F.

IT'S 4.45 P.M. – PEOPLE living around Upton Park football ground hear the final roar of the crowd. The race is on. Those fans would soon be pouring out of the stadium. For the visiting supporters, this is the time they have come to dread. For it's here at Upton Park, in London's East End, that we meet a group of lads who thrive on chaos, disorder and violence – the most feared firm in football.

The InterCity Firm.

In the late 1970s and early 1980s, the I.C.F. were the legend of West Ham fighting prowess. The quest to establish West Ham as the guv'nors among Britain's football hooligans stemmed from the reputation of the original Mile End mob.

The Mile End had emerged as a firm as early as 1968,

when white working-class skinheads began to congregate behind the popular end goal on match days. Our home end was The North Bank, the largest end in the Upton Park ground.

Being heavily into violence and the gang culture was part of youth fashion for many at the time. Most gang members were aged from twelve to twenty, and there was often infighting as the gangs battled among themselves for supremacy.

The Mile End was different. They were one of the few gangs with members beyond this age group. Like gypsy families, they were an extremely tight-knit firm and the main characters were all related – many of them were brothers. To be part of this firm you had to come from the Mile End area of East London. They trusted no one and picked fights with everyone else at West Ham. Now and again they fought amongst themselves; nobody would do anything to intervene.

By the early 1970s, they had earned a fearsome reputation throughout London and had separated themselves entirely from West Ham's other firms by taking up residence behind the goal the opposite end to the North Bank. Their status had reached hero-worship proportions among the West Ham bovver boy following, although our own supporters had every reason to fear them the most. Yet when it came to fighting our rivals, particularly other London clubs, they were often our saviours.

West Ham had become masters of the nationwide bovver boy craze of taking your opponents' ends. Looking on from another part of the ground was like being on a hill watching the spectacle of two big armies clash. But taking part and being among it all was even more impressive. Ex-I.C.F. top man Bill Gardner describes it just right when he says, 'It's that roar. That big fucking roar within the crowd which gets your hair standing up on the back of your neck the moment before the boots go flying in. The shouts of "C'mon then" and everyone steaming in.'

That first skinhead cult of '68 was a great phenomenon. It was a happening time for youth when you felt anti-everything. It didn't matter that you were poor and working class, destined for a life of dead-end jobs, or that you were at an age when you had no say or influence. We were showing the world – 'We're here and we're happening... fuck you!'

* * * * *

On match days, you meet up with your mates wearing your Levi's or Sta-Prest jeans, braces and boots, sporting a crop or outgrown crop, half-shaved fringed crop or long hair, Slade style. You're sporting a Brutus or Ben Sherman shirt in gingham check, perhaps a Slazenger jumper or pullover, Crombie or Harrington coat. If you've got a good enough job, you might have managed to pick up a decent sheepskin from Petticoat Lane.

We travel the Tube, collecting more lads who'd come to join us. They are lads we don't really know, but they know us by the way we are dressed, the Underground route we are on and the silk scarves around our wrists saying

'Super Irons'. You are now in the biggest fucking gang of all time. You are now a West Ham bovver boy. No one – parents, teachers or that horrible prick of a foreman – telling you what to do. We are in a teenage revolution.

We twist off the hand knobs attached to the Tube train ceilings to use as coshes. Flick knives are shown off to intimidate the wanker sitting fiddling with his penknife. The train we're on is rocking as everyone starts jumping up and down, singing 'Knees Up Mother Brown'. That's the cue for mock fights, seat slashing and a bit of train wrecking. The District Line train picks up more of us as it stops at East London Tube stations. Eventually it reaches Mile End station. The mighty Mile End gang swarm on from the platform, shoving anyone not from Mile End from their carriage.

The rest of us are buzzing, the excitement reaches a crescendo. Now the Mile End are on board, we feel fucking invincible.

The chant goes up: 'M.I.L.E. E.N.D.!'

We all sing on our way to take the Arsenal North Bank, Chelsea's Shed or Park Lane, Tottenham – it doesn't matter where. It's only twelve noon, still three hours till the game kicks off. We all swarm through the barrier with no tickets, singing 'As She Wheels The Wheelbarrow, Through Streets Broad And Narrow'. Word comes back through the ranks to 'shhhh' – a reminder that we're on the streets of someone else's manor, heading for the end behind their goal.

The Mile End mob slips away from the rest of us. There's a twinge of regret, which is soon forgotten in the surge of pride that we're West Ham; we can do this ourselves. You follow everyone else, trying to keep up with whoever you think is the hardest in your group, so you've got good company when it goes off.

The next tense moment is here. We're at our rivals' turnstiles to their end. We've got it down to a fine art. The Old Bill's on us, pushing and shouting to get in line. We're showing no colours; scarves and even club badges have been swiftly removed. The plods think we're home fans, which is cool. Up the concrete stairs leading from the side of their covered end – never take the middle set of stairs leading directly behind their end behind the goal – they will be looking out for us there for sure. You come in from the side, controlling your urge to get stuck in to make sure there's enough of us in to hold whatever we gain when we surprise them.

A roar goes up and it's kicking off behind the goal right in the middle of their end. The home lot have either spotted us first or our main faces have kicked off, knowing the rest of us are on our way.

These are terrifying minutes, because you've disturbed the Holy Grail. Nobody is going to allow you just to walk in and take the home end. To do that is to rob the pride of a complete community and not just the wanker you're rucking.

If ever that part of the ground is successfully invaded and run by the visiting fans, it's regarded as the ultimate defeat for home fans. The taking of an end is mentally recorded and remembered always. The home end supporters' morale and pride are badly shattered; it means suffering total humiliation. Being at home, you are meant to have the advantage of the majority. Even if the home fans regain their self-pride with victory in the streets outside, it's only a consolation, forgotten in a few seasons. Everything depends on defending your end and your territory.

The home supporters will lash out at anyone they don't know as you charge around their end to see where your own lot are fighting. In attempting to join them, you move through entire gangs. You grab one by the scarf and nut him, splitting his face to an orgasm of pain as his mates kindly return the compliment by putting the boot in on you.

Somehow it all sorts itself out when the chanting and singing returns. All those around you are singing 'We Took The North Bank, Highbury Again' or 'We Took the Chelsea Shed Again' – or was it Park Lane, Tottenham?

The atmosphere is deafening as the enraged home end regroups. They are still holding advantageous positions behind the sheltered end of the goal, but now they're sharing it with the enemy.

We're a magnet for all the nutters in the ground. Back then you could move freely around the ground, so our numbers are swelled by more West Ham coming to join us. The Old Bill arrive. There are too many of us for them to nick, so they try to separate us by putting a thin blue line between the warring supporters. They link arms to do this, a human wall of police officers hoping to restore order. The only approach the police used in those days was to try to contain the trouble-makers, before sizing up what to do next to eradicate the violence.

Meanwhile, everything is building up to go off big-time again. That early roar and the sound of a row has every home team bovver boy running out of the nearby pubs and side streets to the ground. Nothing works quicker than the terrace grapevine: 'Fucking hell, them West Ham cunts are already here and trying to take our end.'

You can actually see them, all red with rage, thinking, the liberty of it all. Well, it's a liberty they're going to have to try to check, because this is all about territory domination. The West Ham mob had got it off to an art. Normally, away supporters would attempt to take a home end about an hour before kick-off. This would ensure maximum publicity. But we changed tactics to surprise our enemies, sometimes going three hours before kick-off to avoid being detected by the police.

We knew the Old Bill never left the police station until about 1 o'clock. The opposition would be a more manageable size, which would allow us to get a good early foothold on their territory, to establish ourselves so strongly that the Old Bill would have a major problem removing us. In turn, this ensured they had to go for the thin blue line compromise, with the home end that were now baying for our blood being forced to take the fight to us.

It was an unwritten rule that if we held any part of the end behind our opponents' goal at kick-off time, then that area could be declared as taken. It was also accepted as taken if you ran your opposition out from behind the goal and it wasn't them but the Old Bill who finally ejected you.

It would become like a tug of war. Each side used sheer weight of numbers to push through Old Bill's line and force the other firm out entirely. We, the insurgents, would be forever trying to secure the higher ground to make it more difficult to be ousted, while the home end tried to send some of their numbers around our flank to get us in a pincer movement.

Both parties would lob golf balls and coins. Police truncheons bashed those of us unfortunate enough to be pushed into the Old Bill. Then you'd hear the call of another separate ruck somewhere close by, in the heart of the enemy, followed by an echoing chant... 'M.I.L.E. E.N.D.!' It would be the Mile End mob, gate-crashing our party, late, pissed and tooled right up.

Excitement would turn to bedlam, forcing the Old Bill to take tougher action. It was a case of either stay where you were, and be nicked, or join up with the rest of the West Ham boys.

Forced out on to the pitch by the police, lads would be escorted by the Old Bill up the touchline, holding up the game as angry home supporters gesticulated with hand signals. This was what taking an end was all about. This was the buzz.

I'd just love it when everyone had their moment... the big fucking hero for the day. You'd see a geezer you'd not really taken notice of, except to nod your head in recognition 'cause you know he's West Ham. Then later, maybe the same season, you're somewhere where it kicks off big-time and he's the one that's done the star turn. Now everyone is talking about him. Even seasons later, years later, people still remember, 'Oh so and so... right fucking nutter, remember when...'

* * * * *

Attaching yourself to West Ham's East End following was a buzz like nothing else in those days when football violence was sweeping the terraces. It was as dangerous as it was exciting. At one time our following had a bigger reputation than our own team. When the name West Ham was mentioned in conversation, it wasn't the football club that was being referred to, or the names of the players. The fighting prowess of the East End mob was growing on a nationwide scale. We exploded on to the headlines in the 1980s when we became known by everyone as the I.C.F.

Our reputation was built on the respect given us for coming out on top against the odds – usually away from home, where the opposition would have the numbers. Even if we were to come unstuck in a row, we had built a reputation that West Ham lads stood and stuck together, no matter what.

It meant that to have a go or get a result against our little firm, you would seriously have to trade blows. None of those pacts where 'We run you, then you run us and providing nobody falls over, no one gets hurt.' We fought to maintain the expectations everyone had had for us since those early Mile End years. We upset an awful lot of rival teams' supporters, which was one reason why we never mixed on the England scene.

Outside of West Ham, people thought we were all one firm that really stuck together. The truth was, we were split into factions, according to age group and the regular different mobs that travelled away. Then there were those lads who picked and chose their games. But when it mattered, we were together, the top firm around.

In the early Seventies, no matter what we got up to, the antics of Chelsea or Man United's Red Army hooligans always seemed to grab the headlines. Throughout that period, our small travelling army had been involved in plenty that should have made the front page. Still, we knew who was London's number one firm. And clearly another 'firm' also knew, given the extra-special attention they gave us. They were the very folk we didn't want recognition from... the Old Bill.

Throughout the Seventies we continued taking it to anybody, whoever wanted to know, just to show beyond doubt that we were the firm to reckon with in Britain. As the Seventies gave way to the Eighties, the football authorities and the police became determined to get to grips with the terrace warfare that had been going on for over a decade. To beat their desperate clampdown on hooliganism, we would have to step activities up to another level.

The hardcore of every club's firm found it increasingly difficult to perform as they had before inside the grounds. It was fast becoming near-mission impossible. We had become too predictable. Our moves were the same ones that we'd used during previous seasons. You'd come out of the opposition's station then head for the same boozer every time. Drunkenly, you'd attempt to take their end, at roughly the same time you'd entered it the season before. And after the match you'd meet with 'em in the same street you'd had it with 'em in last time. To be honest, we were making Old Bill look wise.

We had to change from a mindless yob army to a thinking thug army; a new era was dawning. What a change. Tired of being searched for the umpteenth time that day, having your old bootlaces removed. Everyone took to going with spare sets of laces, to which Old Bill responded by taking the whole boot. If you avoided that humiliation, you were destined to be gobbing off from inside a police escort all day long. Where was the fun in just looking hard?

We smartened ourselves up and started wearing casual fashions. The Farah strides, Pringles or Gabichis we wore on a Friday night we now sported to matches on the Saturday. Anything to get as far away as possible from the authorities' stereotyped image of what they thought they had to look out for. The other noticeable difference was in the faces that everyone looked to follow for a bit of action. Characters who were unassuming, moderate in their drinking and big on thinking were rising fast in the firm's leadership.

It was funny the way the beer monsters in their claret-and-blue hooped rugby shirts with donkey jackets regarded the new casual look as something tarty. But they gave respect when they saw how quickly the casual in the Lacoste would pull out a blade and squirt. We left the beer monsters to become bit parts, taking the attention away from us as we walked on the other side of the road, watching them get pushed from pillar to post in the escort. We chuckled even more when they came looking for us in the ground to learn of the escapades we'd had with the opposition's top boys after slipping the police escort.

Something else was changing – aggro and violence was not the be-all and end-all of hooliganism any more. Being part of the firm was what it was really all about. Our exploits had become legendary; the I.C.F. was fashionable on the street in a big way. In its early issues, *The Face* printed huge articles on the football casual – and they weren't written as a put-down in any way. The emergence of the football casual was growing in strength around grounds and the I.C.F. gained in many ways from being one of the first casual firms.

Even though soccer violence was on the wane, our numbers actually increased. You were no longer expected to get in a ruck at every game. Going to football was becoming as much about fashion and style as it was about violence. In fact, looking for aggro all the time was almost considered uncool.

The Seventies scarf, kick, boot and punch had been replaced by a quick squirt with a jiffy and in and out with a craft knife, all the time being careful not to get blood on the designer labels. A jiffy was a plastic, squeezable, Jiff lemon bottle full of ammonia. We developed an arrogance that was the mark of extreme confidence wherever we roamed following West Ham. The Eighties was an unbelievable time for football violence and I believe the I.C.F. were at the forefront, taking things to a level never seen before.

Ex-I.C.F. lads of totally different characters, Messrs Woolwich and Animal, bear testament to the unbelievable attitude and arrogance that West Ham had at the time. Woolwich remembers: 'West Ham could do what they liked really... "We're at the Arsenal, so we'll just go in their end", that's how it was. All the years I was a hooligan, the arrogance stayed with me.' Animal reckons we were an army within an army, complete with its own leadership structure. 'Most of us would go to work, where we had proper jobs and decent money,' he recalls. 'They'd go where they want and do what they want. Come the Saturday, they told the world what they were going to do, and it would be pure violence. At the worst of the troubles, you might as well have had no police force. They really didn't have a say.'

Who could forget the image of Prime Minister Maggie Thatcher, the Iron Lady, wringing her hands and saying, 'It's got to stop and stop now' after the Heysel Stadium turnout in the mid-Eighties? As everyone knows, the lady wasn't for turning, and we were now in her sights. Heysel involved Liverpool fans and if it wasn't over for many a fan then, it certainly should have been when Operation Own Goal came along, sending down Chelsea's boys for ten years. I don't think the I.C.F. really saw the end until that bloody ruck with Man United's lot on a ferry in the middle of the North Sea. The brutal mid-sea battle made front-page headlines all over the world. Shortly after that, the police carried out dawn raids in a second Operation

Own Goal, this time lifting the I.C.F. Our notoriety was always going to be the end of us.

* * * * *

Almost everyone in Britain had heard of the I.C.F., and knew that those initials meant terror. But very few actually know how it all began.

The I.C.F. story actually starts with three young lads who went to Villa and ran the famous Holte End. Still no more than youths, they were already hardened football thugs. One was the son of an East End docker; the second was West Ham born and bred; the third had enrolled into the army straight from school. All used to go to football looking for adventure, with soccer violence very much a way of their life. Here is the story of how the InterCity Firm started, as told by those three lads: Andy Swallow, Grant Fleming and Micky Ramsgate.

Grant Fleming: *I knew Andy when we formed the Essex East London firm to go West Ham home games in 1974–75. We were very young and all at school. Before I got into going with lads my own age, I'd been in scraps tagging along with older West Ham.*

We went to Liverpool in '74 on the Special. Everyone was saying how it was the biggest West Ham firm to go to Liverpool. We had three Football Specials full, instead of the usual one that often was just half full. I remember going up with older lads like Sprinty, Northy, Felix and that. But that was a rough one, really rough and we got an absolute hiding that day. That game was a rude awakening for me; I'd say it made me realise what it was all about. Before, we had gone to all the London grounds and we took everywhere. But Liverpool, I couldn't believe it. I think Everton had a game cancelled, because they joined up that day and it was all Scousers together.

It was dark when we came out after the game and all I remember was getting sucked up a side road towards the Kop. The Scousers had done a runner, so we all charged, then we just got caught on Scotland Road. From then on it was everyone for themselves. I remember the train journey back was so much quieter than the journey up. People had their jackets nicked by the Liverpool mob. One geezer sat opposite without his trousers. Another sat there holding his side where he'd been sliced up.

This really brought it home to me: we ain't messing about now. So far we'd walked into Stamford Bridge, we'd walked into Highbury. We'd walked into all these places, but a cold, dark November night running down the Scotland Road really brought it home to me. It was now a case of either shape up or ship out.

We got over Liverpool because that was down to numbers. But another turning point for me was Sheffield United's game of the '75–'76 season. I think it was the only time I'd seen West Ham really take it in an end. They threw everything at us. I had darts, golf balls, bricks and bottles lobbed at me. Again, it was like a wake-up call. I remember outside I got a hiding by a mob of them, but back in that end was far worse. I saw Gardner go down, but he took about eight down with him.

From this point on I would really lose it going to football. I'd gone past nicking scarves, getting involved in little skirmishes and sticking the boot in where I could. Now I was going away a lot, we sort of all drew together. People like Andy, he'd run into Ramsgate, then there were a few connections with Canning Town, a few from Forest Gate and Stratford, like Woody, Johnny Rumble and the Chadwell Heath lot. We were just all young 'uns, basically.

Andy Swallow takes up the story.

We used to follow all the older ones, the likes of Carlton Leach. They all seem to give themselves names like G.L.F., the Good Looking Firm. I'd already started the V.L.F – Vicarage Lane Firm – and when I started meeting others, it changed to the Essex East London Firm. We were all from around Upton Park, Plaistow and the back of Queens Market. We met more and more good lads like Terry Tolson, Neil Taylor, Fraser Jones, Butler. Some good little Townies to go with others we knew, like Shane Hagger and all the Hornchurch, Johnny Turner, Billy Eves. We would meet up in the supporters' club on Sunday night or go down the Denmark in East Ham, which was a strange set-up, as there was Old Bill drinking in there and us lot all underage. But that's how it was. We were definitely becoming a much larger firm and doing our own thing up and down Green Street on match days long before the older ones came bombing round about 12 o'clock to nick all the glory. A lot of the older faces didn't want us with 'em for big games, so one day we just turned round and said, 'Right we'll get our own firm and we're going to have it with the older ones if they want it. If they do want it, we'll fuck them off.'

In those days we'd tag along to be roadies for bands like Sham 69 and we'd collect badges of various pop logos and bands. I remember when we decided to become this new big gang. We were sitting around my flat with Grant and Ramsgate ripping the plastic covers off these badges and spraying them with light blue paint, then painting crossed hammers on them. Grant then Tipp-Exed the initials I.C.F. on them. That was the original badge. The rest is history.

We had the right hump with the older West Ham over being fucked off all the time. Our argument was always that even when the top boys were in charge, and we were back of the pecking order, we were still beating them to the fight. Matthew Thomas said there was now enough of us to make a point.

Ramsgate recalls that although he was a latecomer to the E.L.F., he was in on the arrangements when it was decided that all the young firms were to join up and go to a first away game all together:

It was decided to meet at Euston and make our mark at Villa. Two weeks beforehand we tried to get in the vans outside the market [Cass's old Commer van]. *We got a knock back there and couldn't get on board so the next away game was Villa where we were now determined to make a point. When we all arrived at Birmingham's New Street station, we'd had a laugh with Carlton, Dickle and co., taking the piss when we introduced ourselves as the I.C.F. and sang a song we'd made up. We'd had a series of mock fights running through the carriages, all in good spirits. When we came through that Bull Ring Centre, I think it was the usual – a bit of thieving, with the older ones going their own way.*

So we came to the ground at Villa. It must have been about 1 o'clock when we arrived at the Holte End. We thought, right, we're going in. There was no question, it was just go for it.

We all got in there, climbing up those big back stairs, and as you came to the back and looked at the vastness of it you realised you were standing in the biggest home end in Britain. You could get lost in there because it was so big. I think the South Bank at Wolves may have been bigger, but it was an open end and that wasn't Wolves' home end, they had the North Bank. So the Holte End had to be the biggest end, bigger even than the Kop at Anfield. I think at one time the capacity was 28,000. Funny, innit? That's a bigger capacity than West Ham have had in the past few years, and we're just talking about one end here.

I remember us looking at each other, thinking, 'What the hell have we done here? What have we done? We're in this vast end.' It was early and we thought we'd have some back-up when the rest of West Ham came in.

It was still filling up with home supporters, but with all our claret-and-blue bits and pieces they thought we were Villa and we just blended in, keeping a low profile. We all copped for our programmes and spread ourselves all over the Holte End so as not to attract any unwanted attention. The end was filling up quite quickly and that's when we realised there was only going to be us. We were all in their end, split up in ones and twos and just about scattered everywhere – down by the corner flag, behind the goal, up in the middle. It was real nervy in there, especially when people started looking, but we stayed with the plan, which was to remain low-profile until the big clock at the far end said ten to three. That's when the players would be coming out, the ground would be full up and we'd all meet at the back of the stand and give it this little tune that we had rehearsed on the train up. Clicking the old fingers to a rhythm, we'd sing the words 'We are I... InterCity, we are C.... cool and casual... We are F... firmy-handed... we are I.C.F.!'

Some of us in that Holte End had been sitting down on the floor, but at ten to three we stood up, pulling claret-and -blue balaclavas down over our faces. They were really West Ham bobble hats and we'd cut the eyes out ourselves.

It was great how everyone stayed with the plan of meeting at the back of the Holte. It was a real advantageous position to hold. The Holte End used to have this sort of big platform area that was quite wide before the terracing would drop again. So that was a nice level piece to stand on. Our arrangements were to meet in the top corner of this section, knowing that if we had this it would be difficult for anyone to get around us. When we made that chant of 'I.C.F.' we knew that we would be attracting all the attention, because, first thing, nobody would know what the chant I.C.F. was. Then, all of a sudden, they realised it was West Ham. I think someone said, 'They're trying to come up behind us!' Then it all kicked off. There came a point of no return and when it went off we were all in.

We had a prime position from which to go steaming down. Before you knew it, there were thousands disappearing in front of us and on to the pitch. In their flight they left the biggest gap you'd ever imagine, which of course meant they now realised there was less than fifty of us. For that one moment it was like no other experience, we had just run the whole fucking end. There was mass panic. No one had a clue who we were, including the West Ham at the other end. Only the season before we'd been running out the schoolboy enclosures where they reserved a section of the ground for under-15s. We were getting in all the kiddie ends and running them all – Derby, Highbury – until we realised we could smash the older ones up as well.

Back in the Holte, Villa had realised the truth. The shout went up, 'They're only little cunts, do 'em!' They came steaming back into us real mental, like. They kept coming back up, we kept going down, as the police came rushing in from the sides. We all slipped down to the bottom, then a Villa fan said one of us had a blade. So Old Bill grabbed [one of the us] but could only find a rolled-up programme. He went, 'Look I'm only trying to get out of the ground, I've got into the wrong end.' That's when they threw us out over the terraces and walked us around the edge of the pitch.

Grant remembers the elation they all felt walking along the touchline down on the pitch:

I couldn't believe it. We were still all together and I remember walking round that pitch with Matthew Thomas, who had a broken arm at the time, saying he'd split the plaster cast where he'd whacked so many Villa.

The Old Bill neither nicked anyone nor chucked any of us out. We'd pulled it off big-time. So coming around that pitch, going towards the uncovered Witton Lane end packed with just about everyone who was back on that train all screaming and going mad, we were on top of it. We really felt like we were walking on water. The older ones in our group would 'ave been eighteen, the youngest fifteen. We went in our away end and could see all the faces thinking, 'Who's this lot?' We knew we'd arrived. We were just cock-a-hoop and full of ourselves. The older ones were impressed, but couldn't take any claim. We just give them all loads of abuse.

As far as Andy was concerned, the day was just too good to be over:

After the game we decided to remain together on our own. We got back to Euston, came out the station and went walking down the road as a mob of 100 to 150. All of a sudden, a fucking big firm came up the road towards us. This firm was so massive they filled the whole road. We just steamed straight into them, running them. Turns out it was those South London bastards Millwall. So on the opening day for the InterCity Firm we ran the Holte End, abused the older ones and chased Millwall. How bad is that for a day out? We young 'uns decided to stay as the InterCity Firm and saw the name taken by everyone going with West Ham. It just seemed to fall into place and made sense, for that's the way we'd all been travelling the past couple of seasons.

People still kept to all the different firms. But coming under that umbrella of us all being the InterCity Firm meant everyone had a worth – the elitism had gone a bit and we still kept a structure.

Ramsgate remembers that it didn't take long to realise that they could be on to something with this I.C.F. business:

As the name I.C.F. took on mythical proportions, we started to make money out of it. The following year we had Notts County first game down. We beat them 5-2 and when we went 3-0 up in that game, I remember saying if we get four I ain't going back to the Army. That's when I went AWOL. When they caught up with me on the run they put me in Shooters Hill Hospital. In the end the Army said you've got to do something while you're here, you can either do carpentry or printing. So I said I'll do printing, and that's when I printed up the I.C.F. membership cards, the congratulation stickers.

We were selling them to all the bods coming in from Hertfordshire, from Essex, Sussex, Devon, Cornwall, everywhere – a pound a time in the Boleyn pub. That's how we used to get our money for away games. We'd end up with a great big pot jar of notes. People used to go back home thinking they were involved in this big gang. But I never thought of it other than a money-earning swindle. A pack of 500 I.C.F. calling cards was £500 made in our eyes.

Under Fives

If the I.C.F. marked a new dawn for football violence, then so did the emergence of West Ham's Under Fives. I asked Andy Bowers to explain their beginnings:

The Under Fives evolved out of the period when every little mob had to have a name. There were about twenty of us younger kids who would knock about together with the I.C.F. All we were doing really was a bit of thieving on the back of the football. The older ones noticed us and were the first to use the name. When we turned up somewhere together, they'd go, 'Here come the Under Fives.' It sort of stuck. Me and a mate went and had two T-shirts printed with the words I.C.F.

UNDER FIVES on them. I don't think we ever wore them, it was just done for a giggle, but it meant we now took the name when going to football.

What got me at the time was that a lot of the I.C.F. were only a couple of years older, alright they were a bit bigger, and in the beginning there weren't many of us. Later on we took to hanging around at Kings Cross and Euston and 'taxing' rival supporters on the Tube and taking their clobber as 'payment'. That's when warning bells started ringing with other supporters, who kept asking each other, 'Did you get taxed by West Ham's Under Fives?'

Then other people started going around with us and our exploits got much bigger as we moved into doing shops on away games. It got to the stage where a lot of lads were going to the game because it was one big thieving opportunity. The older ones still took the piss but we never relied on them. We could hold our own and we stuck together, often doing our own thing.

Later we had guys like Richard Wildman, a nineteen-stone amateur boxer, who was just seventeen. Now you try telling him he was an Under Five!

Everyone was I.C.F., but the younger guys were known as the Under Fives. They had some lively characters like Bacon, Peter and Billy Hampton, Lugford, Woody, Sean Pearman, Glenn Appleby, Simon Irons, Little Crapka, Nazi Mick and Mark Hawkins. Later on Jela and Shakesy came on the scene.

Other firms had similar. I remember Liverpool were a firm with a lot of young 'uns, as were the egg and spooners – Gooners. When we started going abroad, that's when we got to know the young Scousers. They were very good at what we were doing.

Chapter 2

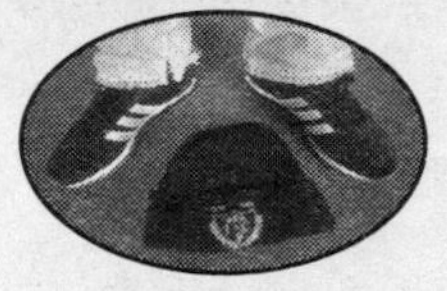

BILL GARDNER

the rock we all stood on

I.C.F.

THE I.C.F. FURORE is at its peak and we've got Chelsea away, which means one thing: we've got to put them Chelsea mugs in their place by taking the Shed. We rule London, always have done, always will do. We're the guv'nors.

Bill Gardner, a six-foot-plus man with a builder's physique and fair hair strolls through the turnstile entrances to Chelsea's Shed end. He goes in without glancing back to see if the rest of our lads, mobbing up in the courtyard, have fallen in behind. As I scamper up the steep, daunting steps of the home supporters' end, I look up. Chelsea are mobbing up along the top of the stairs, just waiting for our predictable entrance. As I look around and realise only a few of us had got clear of the turnstiles, I think to myself, fuck that.' The operators have sussed down on the gate and aren't letting any more of us in.

I turn back to Gardner, who is now just in front. He appears oblivious to events behind. He's locked on a mission, a man who leads from the front. As Gardner nears the top, Chelsea, who've been standing there with their fists clenched, start to back away until he is on top of those stairs with 'em. I'm close enough to hear him utter that by now familiar introduction line: 'Afternoon gentlemen, the name's Bill Gardner.' As soon as Bill announces himself, a big gap opens up around us. Bewildered looks all round, sort of saying, 'Look we're not Chelsea any more, in fact we're nobody at all.' Such is the aura and the presence of West Ham's terrace legend. The Chelsea lot know that when you'd found Gardner you've found West Ham's top boys and all their main firm. It's now an altogether different proposition for the faint-hearted among the Chelsea Shed boys. Yet you can bet your life that only moments before, Chelsea had been scanning the home end for tell-tale signs of infiltration. Looking for unfamiliar faces that wore no colours. You can imagine the whispered comments: 'Where's Gardner?' 'Look out for Gardner.' 'Get Gardner!' Then, the reality. Gardner's here, he's just introduced himself. When he does, it's like disturbing a wasps' nest. The Shed erupts as they all come out from under the covered stand, screaming all kinds, while the Chelsea nearest to us back off. We are the targets now – the name Gardner has ensured that.

While there is some confusion in the Chelsea ranks, we

realise we are in the Shed with no back-up. This allows the Old Bill to get the first move in. Almost as soon as he'd finished his sentence, Gardner got nicked. The remaining few of us put the boot in, only for much the same to come back our way. We take the old backward walk, fronting the whole Shed. Gathered all along the top, Chelsea's bravado returns. 'You'll never take the Shed', they taunt. 'C'mon, West Ham.' They even pick some of us out and call us by our individual names. 'Bollocks', I reply, to myself as much as to them.

The Old Bill furiously push and shove us out, back into the massive courtyard at Stamford Bridge to rejoin the rest of the I.C.F., who've been thwarted at the turnstiles trying to follow us in. Everybody is muttering 'bollocks'; we all know that that's it for the day, unless we can slip the Old Bill after the game. The Chelsea Old Bill now know our intentions and marshal us back up to the North Stand. As we walk I lose count of the enquiries from our own: 'Where's Gardner?' 'What's happened to Bill?' Finally, word goes round that he's been nicked. I thought Bill getting nicked was a shame really, as I chuckled at the memory of Chelsea briefly shitting themselves at the mere mention of someone's name. Yet I'd seen Gardner have that effect so many times over the past seasons.

My first recollection of the legend of Bill Gardner, and the aura of the man, was the battle of 'Boro – Middlesborough away in 1975. It involved every single West Ham fan who made the long trip that day. We reckoned we had a visiting support of just 200 to 240 on the old Football Special, plus forty of us who went by private coach. Basically, two firms called the shots that day: Gardner and the Teddy Bunter firm from the Chicken Run, along with Steve Morgan's South Bank crew, which included Johnny Hampton. After the game, we fought a long-running street battle against such ridiculous odds that it will always figure as one of our top ten rucks. It was during this row that Gardner cemented my view that he was the rock the West Ham firm all stood on.

I was with the lads who'd gone up by coach late on Friday night. We were there so early that morning that we all played football in the park. Bored, we went and looked for 'Boro's end. Old Bill on ground duty looked at our small numbers and actually pointed us in the direction of 'Boro's end – they didn't believe our tiny number would be up to it. At that time, 'Boro were rated. At a service station we'd stopped at earlier, Newcastle fans warned us 'Boro had a firm to be reckoned with. The area certainly looked rough enough. As we got to the turnstiles, the Old Bill saw we weren't bluffing and rushed back over to put us up the other end, which was for away fans.

I don't think anyone remembers much of the game, but you may recall how back then they always opened the gates before the end – sometimes it was ten minutes before, other times it was as much as twenty minutes before the match finished. All the grounds did it to help crowd congestion and to let out those that wanted to leave early. For the away supporter it was always butterflies time. You could give it all you wanted inside the ground, but outside on the unfriendly streets of a cold northern town, you could easily end up as that poor little Cockney...

You wait to see what all the right faces are doing first, before deciding on your own move. Then you get the word, which quickly goes round: 'Boro's firm are waiting outside our end. You immediately look straight to the opposite end and see a lot of empty spaces on their terracing. Now you know for sure. You've come out of your away end as a tight unit, looking to stick together. You don't wanna be split, not up here. They've come to test us, but we can do these. A few skirmishes, but everyone remains together, moving in the direction we'd backed 'Boro off to.

A few streets along and we come into a road with a big park running the entire length of one side of the street. The park has a wall running around it, topped with spiked railings. Through these barred railings you can see an awesome sight – a sea of red and white. It seemed like 'Boro's whole end is gathered in this park – and they'd spotted us first. A hail of bricks whistles through the air and over the railings, landing in the street where we stand, filling the middle of the road and copping direct hits. There are too many to dodge completely; they've got us trapped. Run or go forward? Running isn't an option, as Gardner has copped it with a brick. Several more missiles hit him as commands everyone to stand and visibly show we can take it. We are all getting hit now and began throwing the stuff back. The ambush has served to fuel our anger and the only thought on everyone's mind is going forward. But how? With no park entrance before us, the only thing for it is to climb over the railings. Some are already clambering over. Now we're all doing it. 'Boro remain motionless, as if in total disbelief that they'd just witnessed a firm of mad Cockneys take an inhuman barrage of northern hate.

As we drop and fling ourselves off the railings into the park, the red sea wall breaks and runs. It is an amazing sight: they are a thousand strong and running en masse. We pursue them to the open gates of the far end of the park. You can almost see their fear at the thought of what might happen to them if the maddened Cockneys catch them after what they've just done.

Bill Gardner recalls that amazing day:

Once they threw the bricks and had nothing more to throw, and we were still there, we had them. They had that look of a rabbit caught in a set of headlights. Because we'd stood the barrage and then we had the gear, there was [only] *gonna be one winner then. Everyone had the hump, the adrenaline was up. We'd all been bricked then thought, right you cunts, let's see now.*

We climbed over those railings and for a moment they seemed to look at us in disbelief, then they ran because they didn't know what to do. Their plan had gone wrong. That's what they used to do in those days: suck teams into the park and do 'em. Now every man jack from 'Boro's end who was in that park was running for the furthest end, out of the park.

After the park, we hit the streets. It was grim, but then Middlesborough always was a rough old place. They were coming at us from down side streets. That too was dodgy, for they knew all the alleyways and streets so well. It was a good old walk to the station as well... Two or three miles or so. We'd fight going further and further in the opposite direction. At one time I can recall they came into us from behind five times, twice from the front, and you had to look down every side street you'd pass. Sometimes it was small groups tooled up, other times it was all their main mob. You've only got to look in a man's eyes to tell if he's got the shits up. I looked around and saw a lot of people who were pretty frightened that day at Middlesborough. Better to be frightened with a group of 200 than on their own. We never folded, not once, every one of us fought, including those that were not known to. If you get split up in those sort of places, you've had it. You've got to stick together. A lot of the London clubs used to take far more in numbers than us... Tottenham and Chelsea used to have loads more away supporters than us and they'd go to these places and get walloped. We used to go up there with 200 and do well.

As soon as you came out of the station in those days they used to know where you were from. They didn't have to see what train you came off, they knew by what you wore. What do you do? You stick together. You knew that if you came out of that railway station and they were waiting for you, there were only two choices. You either fought your way out and went to the game, or you got back on the train and went home.

You will never find a Hammers fan of that period who doesn't know, or hasn't heard of, Bill Gardner. Nor will you find one with a bad word about him. The man has the respect of us all. A leader among men; a rock of a man who absolutely lives West Ham. Mention his name to any West Ham fan of the time and the reaction will be an immediate smile, then a grin. Everybody has a big story about Bill, and the first words will be, 'I remember he helped me out at...'

The name Bill Gardner is probably the biggest name in the history of the football terraces. I don't think this book or any other can do justice to Gardner the man and fan. Bill has never written a book. But plenty of leading football books have written about Bill. To quote just a few:

In *Hoolifan*, authors Martin King and Martin Knight wrote: *'The East End boys liked taking the Shed – it was good PR and it kept up morale. At the front of their mob was Gardner, he had been around for years.'*

Writer Bill Buford's book, *Among the Thugs*, was based on the Manchester lads and said *'the trouble started when Roy threw a cup of hot tea at Bill Gardner, West Ham's famous top man.'* Another chapter told of that majestic moment when Bill Gardner stood his ground, flanked by his troops ... *'about five hundred had walked down in three columns. Once they reached the high street they stopped still in formation. At the front was a big, broad-shouldered man, about thirty-five. This was Bill Gardner. He stood there, feet planted apart, crossed his arms and waited. Next to him were his lieutenants.'*

I've lost count of the number of times the main boys from rival clubs would show themselves from across the road as you came out the station, and there were those that would press themselves up to the fences separating supporters in the ground, searching, desperate to be shown where Gardner was. They knew by reputation and the terrace grapevine that Gardner was the man. Find Gardner and you'd find West Ham's boys.

But what of the man himself? I have known Bill for most of my football-going days. The respect I hold for him is immense. I have heard dozens of stories from people who stood alongside him. For the purpose of this book, however, I was more interested in find out about his own thoughts and memories about what made him 'top man'.

Bill gets shy about anyone referring to him as a legend in connection with West Ham:

> *I always found that a bit embarrassing, I just wanted to be me. I didn't want the notoriety. Somebody told me that my name had been scrawled in chalk on a primary school wall in Halifax. I didn't want that. Stories were made up about me. Like the one about me making the phone call to Chelsea – 'Can't make it this week, see you next week.' I never made that phone call, never did it. I can prove it.*
>
> *They put in the* Hoolifan *book that you, me and Swallow were running down a motorway. I was never*

there. We've never been in the same car together. People who know me know I can hardly walk, never mind run, and I've never been very good on my toes anyway. Perhaps that's one of the reasons why I used to stand and have it, because I could never run. I had two choices; if I ran I got done. I think you're better off standing cool and calculated when you've got the numbers against you. Find the high ground or somewhere where you've got your back to the door so you can see what's coming in front of you. Never ever be caught in the middle, where people can get around you. Always get your back to their wall, so at least you know you're only fighting people one way...

I asked Bill if he remembered the time we took the North Bank at Wolves:

The butterflies you experienced the moment you entered the turnstiles of the home supporters' end was unbelievable.

In their end the buzz was brilliant. They knew who you were, but there'd be that look of surprise and shock, then hatred. You knew what would be coming next: taking your opponents' end. There's nothing like that going on nowadays, it was a real Seventies thing for supporters. It was done in the name of your team, to force respect; whether the team could achieve the same on the pitch didn't matter. The supporters at that time had created it that way. The best way of describing it is the roar, to experience the roar of the crowd. Anyone supporting any team would feel the same thing – the roar. That roar of the crowd got the adrenaline going. When the roar went up, that was the moment everyone would go steaming in.

It's different times now. People have moved on, and if you ain't you're a dinosaur.

One of the best-known firms over West Ham was the Teddy Bunter Firm, the mob Bill was always with:

I remember before any other name in gang football took shape, the Mile End were the business. I used to knock around with the Mile End as part of their gang. I was the only one in their mob who didn't come from where they lived. [In] *those days there was a lot of infighting among everyone. Mile End used to wait for the Barking Boys and the Dagenham lot used to have a row with whoever they could. Every week you'd have a mate who belonged to one gang and who'd get a slap off another person who you knew. There were a few years where everybody was at each other's throat. I looked at it and thought to myself, well there's nothing going for this.*

The reason I went over West Ham was because I thought it was like a family. I thought everyone should stick together, and that's what I wanted anyway. If you follow the same team, you've got to stick together. Mile End used to have a party piece at the end of the season. They always used to come round and steam the North Bank. I think it stopped when West Ham all got together and decided enough was enough.

There was a confrontation by the church in Green Street between the lads from Barking, Dagenham and Mile End. There was a lot of heated conversation but no punches thrown. In my mind that was the day West Ham really became united. There's strength in unity. We stayed unified for years after that trouble.

After this, Bill's West Ham mates, whom he'd met through football, became one of the top firms and became know as the Teddy Bunter Firm, or T.B.F. for short.

John Simpson, aka Simo, recalls how the T.B.F. started out in the early Seventies at the time of the Arnie Garnie firm, the Bakers and the Mile End mob:

We knew each other from standing over West Ham and meeting at places like Ilford Palais on a weekend. So we thought, it's time to start our own firm. Without knowing everyone's strengths we decide to call it Teddy Bunter Firm. Simply because Bunter was really well known over West Ham and Ted being the tallest made him easy to pick out, giving us someone to rally round.

The Teddy Bunter Firm was the most active older firm over West Ham. It was Bill Gardner's firm, but it was also something of a mystery for many of the West Ham lads who followed them. A few thought the firm was run by one person, whom they mistook to be the larger-than-life Scoeby, whereas in fact the T.B.F. was run by two people.

Simo explains:

Everyone thought of Gardner as our top man – for me, the rock we all stood on. So if Bill was our rock, who was Gardner's? He doesn't hesitate to tell you it's Big Ted, the other half of West Ham's duo.

Bill Gardner's respect for Ted goes back a long way:

I always had a soft spot for Ted, when I was fourteen he was eighteen and he took me under his wing. We've been friends for a long while. One of the nicest fellas you're ever likely to meet… Me and Ted knew one thing: I'd always stick by him and he'd always stick by me. That's the way it always was. At the end of the day he knew he could rely on me and I knew I could rely on him. We had a good relationship.

If Bill took the plaudits, we in the I.C.F. knew that Ted was the equal of him. They were a formidable partnership. I remember one occasion when about a hundred Leicester caught up with us on the walk back from their ground. There was just three of us – myself, Johnny Butler and Big Ted. We realised we'd got too far behind the escort, so we just looked at each other and thought, fucking hell it's on top for us. None of us had any respect for Leicester, but we were talking numbers here. The Leicester boys came walking along the pavement in a long ant trail behind us. It was a bricking party to see the Londoners off home.

Ted just stopped dead on the corner of the road. I

looked back to him and his reply was classic: 'I'm too old to run. I'd never make it, but you two will.'

'Bollocks!' we both replied.

'Right turn, now,' said Ted.

And the three of us did. Surprised and startled that we weren't heading in the other direction, the Leicester backed off. We scuffled with what could have been no more than half a dozen coming into us. These Leicester had no bottle.

For a man that was always out front, I was interested to find out whether Bill respected his rivals. Here's what the man himself says:

My answer would be: none of them. Not as individuals – two bob the lot of them. That's all they are. They can look deep into their souls, but can they really say, 'I was a hard man'? No, they were bullies.

Millwall, Manchester United, Stoke, Man City used to have a hell of a row with us... Forest were always game. They are the ones that come to mind for me.

Midlands – hopeless place. It was just somewhere you went to get back home early.

On most of our trips we were always outnumbered, and always going to be when you're playing against 40,000 at Liverpool, Manchester, Leeds, Newcastle. But if we were going to go anywhere and hold our own and stick up for ourselves, we had to stick together. And that's what we were good at. The people in your own individual groups, you could rely on them. Even if they couldn't have a row or nothing, you know they'd always stand there and be with you, to save face, and you got strength from that.

Now, what I would say about us rather than others? You never had a West Ham mob that used to go and turn up at a ground at five to three. West Ham was always around the ground early.

Twelve o'clock, half-past twelve. Always there early in the morning, two or three hours before the kick-off, drinking in the pubs. A lot of these mobs now, they get out of the station at five to three, rant and rave, make a noise, police get round them, [they're] escorted down the ground; same at the end of the game. Big roar, police round them. They get escorted back up the station.

Millwall? I've been every game that we've played them. I remember we were over there and in their end. All credit where credit's due, Millwall were a lot like West Ham. They had the same values, they stuck together, they stuck with their team. They stuck with their mates. To be truthful with you, I hate the sight of them, always have done, always will do. But I admire them for being different.

I shared a journey with Bill as we talked of many rucks we'd been in, confrontations that those outside our world would find hard to believe had taken place. Somehow, we'd been kidding ourselves as to what was our last battle. Most of our own had long considered us as retired after the I.C.F. show trials, Operation Own Goal and a dawn raid. Bill will never forget that day:

Twenty-past six they knocked on the door. There was eight of them. I had been doing nothing at the time and the day they came, I had a broken leg. They came in and said, 'We're arresting you for being a general of the I.C.F.'

I knew it was serious when they said I'd be looking at ten years. You'd have thought they had captured somebody big-time when they got me to East Ham police station. When the sergeant who arrested me walked into their control room, I heard applause. He got a big round of applause for arresting me. I suppose if it takes eight of them to arrest some bloke, he deserves a round of applause. That was the highlight of his year, so good luck to him, made him a hero for the day. Ain't no grief from me, it's water under the bridge now.

Without a doubt the trial frightened the life out of me, but adversity can sometimes bring the best out of you. When you had so many people telling so many tales, there had to be a time when one of them told a lie, as they hid round corners and pretended they were places they weren't. If you're going to fix people too, do it right…

At the end of the day, it was a political thing. Margaret Thatcher wanted it to be part of her law-and-order campaign. I think those things might come again with the 2002 World Cup. Banning people from travelling and that. It's a whole different climate now. When we were in the Inter-Toto Cup with West Ham, I went to all five games and there wasn't one arrest, there was no trouble and everyone had a good time. That must really grieve the Old Bill.

Chapter 3

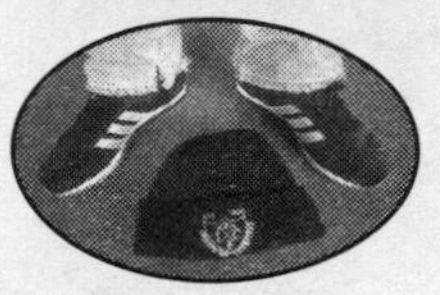

GOING STOKE AWAY

I.C.F.

ANY DIE-HARD West Ham supporter will have vivid memories of going to Stoke, particularly when recalling the epic encounters we had with them in the early Seventies. It was the era of Geoff Hurst, Pop Robson and Clyde Best, when we clashed with the Potters in the league, FA Cup and League Cup. In the 1971–72 season, West Ham played Stoke four times before the outcome was decided in their favour. How we never got to Wembley that season, West Ham fans will never know. The games from then on between West Ham and Stoke City were always classics.

Off the pitch, things were no different, and just as lively – we had some right tussles whenever we rucked Stoke. I think everyone had a story about going there. You'd hear of Chelsea and Tottenham taking big mobs to Stoke and taking their end. So when your time came to play them, you just knew everybody would be thinking of doing the same.

I remember as a teenager, lads from other London clubs would tell me, 'Watch out at the graveyard, Stoke always meet you there.' They were absolutely right.

After the game ended at Stoke's Bootham Crescent ground, the away supporters would always walk back towards the station the same way they had come. I later learned the home fans would deliberately walk down a route running parallel to the road we were on and they'd lie in wait for us at a graveyard, where the two roads met. It was the same move every time, so that must have been the ploy they used for all away teams. Once you got wise to this, the race was on as to who got to the graveyard first.

It used to really go off with Stoke – proper old-fashioned tear-ups all the way through the Seventies. I had them down as bit of a boot boy army, not enough men and not enough class. I thought we always had an edge, but it was never the walkover we had against most Midlands clubs. It was still going off with Stoke into the early Eighties, until the Potters disappeared down the divisions. I listen with interest to everybody else's experiences of going away to Stoke. They were gamer than a lot of people gave them credit for. West Ham put Stoke boys right up there.

Don't take my word for it. Listen to Gardner, Swallow and co. recount their Stoke tales:

Bill Gardner: *I had a lot of respect for Stoke City. They were always fair when you went up there, and if* *you had a row with them, it was done and dusted. There were never any weapons involved, it was man against man. Look, I say anybody can fight with a lump of wood or a knife. But it takes a man to hold his hands up and have the front to look a man in the eye if you're going to have a fight and 'ave it. It was something I felt was totally lacking with a lot of firms for a lot of years. A lot of them would run in slap, [then] run out or try and do you with a weapon. Or maybe five, six of them would jump on you and give you a good hiding. But when it comes to actually standing there man against man, I found there weren't too many like that in all my experience.*

Brett Tidman: *Probably the worst row I got involved in was Stoke. In the mid-Seventies you had to be a right nutter to bother going to any away matches. In those days it was a 2p bus ride from Canning Town to Trafalgar Square, 5p from there to St Pancras station, where there would be a sign on the ticket office saying 'Football Special: Stoke-on-Trent £1.30 return'. We'd have up to 400 fans on a full train going to Stoke. When you arrived there, you'd never get a police escort, the Old Bill would just point and say, 'The ground's that way.'*

We'd get to the ground all right, as there was never ever much trouble before the game at Stoke – it was always afterwards, when they had all their mob together and you had fights in the streets around the ground. About sixty of us got in their end – the Bootham End – by a side entrance. Once in the ground, we'd meet up in the middle behind the goal. [I remember once when] *it didn't take long for a great big northerner to come along and ask one of us the time. The lad he asked was eating a pie and his cool response of, 'Oh not this again', was immediately met by a northerner's fist smashing him straight in the mouth, sending splatterings of pie everywhere.*

I ended up running around the barriers being chased by three or four of these Stoke 'erberts. Every time I looked I could only see West Ham getting bashed and fighting for their lives. I remember hitting the deck, getting up, bashing a few of them, getting knocked down again, all the way to the bottom of Stoke's end. I'd get up, lose my fucking temper then run back up at 'em again.

You're totally unaware who's around. Then you realise there's about ten West Ham left. Oops... time to go. Too late, I've got spanked. I'm on the deck, then I'm up an' out on to the pitch. The Old Bill's there – 'C'mon lads, we'll walk you around.' The scene they encountered was a regular occurrence for them.

I wanted revenge for that kicking in the Stoke end and a few seasons later I was back at Stoke. Ten of us got broken up from the rest of West Ham and decided to slip down the side entrance that leads to the Stoke end.

I was a bit of a Jack the Lad then, and I'd go to football wearing one of those American parka coats. I also took to wearing a gumshield on this trip. Before we'd got to the Stoke end, we were spotted by about thirty or forty Stoke. They'd clocked us, but I wasn't about to start running. About five of them jumped on top of me and started kicking the granny out of me. Looking something like the green Hulk in my parka coat, I got up fighting. I'm struggling away as the older Liddy brother, Terry, jumps in, dragging two of them off me. Both of us were now kicking the shit out of them. Everyone was having individual fights. I saw Guildford come unstuck. Then we turned it, now it was the Stoke mob who were coming unstuck. It was a naughty fight. Even with the gumshield in, I had blood trickling out of my mouth.

Suddenly I was dragged off, along with other people, by a copper on a horse – 'You're nicked.' The cops had a newly built police station opposite the ground. At the time I was sixteen and would have been a juvenile going along to that police station.

The police put us all into separate cells. 'Take your shoe laces out, take your belts off and empty out your pockets'… all that routine stuff. So when I emptied my pockets, the copper at the desk announced out loud, 'One gumshield, still wet.' All the officers laughed as he wrote down the word 'gumshield'.

We were all down in the cells and I remember Guildford shouting, 'We'll be out of here soon.' But come 9 o'clock I was still there with about thirty others, who'd all missed the game. A copper who'd kept looking through the spy hole in the cell door unlocked it and a detective came in. He said, 'Right, you've got fifteen minutes to get to the train station.'

Now, anyone who knows Stoke will tell you it's a half-

an-hour walk from the ground to the station. I remember running through that cemetery – I dunno if I was more scared about that graveyard or the possibility of Stoke fans hanging about for me. When I eventually got to the station, all the others were there, including Terry Liddy and Guildford. That's when I realised I must had been the last one out of that nick. I'll always remember Stoke, because I didn't see the game, it cost me a fortune and I got nicked.

Mouthy Bill: *Before we were a real big away mob, I remember how Stoke came round and steamed us outside the away end before the game. The fucking cheek of it. We done 'em proper and chased 'em all the way up that big Boothen End of theirs. We all paid again at the turnstiles and followed them in. We thought the muppets would all run from us. When they saw us coming through their turnstiles, they all ran again. But this time we could see all their main boys, the old mob, coming through. We held and run them at first, then they came back again.*

Andy Swallow: *Stoke seems to be a bit of an unlucky ground for me. I've been going there since '73 and always end up fighting with people or getting hit on the head with a brick and such like.*

This particular year we talked up going to Stoke and a big mob of us gathered outside the Stoke end, but only about fifty or sixty of us got in to the middle of their end. We were about halfway up, with Stoke mobbed all around us. Bill was there, so was Vaughny. Gardner came up to me at half-time and said, 'Listen Andy hold the fort. Look after all the boys I'm going to get a drink.' No sooner had Bill popped downstairs than the Stoke mob came up bouncing in front of us. It's on again. At the time I was leaning on a barrier with Vaughny standing just in front.

Now they've picked on Vaughny, giving it, 'Come on then, Cockney.' So I leant across and smashed this Stoke geezer straight over the head with a little umbrella I had. He was gone, the fella was spark out. We all just jumped over the barrier and had it right off with them.

Weight of numbers told in the end. The sheer force of Stoke's numbers had us backed up into a corner of their end. Luckily for us we all managed to slip out. It really did go off that day, I mean right off.

In the Seventies you could always have a row with Stoke. There were two roads back to the station and after the game we went down a side road and found we were on the move with all the Stoke crowd. We kept really quite, as they hadn't noticed us. Then someone went, 'NOW!' and we all steamed into them. It went right off and we chased them. This was the row when Richard Wildman got nicked and nobody saw him for three months – they kept him up there.

Vaughny: *We passed the Stoke end, had a look and decide to go in. The Old Bill chucked a load of West Ham out but about thirty of us got in there. We were in when West Ham scored. We started jumping up and* *down and that's when the Stoke mob started gathering up in front of us. We all started fighting when Andy Swallow did this geezer, knocked him spark out with the umbrella.*

In the end, there was only me and Andy left fighting. Bill had fucked off earlier, gone for a piss or something. The next I saw of him was when he was fighting in their side, rattling them off left, right and centre. The fight had been going on for quite a bit and we'd both done quite a few of the Stoke between us, when two Stoke geezers in England shirts tried to stop it. This gave us the chance to slip off through the crowd.

Woolwich: *It was a pouring rainy day when we travelled up to Stoke. It in the early years of the I.C.F., soon after the season we took the Holte End at Villa. We had got there right early and a whole coachload of us went running up the stairs of Stoke's Boothen End. We went steaming in there shouting 'United!... United!' I think there were three Stoke fans, a dog and a bloke smoking a pipe in there. It was so empty it was really embarrassing, almost disgraceful. We got taken out straight away with everyone laughing at us. I've never felt so embarrassed.*

So how did we rate Stoke? Well, in our unique league they were above the better Midland clubs' firms but below the big northern clubs. You could say Stoke had a decent mob: you weren't going to come unstuck, but at the same time, you couldn't go around up there taking the piss. But we never saw Stoke as real rivals. There simply wasn't any real hate between us. A Stoke v West Ham affair was never a vendetta.

Stoke never did anything worthy at Upton Park, and when we went up there, we had our punch-up, said, 'See yer next time,' then went home. Unless your name was Richard Wildman.

Chapter 4

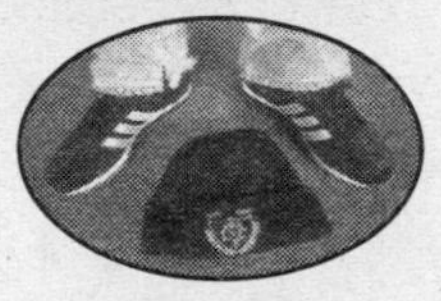

WHY DID YOU LEAVE AT TEN TO THREE, FOREST?

I.C.F.

BRETT TIDMAN and Ramsgate reminded me of the day Nottingham Forest dared to come down to Upton Park as a firm. This is their favourite account of the day. It's a real classic:

The previous season we had it twice with Forest at Orient, but we never had the numbers to give them a really good go. I remember one was a night game in the Anglo-Scottish Cup. Forest were down mob-handed for both games. At the other game, the Old Bill nicked about forty of us and put us on in a little pen. Our pictures appeared in the Sun newspaper the following Monday. [They wrote] *that this is what the police do to football hooligans, lock them up and keep them caged while the game is on.*

The following week, speculation was rife that Forest were going to bring a big mob to West Ham. We knew they had a mob. They'd just been promoted to Division One and were going great guns under Brian Clough. But as for their firm, they were living in the past, back to the bovver boy years of Crombie coats and sharpened metal combs and those original skinhead years. In those days, all the London clubs went up there with a bit of respect after they turned over a decent Tottenham mob in a big Cup match.

Forest's feared reputation stemmed from their practice of deliberately engaging and trapping visiting fans to throw them in the River Trent. The Tottenham boys retold that experience like a real horror story. Since then, Chelsea had sorted them out and Tottenham got their revenge years later. As for West Ham, we never really played them much, and when we did, our reputation was too big for them to be up to much. That's why no one believed they were going to come to Upton Park. To date, we had played Norwich, City, QPR, Everton and 'Boro, and not one firm had been seen. Upton Park had become a no-go area.

Come match day, as usual, we hung about in and around Green Street from as early as 10 a.m. By 11 a.m., people were actually walking around the streets in red and white. You would have thought it was a day out. They didn't have a care in the world, but that soon got knocked out of them. We just picked off the stragglers from this main fucking firm we'd been hearing about.

At about 2 p.m. we were in and outside the Queens pub, by the market, which is literally ten yards from the Upton Park station. A group of our snipers came out, they'd been down the line to Barking. Barking was on the route that the Old Bill made those travelling down on the Football Special take in order to organise the police escort to get them to the ground. Some West Ham young ones told us that hundreds of Forest had arrived at Barking station, saying excitedly, 'They've got two Specials.' 'You sure?' we quizzed in disbelief. We still thought it was a wind-up. Our last two home games against Everton and 'Boro had both been a no-show, so we didn't think that Forest would give it a go.

Ten minutes later, a big mob of Forest fans came out of Upton Park station. They had come from Barking, two stops down the line. They were a tidy firm of 500 to 600 with plenty of geezers – their old firm with all the new bloods. The Old Bill marched them along Green Street under escort. Among them was one particular Old Bill, nicknamed The Muppet, who was a trained hooligan spotter. He knew every one of us by name, but it was going to take more than The Muppet to deter us. We mingled in with them in small groups, while others had come off the train with them and remained in the escort. There were also little mobs on street corners who kicked the fuck out of anyone they could lure into side streets.

At last, a firm had dared to show at Upton Park. The lads were all buzzing big-time. Everywhere you looked there were grinning West Ham faces, like it's gonna be party time. The Forest never said a word. They had that worried northern look about them that just said, 'Concentrate on staying together and getting in that ground.' They were escorted to the South Bank via the Castle Street Road entrance. The West Ham that had mingled in the escort went through the turnstiles with them.

The South Bank end was behind the goal and faced the North Bank end. It was segregated by a fence railing, leaving two-thirds for home fans, situated behind the goal, and the remaining third, nearest to the West-Side enclosure, for visiting fans.

Those of us who hadn't got inside the South Bank with the escort turned off from Green Street and jibbed our way through the turnstile by either doubling up with the guy in front or just jumping over after tipping the turnstile operator a quid. You never had to worry about any watching stewards, as there weren't any. Once inside the West-Side enclosure, the lads jibbed again, this time bunging the old boy on the dividing door underneath the stand, which gives access to club staff or the Old Bill to the South Bank. Another quid and we were in the South Bank.

Forest, all together in their own section in the ground, decided to get brave and let their team in the dressing room know they were there. A chant of 'Forest! Forest! Forest!' went up. That was it. All the West Ham in the visiting enclosure gave 'em a tunnel death, all the way to the front of the pitch. They were literally diving into 'em. The Old Bill had no control, because they hadn't been prepared for any West Ham to be in that part of the ground and with West Ham steaming in from all angles they weren't going to get any.

People were getting chucked out on to the pitch as Forest were getting forced out. They tried running on to the pitch, but the Old Bill put them back. However, within five minutes West Ham had steamed them all back on to the pitch again. This time it was like an avalanche. At first, it started with a few and then quickly become the entire Forest travelling support clambering to seek safety on the pitch. A loud cheer went up from the crowd. This was followed by laughter as four guys from the Chicken Run East enclosure ran across the pitch, kicked and punched a few Forest, then ran all the way back to the Chicken Run.

The confidence of the Forest mob that had dared to show up at Upton Park began to evaporate. You could see the look of bewilderment on their faces. The Forest boys sort of looked at each other as if to say, 'What the fuck are we doing on the pitch? Do we have a go back at West Ham?' The West Ham lads on the South Bank were calling on Forest to come back for more, with their neck veins popping out, arms gesticulating wildly and faces full of venom. When it looked like West Ham were getting ready to follow Forest on to the pitch, Forest decided there and then that they had to get into a neutral part of the ground without a mob in it.

With survival their main thought, it was every Forest lad for himself. They ran over to the West side looking for sanctuary, only to find another West Ham mob, a skinhead mod revival called the West Side Boys. They surged towards the pitch, beckoning the Forest boys to come and join them. Forest backed off as the first few that had jumped in got slapped for their troubles. All eyes were on Forest as they all huddled together, stuck along the side of the pitch, under threat from both the West Side and South Bank. The North Bank also began to ring out chants of 'Come Up The North Bank', clap, clap, clap.

When the police found that the St John's Ambulance had treated several people for stab wounds, they decided the only real protection they could offer was to take Forest out of the ground for their own safety. As they were being shepherded out of the ground, their humiliation became complete when West Ham started singing the North's favourite song, usually sung when dreaming of going to Wembley. The old favourite, 'Que Sera, Sera', was adapted to: 'Why did you leave, you leave? At ten to three, o'three, Why did you leave, you leave?'

The last anyone ever saw of Forest at Upton Park was the sight of them all put back on the coaches, trains and sent packing back up the M1, all before the game had kicked off... see ya later, Forest.

Chapter 5

BRIGHTON RUCK

I.C.F.

We were down in the old Second Division with a fixture full of teams without mobs to fight. It really hit home when we had to endure going to games at the likes of Notts County, Palace, Fulham and Cambridge – we'll excuse Orient. But Brighton brought out a lot of interest, based purely on the strength of its location rather than on its reputation as a mob.

I don't know what it is about seaside towns and football supporters, but being by the sea always brings out the siege mentality in everyone. I suppose it's a tradition going back to the working-class roots of the English, but for most of us a day at the seaside conjures up thoughts of beanos, mods and rockers and birds in 'Kiss Me Quick' hats.

There's definitely a different buzz about, and all the ingredients are there to light the fuse. Every now and again one of these resorts would say, 'Enough is enough, we're fed up with invading supporters coming into town and taking the piss.' That's why on occasions fancied firms have been turned over. Seaside town clubs' fans were never really rated, because their firms were inconsistent. The locals often move out to find work and those who do work there are mainly outsiders anyway. But as I said, the ingredients are all there and it's not unheard of for mobs to come unstuck at the likes of Brighton, Southend and Blackpool. All too often things escalate, and before you know it, you've got a riot on your hands.

A riot is more than just a bit of aggro. Surprisingly, there haven't been too many football riots, but it would be interesting to see how many soccer riots involved a seaside resort. My guess is that it would be half of them.

The difficulty for a seaside resort fixture is for the police to gauge how many supporters are expected to turn up. You can't calculate it on what the current away teams' travelling support figures are and neither can you control it by making the game all-ticket. The resort alone will have enough attractions and alternative sources of entertainment for supporters not to worry about whether they've got tickets or not.

The Old Bill will have problems because there's more than one firm out and those firms will be swelled by more than the usual amount of nutters. As the two songs go, 'The Boys are Back in Town' and 'Saturday Night's Alright for Fighting'. Jimmy Smith recalls a Friday night in 1978, the night of the Brighton riot:

Brighton away was a game we all looked forward to when we saw the fixtures in our first season down in Division Two. Everyone had the idea of going to Brighton on a Friday night. I came home from work as soon as I could and headed straight to my nan's. I got there about 5 o'clock and two of my mates were already waiting, including one pal who had a brother doing life for murder. He said, 'C'mon, we'll go tonight.' It was October 28th, it would hardly be a summer's night down there. When we got to Victoria I was really surprised to find at least 200 West Ham all on the first train out. I thought then we could be on to a decent weekend in Brighton.

We were a right cheerful crowd walking out of Brighton station to see where we were going to have the first drink. We walked past this pub, The Bosun, and as we got past it bottles and glasses came flying out at us. Brighton must have expected us. We tried to dodge the bottles and get at them. Someone took a crate of milk bottles from outside a shop and as the Brighton mob came out we aimed an avalanche of glass at them. Within ten minutes of what was a decent row the Old Bill came along and we ended up walking off down to the seafront. By the end of the night the mob that was originally 200 strong must have been nearer a thousand. That was no exaggeration, because 150 of them were later to get arrested.

Our next port of call was an Indian restaurant. About ten of us went in, ordered a big meal, drinks, you name it, then walked out without paying. We even remembered to thank the bloke on the way out. By now we were ready to go back to The Bosun and this time we were tooled up. The difficulty of trying to attack this pub is that it's up on a hill at the top of really steep steps. So we did the same thing again, got the milk bottles and aimed them. Just like before, we had a ten-minute killing match, which was a great fight but no joy, as West Ham couldn't say they had it all their own way. Locals were involved in this thing and I think Brighton had some real bad bastards in town that night.

As Brighton filled up with more and more Londoners, a real bad atmosphere came over the town; the mood was definitely ugly. No fucking guest houses would entertain us. At 1 o'clock in the morning we tried to get into a nightclub. We kicked the fuck out of anybody who walked in there, then we attacked the bouncers.

Moving on now.

Some geezer I'd never seen before at West Ham latched on to us. He had a West Ham scarf hanging off his wrist and a swastika tattooed on his forehead. Now he's into ordering us around. He definitely wasn't one of us, I thought he'd escaped from St Clements hospital for the night. He came over to us and said, 'You lot are going to go in that pub over there and wreck it.' I couldn't believe it, nobody had ever seen this geezer before that night. Livid, I said to him that if he didn't fuck off I would cut his throat... later this loon was one of the first people to be nicked and never seen again.

My balls were freezing. It was three in the morning and we were down the seafront. We'd all had a right drink and were hungry, but Brighton was closed, no food places open, nothing. A couple of the Under Fives had the idea of breaking into a café. They came out with box upon box of frozen burgers. I don't think they gave it a thought that nobody had a cooker or microwave on 'em. So one of the young 'uns said, 'Don't worry about that... there's a little boat on the beach.' The boat must have had a gallon of fuel aboard, because he set it alight. From being pissed, cold and hungry we've now got a flaming barbecue! Great.

Next thing, a copper comes along who looked like he was only a couple of days off his retirement. There were about sixty of us spread on the beach enjoying the barbecue, sat there holding our burgers on bits of stick. The old copper took a good look around. Now he's seething. 'Fucking bastards coming down from London and wrecking the place.' Nobody took any notice, we just carried on munching our burgers. But when he started to get on his radio, we quickly finished our meal and fucked off in all directions.

The barbie on the beach actually made a big headline in the Sunday papers. One headline read: 'West Ham supporters set light to a yacht.' Now, if that boat was a yacht, then it probably only needed two paddles to row it. But if the headlines were exaggerated, the events of that night weren't. Some nasty things happened that night. It was inevitable when you had a thousand young men down for a football match with nowhere to stay and nowhere open.

After escaping Old Bill's attentions on the beach, we were later to be caught and trapped by the police down a subway after another fracas. About a hundred West Ham became trapped, but three of us managed to slip out. It was well into the wee hours before we at last found somewhere to crash out. We met a bird and bloke who were local, and for some unknown reason they offered us the use of their flat on the seafront. Needless to say, we showed our appreciation of their generosity by guzzling the spirits cabinet dry and trashing the flat. The bloke was so pissed he was half joining in while the bird, who we all thought was a bit odd, was going mental. In fact, she was like a fucking animal.

As for the match itself, there were thousands upon thousands of West Ham supporters in the Brighton ground. It went off in one end, but we couldn't get in there. Brighton was another one of those grounds where you could walk all the way round, but the police had it cordoned off. There must have been a couple of hundred West Ham in the Brighton end and there were running battles throughout the match, but the rest of us couldn't get anywhere near it. So when we got the first train out of Brighton and were back in London we went and had a drink around Kings Cross. There were about twenty of us looking to see if there were any other teams about. Brighton had been such an exhausting experience we must have been home and back in our beds by 11 o'clock!

Woolwich backs up Smith's account in his own account of just how mental that day was down at Brighton:

> *We had gone down to Brighton like everyone else on the Friday night. There were about thirty of our crowd, all seventeen to nineteen years of age, who'd thought we'd have a laugh until we went to the match the next day. No one gave it a thought; it was the end of October and the coast was freezing. If that was no laughing matter, we had a nutter with us who would have had us on the beach at 5 a.m. doing training for the day ahead. He was a character who probably couldn't even name the team, he'd be there purely for the day's events. He wouldn't drink or anything, he just wanted to go for the row and to be the best.*
>
> *We terrorised the whole town both Friday and Saturday, there was West Ham everywhere. I remember thinking, 'Where's our nutty mate?' when all these Brighton blokes came out of a pub, proper geezers in their mid-twenties. I don't think any of them were Brighton's firm, more like locals who supported everyone like Man United and Chelsea. They came across the road at us, and, being West Ham, we just steamed into them. They ran back into the pub, then the whole boozer emptied, tooled up with pool cues and weapons to run us down to the seafront.*
>
> *People think Brighton and laugh when you tell 'em about it, but back then it was a period when every town with a football club had their boys. Brighton was a big game.*

The Brighton match was always going to be marked by a siege mentality. As much as the boys liked to think we were a cut above firms like Chelsea and Man U's Red Army, when it came to conducting our business, we couldn't say that about the Brighton affair. Not even those involved can control a riot, there's just too many people involved, each with their own agenda. It's interesting to learn what the better-known faces among us were up to that weekend. Brett Tidman takes up the story:

Quite a few West Ham went down on the Friday night and created bedlam. Some had nowhere to kip, others had been thrown out the hotel for fighting, so they were all on the beach, sleeping underneath the fishing boats. We heard all the stories when we got there after driving down on the Saturday morning of the match. Stories of a few rows, people being set about, boats being burned. It all carried on around the ground, but [there was] another little story [about what] occurred on the way back.

A few of the boys suggested going to Tonbridge. Why Tonbridge, a Kent town with no proper football team? Because: 'It's a nice little place to have a beer, it's out of the way and, you know, "Chelsea" Hickey should be there. It's his local.'

This was one of those little scores that needed settling. Things had been brewing for a while with us and Chelsea. Although no longer in the same division, there had been more than the usual clashes in and around the Underground. The root of this personal feud went back to a West Ham supporter who lived in Tonbridge and got rather a lot of flak because of it. Some of the real heavy stuff came from Steven Hickmott's Chelsea following, who appeared to be the main firm out of Tonbridge. They had singled out this West Ham supporter, believing him to be some kind of mole. We bumped into Chelsea on the Tube and embarrassed them. They reckoned we only found them because of the Tonbridge Hammer. After that battle on the Tube, he got a right slapping in his home town. He decided to go back at them, so it was only right he had some back-up.

A good twenty of us were in a particular boozer in Tonbridge. We were getting a few beers in, ordering a pub sandwich or playing the one-armed bandit, when in he walked with a dozen Chelsea blokes. Nothing was said, it all went quiet as everyone looked at each other.

Hickey sat down with his pint among his Chelsea mates, then big fat Scoeby from the T.B.F. got up. He sat down next to Hickey, put his arm around him, giving him a good old squeeze, then leant over and said in his ear, 'Hello mate, we're here.' As he said that, everyone started cheering West Ham. There was a little scuffle and some running around the pub for a while. Someone said, 'Make 'em dance!'

One of the Chelsea mob went, 'I can't dance', which was not the thing to say, because back came a very serious reply: 'Fucking dance or get a dig.' One or two slaps and the Chelsea in Tonbridge were up dancing as our people clapped along. It was pitiful and one-sided, but there was a message in all of this. Some of the others with us came back into the pub after having a conference in the car park. There was one more final humiliation for the Chelsea backed up in their own boozer. Our mate Hickey was singled out after he said he couldn't dance any more. 'So do a little shuffle,' said West Ham. More whooping and cheering, as he did first a shuffle, then a sing-song.

It was becoming boring, so we just upped and left, satisfied that if Chelsea ever wanted to make things personal with West Ham, they knew how far we would go with it.

Chapter 6

COCKNEY REJECTS

– Oi! Oi! Oi!

I.C.F.

IN THE SEVENTIES, **football fans – so often the leaders of new trends and fashions – began following bands and brought mayhem to concert halls all over Britain. After the punk explosion of '77 – sparked by the Sex Pistols – the skinhead movement emerged again. Bands like The Specials from the Two Tone label, UB40 and Bad Manners, who played to the skinhead following, dominated the charts.**

They were quickly followed by the metal punk sound of Sham 69, with lad supreme Jimmy Pursey fronting up. Sham 69 were in tune with the terraces. They sported the fashionable green MA1 jackets we all wore and had a massive hit with 'Hurry Up Harry' – a song all about going down to the pub. Sham were the leaders of football music and young Hammers fans soon began to appear at their concerts all over the country. Some fans became very close to Sham and the bands that were springing up around them, and ended up working for them as unpaid roadies.

Trouble quickly followed. Fights broke out at concerts, sets were abandoned and concert halls wrecked. The press latched on to it and some record companies even considered dropping bands that were now finding it hard to get venues.

The bands appreciated the football following, but didn't share in some of the more right-wing political views. Some declared that they stood against racism and violence and performed at a series of rock against racism concerts around the country.

Fed up with the new political rantings of their heroes, the fans formed their own bands. The first and most successful were the Cockney Rejects, who had a Top Forty hit with a rocked-up version of 'I'm Forever Blowing Bubbles'.

The Cockney Rejects are well remembered over Upton Park, because they were West Ham. Going to the Rejects' gigs was better than buying their records.

The story of how the football terrace circles moved into the music industry is best told by three people. A music journalist, Garry Bushell, a fan, Lol Prior, and a band member, Vince Riordan.

It's a little-known fact that *Sunday People* TV columnist and Charlton fan Garry Bushell was closely involved with the launch of the Cockney Rejects. Here's how he remembers knocking up with the band:

I didn't discover the Cockney Rejects – they found me – and I got roped in to being their first manager. Mick Geggus and his brother Jeff tracked me down to the White Lion pub in London's Covent Garden. They burst in looking like refugees from Fagin's urchin gang, covered in West Ham United badges, and thrust a cheap demo tape of their song 'Police Car' into my hands. It was a revelation. 'Freedom?' Stinky hollered. 'There ain't no fuckin' freedom'. And the band kicked in – raw, wild, brutal, exciting… and as welcome as opening time.

It was May 1979 and the first wave of punk had gone pear-shaped. The New Wave had become the new Establishment. We had a Top Ten full of Tubeway Army, disco queens and The Boomtown Prats – dramas, charmers, and men in pyjamas. And ours was not to reason why, ours was just to clap and buy…

For punk writers like me and Dave 'Dave Angry' McCullough, it seemed like the hippies were taking over again. Even John Lydon was playing the prat on Juke Box Jury. *And all 'the stars', 'our heroes', the 'kids off the streets', all turned out to be phoney baloneys. Billy Idol was telling the* Daily Mirror *about his nice middle-class upbringing. The working class can kiss my arse, I've got the pop star job at last. No wonder Mickey Geggus felt betrayed. But the Rejects stood for something different, a New Punk. In the East End, as in South Shields with the Angelic Upstarts, the spirit was coming back…*

The Cockney Rejects were the real deal, dockers' sons whose songs were about East End life, boozers, battles, police harassment and football. I put them in touch with Jimmy Pursey, who produced their Small Wonder debut EP 'Flares and Slippers'. It sold surprisingly well and earned them the NME *epithet of the 'brainstorming vanguard of the East End punk renewal'. The music was tough and hard, a right kick up the Khyber. 'But that's what punk should be,' Mickey exploded. 'It should be bands like us. It should be raucous and a fuckin' big shout and a bang in the mouth.'*

Rejects only emerged as a real group after council painter Mickey recruited twenty-one-year-old Vince Riordan as bassist in 1979. Previously a Sham roadie, Vince (whose uncle was Jack 'The Hat' McVitie) looked as though he had spent his early years on Alcatraz eating gorillas for breakfast. He was also witty and drank as fast as Mick talked. Drummers were to come and go with the regularity of a high-fibre diet until Stix transferred from the Upstarts in 1980.

Live, the band hit like a mob of rampaging rhinos, with Mickey's sledgehammer guitar the cornerstone of their tough, tuneful onslaught. Gap-toothed schoolboy Stinky was a sight for sore eyes too, screwing up his visage into veritable orgies of ugliness, and straining his tonsils to holler vocals best likened to a right evil racket.

Their second EMI single, 'Badman', was superb, like PIL on steroids, but it only made the fag-end of the charts. Their next release, a piss-take of Sham called 'The Greatest Cockney Rip-Off' did better, denting the Top Thirty. Their debut album Greatest Hits Volume 1 *did the same, notching up over 60,000 sales.*

The Rejects' first following wasn't largely skinhead; in fact, at first skins didn't like them. The Rejects' crew came from football and consisted largely of West Ham chaps attracted by Vince's involvement, and disillusioned Sham and Menace fans. Famous faces included Gary Dickle, Johnny Butler, Carlton Leach, Andy Russell, Andy Swallow, Gary Hodges, Hoxton Tom (who was Spurs), Binnsy, H and Wellsy. Even as early as November 1979, their Hammers support was so strong that mass terrace chants of 'Cockney Rejects, Oi! Oi! were clearly audible on televised soccer matches – to the tune of Gary Glitter's 'Hello! Hello! I'm Back Again'.

Many of the East End Glory Boys swelled their ranks a little later, realising for the first time that here was a band exactly the same as them.

The first stand-alone Oi! scene developed around the Cockney Rejects and their regular gig venue, the Bridge House in Canning Town, East London. It became the focus for an entire subculture. In 1980, this was the LIFE!

None of these faces were 'Nazis'. Most of them weren't political at all, beyond the sense of voting Labour (if they bothered to vote at all) out of tradition. A tiny percentage were interested in the extremes of either right or left. As a breed they were natural conservatives. They believed in standing on their own two feet. They were patriotic, and proud of their class and their immediate culture. They looked good and dressed sharp. It was important not to look like a scruff or a student. Their heroes were boxers and footballers, not union leaders. The West Ham I.C.F. were fully represented at most local Rejects gigs.

Outside of London, football trouble was their undoing. They would deck the stage out with a huge red banner displaying the Union Jack, the West Ham crossed hammers and the motif 'West Side' (which was that part of the West Ham ground then most favoured by the Irons' most violent fans). Their second hit was a version of the West Ham anthem 'Bubbles', which charted in the run-up to West Ham's Cup Final victory in the early summer of 1980. On the B-side was the I.C.F.-pleasing 'West Side Boys'.

It was a red rag to testosterone-charged bulls all over the country. At North London's Electric Ballroom, 200 of West Ham's finest mob charged less than fifty Arsenal and smacked them clean out of the venue. But ultra-violence at a Birmingham gig really spelt their undoing. The audience at the Cedar Club was swelled by a mob of Birmingham City skinheads who terrace-chanted throughout the support set from the Kidz Next Door (featuring Grant Fleming, now a left-wing filmmaker, and Pursey's kid brother Robbie). Grant Fleming, a veteran of such notorious riots as Sham at Hendon and Madness at Hatfield, described the night's violence as the worst he'd ever seen.

Brum had meant the end of the Rejects as a touring band. However the band's second LP called, surprisingly enough, Greatest Hits Volume 2, *reflected their apparent death wish with sleeve notes boasting*

'From Scotland down to Cornwall, we dun the lot, we took 'em all.'

On the song 'Urban Guerrilla' they spoke these words: 'Some folk call it anarchy but I just call it fun. Don't give a fuck about the law. I wanna kill someone.' Me? I think he meant it.

But the fuse they and fellow bands like The Upstarts lit was to inspire a whole new scene. Bands as different as The Exploited, Blitx, The Business and Splodge became part of the movement they spawned. I called it Oi! It is still going today.

* * * * *

Lol Prior was born of working-class parents living near Millwall Football ground, but he went against his father's advice and supported his mother's East End team – West Ham. It wasn't hard. Lol was six years old and West Ham had just won the FA Cup. He says he has suffered ever since for his loyalty to the Hammers.

The other love of his life is the music scene. He's forty-two now and still involved in it, running Harry May & Link Music record company, which revives music of the Oi! movement of the early Eighties. Lol recalls where it started for him:

I remember the original punk scene in 1976–77. Although I went to live gigs to watch punk bands like the Buzzcocks, I just thought it was all trendy middle-class pretence. I didn't feel part of it. Then a couple of years later I heard and saw bands like Cock Sparrer and Menace. Now instead of punk bands like The Clash and their famous 'Sten Guns in Kensington' slogan, we had the real voices of angry youth singing about trouble on the terraces. So much anger and energy.

Then Cockney Sparrer's track 'Running Riot' came out. On the sleeve was a picture of a football riot involving Man United fans. A cover like that seemed to me to be more what punk was really about than bands singing about guns in Kensington or problems in Nicaragua. That was the first of what was later to become Oi! – a genuine working-class punk movement. That Running Riot picture sleeve is now worth about two hundred quid today!

Cockney Sparrer were the first terrace band I knew – Colin McPaul, singer; Steve Burgess, bass; Micky Boothby and Spider on drums and Gary Lamming, guitarist – he later became an actor. These lads were all from Bow in East London. They were signed to Decca, had two records that did nothing before moving to a major label in France. Eventually they ended up with my label, Link Music. I remember a classic live gig in '78 or '79 when they played the Tidal Basin in Canning Town. At the end, the whole audience were singing and chanting 'We hate Millwall!' Even the bouncers on the stage were joining in. There were only about 200 people there but the atmosphere they generated was electric. It was around the time everybody was moving away from punk fashion with its pins and mohicans into Harringtons, green bomber jackets and going back to a boot boy look. Everyone was turning up in Doc Martens and Fred Perry shirts.

The boys on the terraces were into going to gigs. The West Ham boys took to Sham 69, particularly after they played The Roxy singing about George Davis – an East End bank robber. Sham had a famous phrase – 'The East End is all around'. It didn't matter whether you came from – a council estate in Hersham in Surrey, like they did, or a council estate in Bow – you were still a council estate kid.

The East End connection following Sham around led to the arrival of the Rejects on the music scene. The Rejects' guitarist Vince Riordan was a West Ham face and soon Swallow, Grant and all the boys were going to their gigs.

* * * * *

Vince Riordan was born in West Ham and first began going to West Ham's matches with his sister. They'd stand up by the rafters at the back of the North Bank, where they could only ever see three-quarters of the pitch because the North Bank roof obscured the South Bank goal. This is Vince's story:

By my early teens, my pal Johnny Page and me would be going to Upton Park on our own. There was always a lot of bovver in those days and we'd watch Joey Williams, Bill Gardner and all of the rest of the Upton Park Mafia, as they were known then, going into the

South Bank and kicking off.

We used to walk behind them to Upton Park station and watch them fighting on the trains. Eventually we joined in. I remember one great big ruck with Wolves fans in the South Bank. From then on, everybody stood in the South Bank end to watch or take part in fighting with away supporters. I loved my football-going days, they were great days.

Going to away matches was how I got into music. Me and a mate Gary were going out with a couple of girls from Coventry. On most away matches we'd stay in Coventry on the Friday night and we'd go to a club called Mr George's and see bands like XTC. One night the Pistols were there on a SPOTS tour – Sex Pistols on the Stage.

From then on we'd travel down the motorway from away games and stop off on the way to check out bands. After seeing Sham 69 three times, I ended up as a roadie.

Although they were from Surrey and not the East End, they did brilliant stuff like 'George Davis' [and] 'Borstal Breakout'. Maybe the 'George Davis' song was the link with the East End, but loads of West Ham started turning up at their gigs, acting as the band's unpaid security. Trouble followed them everywhere. One gig, in Hendon College, went off proper and turned into a riot, with cars turned over in the streets outside.

I went from roadie to being a band member after a five-a-side tournament in Leysdown, Kent. A geezer came up and asked me if I wanted to be in his band. It was Mickey Geggus. He knew me from Sham.

A week later I was in the Cockney Rejects. The band had been formed by Mickey's brother Jeff Stinky. The brothers came from Custom House and supported West Ham. I'd never played a guitar in my life – I'd only ever handled one while tuning up and sound-testing for Sham. But I became the bass player. I just thought, one finger up and down – here we go. A fortnight later I was signed to EMI on a five-album deal! We were singing street songs: 'I'm Not A Fool', 'East End Bad Man' and we kept on going to West Ham until we started touring.

Things started quietly enough and then in 1980 we released our single 'War on the Terraces'. We wanted a picture of the battle with Millwall at Upton Park on the record sleeve but EMI bottled it – they thought it was going a bit too far. Later that year we released 'Bubbles' – it was massive. It was the rock alternative to the football club's official version for the club's victorious appearance at the 1980 FA Cup Final, where we beat Arsenal 1-0. And, would you believe it, Trevor Brooking scored with his head.

Originally, Iron Maiden's Steve Harris – a big Hammers fan – suggested we could do it together with them. We were both with EMI, so it made some sense. But we'd always wanted to do 'Bubbles', so we said 'Bollocks, we're doing it.' There was a bit of an argument. Steve weren't too happy, but we ended up getting our own way.

The B-side was 'West Side Boys', a right football thuggery song with these lyrics:

'Steel toe-cap Dr Martens and iron bars,
Smash the coaches, do 'em in the cars.'
Come on:
'We've got the North Bank,
We've got 'em in the South Bank,
We're the West Side Upton Park!
West Side Boys! West Side Boys!'

That year everything was claret and blue and our A-side, 'I'm Forever Blowing Bubbles', was a big hit. We were back on Top of the Pops *– but that's when our troubles started.*

Straight after we beat Arsenal we went on tour around the country, playing proper venues with a hit single that was a West Ham song. As soon as we went north people were waiting for us. We were playing Liverpool and the local Echo paper printed [the fact] that we were bringing four coachloads of West Ham supporters with us. We had to have a police escort from the hotel to the gig at a club called Eric's.

I was in my room at the Holiday Inn getting ready when two West Ham lads – Danny Meakin, from East Ham and Kevin Wells from Grays – who were working as roadies burst in. A huge gang of Liverpool and Everton supporters had given Danny a good hiding in the hotel foyer. I charged downstairs with Wellsy. Forty geezers milled about outside the hotel, screaming for our blood.

We stayed inside and a geezer we didn't see slipped up the side of us. He was after my bomber jacket. He spat:

'Gizz yer fucking fly, you Cockney bastard.' I'm standing staring out this Scouser as another one lunges at Kevin with a Stanley knife. It missed his face by half an inch. I caught the Scouser with a couple as he ran past. Just as I was doing him, the management walks in, calls the cops and the band ended up with a police escort.

We walked into the gig to meet a wall of Everton shirts – it was all the geezers from the hotel waiting for us. A six-foot high metal barrier divided the stage from the audience. A collection of off-duty Old Bill armed with pool cues and baseball bats were the security for the night.

We opened with 'Badman' and did three more songs before it all kicked off. A bottle hurled from the crowd showered the band with glass. Mickey leapt on top of the barrier, waving his guitar above his head and brought it down with a smash on a head in the crowd. It kicked off proper, then.

A huge lump of a security guard dragged us off stage. Then the security threatened to do us if we went back on and played. We were left backstage – going 'Bollocks' and abusing everyone in sight: 'Fuck off you Scouse cunts! Come and have some if you want some!'

A couple of nights later we were playing the Cedar Ballroom in Birmingham. Word of the trouble in Liverpool spread like wildfire and a few of the boys came up – Dickle, Swallow, Brett, Bruce and a few good lads were along then. We were playing to 2,000 – even Dexy's Midnight Runners had come to see us. Our record company advised us to drop 'Bubbles' from the set to avoid inciting any more trouble. But we had other songs that were just as bad – 'West Side Boys', 'We Are the Firm', 'War on the Terraces'.

As we were playing, I saw a guy from the crowd trying to hurl a glass at our singer Jeff, alias Stinky Turner. I watched him coming round the side of the stage to launch it. As he approached I took off my nine-hundred-quid Thunderbird Gibson guitar and smashed this geezer right over the head with it.

The whole place erupted. That was it, glasses and ashtrays came from all directions. We all piled into this mob of about 200 Birmingham City supporting skinheads who had been giving me the abuse at the front of the stage. People were getting proper hurt, the marble dance floor was red from blood. Although outnumbered more than ten to one, together with all our entourage we drove the Brummie mob right across the hall, and finally out of it altogether. In under half an hour of mayhem we had mullared the whole hall. We weren't finished – the missile attack back in that hall left Jeff's eye and the side of his face pouring with blood and his brother Mickey sustained a head injury that needed nine stitches, leaving him with what looked like a Fred Perry design above his right eye.

We left Mickey at the local hospital for treatment while we got back in the crew van and drove around, jumping out on every skinhead we saw. Meanwhile, Geggus had to bunk out of a twenty-foot high window after tooled-up mates of the injured Brummy lot came looking for him.

We all met back at the gig from all the fighting to discover all our gear and equipment – total value, two grand – had been ripped off.

The next morning our contingent split into two vans – one went on to the next gig at Huddersfield, leaving the rest of us to go cruising round the city looking for the bastards who might know the whereabouts of our stolen gear. Along Wolverhampton Road, we spotted a big gang of Birmingham fans riding out of the town centre on scooters. We jumped out of the motors and hurt 'em proper. We forgot all about it. A month later I was lying in bed in a hotel in Northampton when all these coppers kicked the door in. We didn't know what was going on until the Old Bill took the whole band back to Birmingham and we were charged with GBH. It got splashed across all the papers, but we came through and we were still making albums.

Our live gigs were a battleground. In the end, we were banned from playing on the college circuit and from every Odeon in the country.

Another bad day at the office was at the Electric Ballroom in Camden, north London. We'd played there before, but this night was murder – all the I.C.F. were up. Trouble started at the back of the hall and spread like wildfire. Pure football violence – Arsenal v West Ham. More bad publicity – the Rejects at it again! This time the former GLC put a ban on us. Now we couldn't play in London or up north after problems in Leeds and Huddersfield.

The Huddersfield gig was in a black club called

Cleopatra's. The doormen were black and they were so worried about trouble from skinheads that they asked if our roadies would do the door. Carlton Leach went down to see what the problem was. He said, 'Fuck 'em – just do 'em.' And that's what he did to Huddersfield's skins.

In Leeds, the skins were into the heavy 'Sieg Heil!' stuff. We knew they were all talking bollocks and it was more a case of copycat syndrome – but these were the times and some places were heavy into that scene. The media said we attracted that sort of crowd, and so that was another town we were banned from.

Another time we turned up at a club in Plymouth, which during the day was a boxing gym. A bunch of guys were sparring as we arrived with our roadies to start setting up. Unknown to all these lot, Jeff Stinky and his brother Mickey had boxed for West Ham in their youth. In fact, Jeff was good enough to have fought in the ring for England.

Jeff, who isn't a big fella, stepped up and said, 'I'll spar with you, mate.' Seconds later, blam!, blam! blam! He tore the geezer apart. The locals weren't happy. It turns out Jeff has just beaten the head doorman!

As we got off stage after the gig, I was in the dressing room when Mickey came flying through the door and stood behind me as all the club doormen stormed in. As I held up my fists, I thought, fuck me what have you done?

These eight bouncers wanted nothing with me. They said, 'It's the little guy behind you we want.'

I was first off stage and I didn't know one of the

doormen had pulled Mickey and snarled, 'You're gonna get it outside.'

Mickey stepped forward and dropped him with a punch. He fell where he stood. He lay there choking on his tongue. So now, as the rest of the bouncers were about to set on me and Mickey, the guv'nor of the club walked in.

Outside the dressing room, he'd stepped over the geezer on the floor still trying to get his tongue out of his throat. The boss pointed at his blokes and said, 'You must be fucking joking. He's just done that to your top boy.'

He ordered everyone out and walked back out, stepping over the bouncer still struggling on the ground!

Unable to find a venue willing to risk [having us], we looked abroad, but skinheads reared up again in Germany. German skinheads sporting West Ham shirts started turning up at our gigs, thinking we were a skinhead band. We played the Black Theatre in Paris and after just three songs a riot broke out. The house lights went up, we were dragged off stage and told we weren't playing again. 'Who the fuck says so?' we asked. 'The CRS', came the reply. 'Who's the fucking CRS?'

We looked out of the window, saw dozens of blokes carrying long truncheons and rifles pointed at the crowd. The CRS – France's elite riot squad – simply escorted everyone out of the theatre. The band had played no part in that riot. The crowd, a mixture of Euro skins, punks and no dress sense, had kicked off among themselves.

Berlin was the same. We played a club as a favour to the owner – totally unannounced – and trouble still kicked off – the four band members against the whole audience. It had started with the German skinheads. We didn't like their attitude. It wasn't what the band was about. They had heard about the band's reputation, read about our football scene, so came along thinking we'd approve of what they were about.

It was the sort of hassle that disillusioned Jimmy Pursey and led him to break up Sham 69. I now understand why Pursey just quit. Me and Mickey would go into pubs, people would look at yer and go, 'Well you're supposed to be on our side. You're supposed to be right... or left.' I'd reply, 'No we just go to football.' The publicity became a monster. We wanted to keep politics out of football. The Cockney Rejects was how we lived our lives. East End and football.

A lot of fans related to our music because the East End was in every town, from Liverpool to Portsmouth. We all lived downtown.

Unlike a lot of pretentious uptown art college punk bands, we made records that were true to the life we actually experienced in the street.

Lol Prior agrees:

The Rejects really got up the music industry's noses. Unlike Sham and the other bands before them, they didn't have to suffer what I'd call the West London music industry bollocks.

Because of Garry Bushell's connections as Features Editor on Sounds *magazine, and because they'd already had a minor hit, 'Flares and Slippers', on an Indie label, they walked straight into a deal with a major record label – EMI. What made them interesting was that they didn't have to compromise. Here were four East London geezers who thought, fuck you, we're going to play this, we're going to do our own songs.*

If you think of some of their songs like 'Shitter', 'Are You Ready to Ruck?', 'Running Down the Back Streets' – I think nearly every song is about doing somebody!

As a band I think they were important for their uncompromising attitude to the industry about [staying true to] their music. The other thing I admired was that they weren't scared to nail their West Ham colours to the mast. They played on Top of the Pops in their claret and blue. Crossed hammers were everywhere and people who weren't West Ham supporters were buying the 'Bubbles' single.

I believe that was the start of so many people around the world supporting West Ham.

Lol looks at the other bands that were spawned by West Ham:

West Ham – or more likely the I.C.F. – had actually influenced the punk movement, which is now one of the biggest music scenes in the world, although living in the UK that's sometimes very, very hard to believe. What's really strange is that there can be no sporting team, let alone [a following of] *notorious fans, who have had such an influence on a style of music.*

SKREWDRIVER: *To the best of my knowledge they didn't include any West Ham fans. Although in their original (pre way out, right-wing) days, they did have a sizeable West Ham skin following.*

THE 4-SKINS: *Strange as it may seem, The 4-Skins have probably sold more records around the world than the Rejects... mainly due to the band's notorious reputation, which was only enhanced by the July 1981 Southall Hamborough Tavern gig, which resulted in the Southhall riots. The gig also featured The Business and The Last Resort, although it was The 4-Skins who seemed to get the blame. They broke up after three albums and never 'sold out' or moved on to other musical styles like the Rejects or the Upstarts. The West Ham connection was that Scully had been their original manager and Gary Hodges was a well-known 'character' over Upton Park. Their entourage and hardcore following included loads of West Ham. So much so that many other teams' fans decided to give their Bridgehouse gigs a miss!*

COCK SPARRER: *These boys were really the ones who set off the whole street punk (i.e. working-class punk, unlike The Clash and the Buzzcocks) movement before Garry Bushell christened it 'Oi!' after the Rejects song 'Oi! Oi! Oi!'.*

The band were all from East London and unashamedly West Ham fans, when it wasn't trendy to mix music and football. They were also about before Sham 69! There are famous pictures of them being photographed outside and inside West Ham's ground, which even included them deliberately posing around a lamppost outside Upton Park [that featured] *the graffiti 'DAF Rule East London'. That proved they were real West Ham, as at the time only certain people would have known DAF stood for Dodgy Area Firm.*

They even used footage of West Ham fans at the 1975 FA Cup final in their 1977 video for their Decca Records single 'We Love You'. They also had pictures of Hammers fans rioting on the cover of their 1979 'Runnin' Riot' single. Their 1984 Syndicate Records album sleeve pictured crowd violence at the 1979 West Ham v Millwall match at Upton Park. Their huge West Ham following included people like Terry Hayes, Terry Adams, Barney Rubble and the Ancient Brit crew.

THE BUSINESS: *They are probably the biggest UK band to have come out of this scene and are now signed to the world's biggest Indie record company, Epitaph Records. Their last two records, on Indie USA label Taang! Records have now sold over 250,000 in the USA alone. They are one of Epitaph's priority acts and will probably sell 10,000 copies of their new album over here in the UK! Their influence on the Oi!/punk scene cannot be overstated. One American mag described them as 'the most significant Oi! street punk band ever* *to come out of England' and as the 'most crucial Oi! band'.*

Strangely enough, only vocalist Micky Fitz is a West Ham fan. But the band has always had West Ham connections through managers, roadies and labels, plus their entourage which, at times, has included people like Pompey, Lanky Paul, Lewisham, Bear, Scully and others.

For ten years Micky Fitz made a habit of wearing a West Ham shirt every time he played. The band's Business Crew merchandise logo includes a crossed hammer over a London skyline and the words 'South London'. This logo must be on the back of 20,000 kids in the USA. And at any Business gig in the USA and France or Germany there will always be a large number of people sporting West Ham colours!

THE LAST RESORT: *Although The Last Resort is known as a Millwall band, mainly due to vocalist and Lions face Roi Pearce, the original singer was Saxby from Herne Bay, who still frequents Upton Park to this day. Since The Last Resort split up, former members still tour and release records as The Warriors in USA, Japan and Europe. Saxby is The Warriors' vocalist and still wears a West Ham shirt on stage wherever they play. Unfortunately, bassist Bilko also wears his Millwall top at the same time, which looks kind of odd.*

Bits and pieces:

It's [been] *rumoured that Harley from one of America's top Hardcore bands – that's an American heavy punk sound not unlike British Oi! – 'nicked' the crossed-hammers I.C.F. logo he saw on a visit to London back in the late Seventies to invent the now world-famous New York Hardcore cross. Steve Whale from The Business recently asked Harley if this was true… and he confirmed it!*

Scully and Terry Hayes were in a short-lived Oi! band called The East End Baddoes, who did manage to frighten the lives out of a London punk band while supporting The Business at Skunx. Their track 'The Way It's Got To Be' was featured on the Top 50 Secret Records album Oi! Oi! That's Your Lot. The album also featured the track 'Fight For Your Lives' by Angela Rippon's Bum, who had Tilbury's own Tony 'Boozy' Barker on vocals and the Tilbury West Ham firm in support wherever they played. The record's inner sleeve featured a picture of The Britannia Disco Groovers featuring Carlton Leach, Paul Dorset, Johnny Butler and Gary Dickle in their West Ham United T-shirts!

At one time, Grant Fleming had been in Kidz Next Door – who I think were signed to EMI – and also featured Jimmy Pursey's brother. They supported the Rejects on one of their major troublesome tours. Grant also recorded some tracks with Rejects guitarist Mickey Geggus as the Terrible Twins. One of their tracks, 'Generation of Scars', appeared on the now-legendary first Oi! album on EMI, Oi! The Album. Obviously, Grant and Gary Dickle featured on Sham 69's second album, That's Life, as well as appearing in the BBC2 Arena TV special, which in effect brought the album to life on film.

Cockney Rejects hit list

Singles	Top 75 Chart Position	Release Date
'I'm Not a Fool'	65	Dec 1979
'Badman'	65	Feb 1980
'The Greatest Cockney Rip-off'	21	Apr 1980
'I'm Forever Blowing Bubbles'	35	May 1980
'We Can Do Anything'	65	Jul 1980
'We Are the Firm'	54	Oct 1980
Albums Top 30		
Greatest Hits Volume 1	22	Mar 1980
Greatest Hits Volume 2	23	Oct 1980
Greatest Hits Volume 3 (Live and Loud)	27	Apr 1981
UK Indie Singles Chart		
'Flares and Slippers'	24	Feb 1980
'Til the End of The Day'	25	Dec 1982
UK Indie Album Chart		
The Wild Ones	7	Sept 1982

Chapter 7

WHEN THE BOOT GOES IN

– War on Geordies

I.C.F.

MARCH 15, 1980. Newcastle away. That was the day the fuse was lit – literally – between West Ham and the Geordies. The day a Geordie bastard threw a bomb.

We were all bastards that day. We were used to being called Cockney bastards, but believe me, when the Geordies say it to yer, they mean it. Mind you, the thing with Geordies is that you could never understand what the hell they're saying anyway, especially when you hear 'em singing in the ground. The West Ham lads used to say that the Geordies were Jocks with the shit knocked out of 'em, even going so far as to taunt them with the words 'Are you Scotland in disguise?' This could not be further than the truth, but we didn't care because it always got the Geordies going ape. Our fans would also refer to 'Boro and Sunderland supporters as Geordies, which would get all the North-East having a funny turn.

Until this match, it had never gone off between us and the Geordies on a scale worthy of a vendetta. In all fairness, they were one firm we had always given some amount of respect to. Over numerous seasons they would show up at our ground, sticking close to the police escort. They would stand up for themselves without ever truly calling it on. We used to infiltrate the Geordies in the South Bank, back along Green Street and along the Tube stops. Although they came down a few times, they were always pretty quiet at ours.

However, it was a different story when they went to the grounds of some of the other London clubs. They took far bigger numbers and would put it about a bit. Tottenham was always a fierce street battle with them, both before and after the match. We used to slip over Tottenham with Steve Morgan's South Bank crew as we got along with Spurs, or the Yids as they were known at the time, in the early 70s. The Jewish connection at Tottenham dates back to the sixties, when they won the double and were considered a rich and glamorous team. In the 70s and 80s, rival fans used the term anti-semitically; Arsenal, West Ham and Chelsea being the worst offenders. As the yobbo element of the clubs emerged in the 80s, they each had to have a name and the Tottenham yobs called themselves the Yids. The name stuck, and the fans named their team and their firm the Yids, a name that still stands today.

The Geordies also had respect in London when they used to come down for Wembley cup finals. They would come down on the Friday night and hang out in the West End, just like the Jocks would. The London lads would form various alliances and carefully pick the pubs to hit.

The one thing I could never get over with the Geordies was the size of 'em. They were pretty big lads, all seemingly living in a time warp. Long after the world had gone casual and started wearing designer labels, Geordie geezers could still be seen on open terraces sporting a threadbare faded jean jacket with badge patches sewn on or going to football matches in donkey jackets. As far as the Geordies were concerned, clothes and style were for southern poofs, along with our bottled lagers. Where else but Newcastle could you still get a brown ale, long after it had disappeared from our pubs? It flourished so much up there that they put it in special bottles and named it after themselves.

While they left themselves wide open to have the piss taken out of them, you couldn't deny the fact they were a game lot, as up for it as anyone. If fighting had been as high on their agenda as worshipping the team, getting another tattoo and drinking, they might have had their own shout as to who the number one firm in the country was.

For teams with half-decent mobs, it was a sad joke to be stuck in Division Two. The only two firms doing the business were Chelsea and Newcastle, and we had terrorised Chelsea all season for it. We had quite a travelling support now, so it was time to have a proper go at the Geordies at theirs. Now that would be something. None of this 'Put your scarf away in your pocket and just go up there to keep your mouth shut' rubbish, as many a Hammer had done in the past. If we were who we thought we were, then we had to take a mob to Geordie land. And we did.

There was no one in the firm that turned up at Kings Cross that morning to jump on the InterCity who wasn't up for getting involved, apart from two old ladies who would travel everywhere away covered in badges and old-fashioned rosettes. We were the advance party. The Geordie Old Bill weren't aware that West Ham were coming ahead on the inter-city train. A good 250 of us arrived at about 1 p.m. and began chasing off groups of Geordies hanging round the station. Loads of us had never been up there before, but we knew from those who had that there must be more Geordies than that.

By now the Old Bill were already on our case. The last thing that any of us wanted was to come all this way only to be rounded up and held somewhere or put in the ground with over two hours to kill before kick-off. In order to keep in front of the Old Bill before they had chance to call back-up to round us up, we did the usual thing of spreading on to both sides of the road and panning out into smaller groups, all the time keeping moving. This way the Old Bill couldn't contain us all or gain control. Each group would be in sight of each other or know that the other group were further up the road somewhere. Everyone recognises the sound of a row and if one group found themselves involved in one, they knew that the rest would soon be coming up behind them.

This was how it was for us. We could feel the buzz and adrenaline running through us, all cock-a-hoop from catching out the Geordies waiting for us at the station. We knew we'd caught the Old Bill on the hop; we were now on the Geordies' manor, and they knew it too. Sooner or later we all knew that we were going to find each other again.

Then we heard it. Just a small roar at first, and immediately we all went from a fast walk to a jog, then a trot, until running full pelt. It was going off somewhere up ahead and we were in pursuit. We were in front of most of ours, along with whatever Old Bill were in tow, just the right position to be able to do something before the Old Bill were on top if we were fast enough.

The roar was becoming louder. We had to get there fast. I turned a street corner with the rest of my group, lungs bursting, yelling and screaming as we ran after our own lot that had got ahead of us. We came across them attacking the Geordies' main boozer, The Geordie Pride. They had confronted the Geordies in the street and had run them back inside the pub. Everyone was oblivious to us turning up because they were already going at it hammer and tongs. I recognised Jono, Swal and Harrison in the crowd. There were no more than twenty and we had about the same number of people, with more coming.

The ones already there were attacking the pub doors and windows in a desperate attempt to get in, but they seemed focused on something preventing them from entering the pub. As I went to join the struggle I saw what the problem was. They sprang back and there was a fucking great big Geordie skinhead with a cropped, shaven head, dark Crombie, the lot. They still had skins up here. They were obviously having a pitched battle with the Geordies here and the big skin was all that was stopping them from doing the pub.

As I moved in along the side wall to the entrance, I saw why the others were steaming. The skin had a Bowie-sized sheath knife. All I had was a plastic carrier bag in my hand, which I had been holding on to since I got off the train. Harrison, Jono and the others glanced at me as I moved in, which made the skin do the same, but it was too late. I swung the carrier bag and the big Geordie buckled as it hit him – I think more out of fright than anything else, as they don't see too many black men up in those parts. I hit him again and he crashed on to the floor near the doorway floor, as the big Liebfraumilch bottle inside the carrier bag shattered...

The others didn't hesitate. They trampled all over the fallen skin as the Geordies that were behind him fled back to the bar and over the bar counter. They made a desperate attempt to resist by hurling beer glasses back at us, but by now we were inside the front of their pub, dishing it out. We knew the others had arrived too, because all the pub windows started to cave in from the outside.

Then, as always, a shout came from behind warning us that the Old Bill had arrived and everyone raced out of the pub and tried to slip down the street, looking innocent. The Old Bill weren't having any of it and rounded everyone up in an escort. They got a bit rough with us, but they didn't nick anyone. The Old Bill seemed pretty fair up there – they didn't appear to be interested in making arrests based on guesswork.

By now, everyone was full of themselves. Word began to pass through the ranks that we had done a main Geordie boozer full of their boys.

After the incident, in what seemed like no time at all most of the 200-odd that had come on the inter-city train had gathered outside the ground. The Old Bill had escorted us to the ground and then left us. This was a foolish thing to do, but I guess they had been assigned to different areas and the train with the main travelling support was also due in. With just the Old Bill who control the outside of the ground looking over us, we were basically left to our own devices.

Various groups then began splitting and going walkies in the hope of confronting more Geordies. We were on a roll. Most of us went around the ground a few times and everyone had little skirmishes to tell of, which – because the Old Bill was about – amounted to nothing more than giving people the odd slap. The most interesting tale came from the lads who had got to The Geordie Pride first, who claimed to have had a good little pop at another one of their boozers, The Strawberry. Later, the stories all got a bit confusing because everyone had a tale about doing a top Geordie pub. Whatever stories were flying around, the fact was that we'd taken liberties by even turning up at Newcastle that day and had hurt many a Geordie's pride in the process.

This wasn't the first time I'd been up to Newcastle. I had come up some five years before to see why the Geordies on their own manor were respected by Londoners. In retrospect, I was surprised that it had taken so long for me to come back again, but there always seemed to be some reason why we hadn't taken a good-sized mob before. On one occasion it was cup final week and, as with the previous season, we nearly always met Newcastle in a mid-week night match.

We decided to go inside the ground. I must admit, once I stepped inside St James's Park, I had to marvel just at the experience of being there. The atmosphere at that ground really is something else. The people are absolutely fanatical about Newcastle United Football Club, and about being Geordies, and you can feel their passion.

We were put into a corner section of the ground. To the left was a long-sided terrace with a half-covered roof, which I believe is called the Leazes Terrace. To our right was the area behind the goal, which had a long open end like the one behind the opposite goal at the big Gallowgate End. I looked around at our own support and counted around a thousand people, mainly from the firm, all crammed into this corner bank. We looked like a fucking army, as everyone seemed to be wearing these shiny green bombers. We looked a proper firm, but with Geordies crammed on all sides, the rest of the ground looked like the land of black and white.

We started chanting 'I.C.F., I.C.F.' repeatedly. It was like we had stirred something in the crowd and from then on it was all happening. Judging by the noise coming from the Geordies all round the ground, you would have thought we were playing a local derby. You could feel the passion and hate and it made the hairs on the back of your neck stand up. Forget what had happened earlier outside the ground. You just knew that before the day was out you'd be fighting the whole Geordie nation.

The whole ground shook with hostility. I even saw these Geordie nerds, characters that looked like the puppet Joe 90, taken out and dragged around the pitch, fighting and resisting all the way and spitting at us as they were dragged past our section. I looked at one guy and thought that there was no way he could be a football thug or one of us. He must have been a loopy student or something, but he was still so passionate about his team that he couldn't handle being taken out and missing the match before it had started. There he was, struggling away and giving it to the Old Bill like a pro.

I was standing alongside Bill Stokes, a seasoned campaigner – his mates always called him Mouthy Bill. He believed Newcastle was one of the worst grounds to go to. He had been a few times before and said he was glad we had taken some numbers with us. He remembers that day in the ground vividly:

Every now and again small groups of Geordies would somehow find a way of getting in to our section. The Geordies that tried were complete nutters, but we beat the crap out of them. One group that I remember clearly even came around in fancy dress, one wearing a lion suit and the other a cavalier's suit.

The situation became worse after the game started. Me and my mate Alfie Barker stood and watched as the Geordies threw a dart over into our section. Someone picked it up and threw it back, hitting a Geordie in the head. You can imagine what everyone shouted out next… 'One hundred and eighty.'

Soon after the dart was chucked back, we saw what looked like a box of matches that had been set alight, only bigger, spinning over us. At first I thought it was just lighted rags, but as it smashed just in front of me, flames flared up instantly from blacked, broken glass. Everyone ducked and it caught this geezer's trousers on fire. He ran to the back as if to get out of the ground. I managed to drag him down as everyone started to pat him out in an effort to put out the flames. The poor chap's shirt was catching alight because of the petrol, but we patted it all out in the end and it turned out he was hardly injured. I think at least two other West Ham fans caught on fire, but it was quickly put out. They didn't suffer any serious injury, but they would have been in a bit of shock. However, the rest of us weren't in shock and now it was our turn to go mental.

The whole of West Ham's support was in this corner, so we all knew what we'd seen. It was a petrol bomb and a Geordie had chucked it. It had come from the group packed next to us in the Leazes, where there was only a fence separating us. This wasn't in the street, this was in the ground and could have injured any women or kids who may have been with us. At that point everyone had the same thought… kill the Geordie bastards. We meant it.

We began to steam the fences, with the more intent ones climbing on to the pitch. They were already punching and kicking Geordies at the front of the

Leazes terrace. But all credit to the Old Bill. They knew straight away what the ball of flame they had seen flying through the air was. The West Ham lads attacking the Leazes didn't get much of a foothold before the Old Bill were on them, pushing them back. They didn't need to worry though, as the Geordies had all backed off from the front of the pitch. They knew what they had done.

For the entire game we just wanted to get the Geordies. We thought of nothing else and no one even watched the game. Penned in by a ring of steel, the Old Bill watched our every move. If a Geordie got too close to the fence, we would try to rip his arm off, but the Old Bill were always between us. Whoever took charge of the Old Bill after the bomb was thrown did a good job. Not once did they go against us or take sides, [it was] as if they'd been told not to further agitate the feelings of the Londoners. It was a good move, because it prevented a riot inside the ground. The West Ham supporters directed their hatred towards the Geordies and not their Old Bill.

Once we had resigned ourselves to the fact that the Old Bill had us well contained inside the ground, our thoughts turned to [what we'd do outside] *after the match. That would be the real test.*

Any West Ham supporter there that day would remember the events that occurred only too well.

Woolwich:

Everyone was fuming. They'd taken a liberty

in throwing the bomb, because we could have had kids there. Everyone was really up for it. I mean, we were 'orrible anyway, but we was double 'orrible that night.

After the match they kept us in ground until everyone had gone. The Geordies and West Ham were all raring for it but there was loads of Old Bill lining every street and road. They even had them on tops of flyovers. [It seemed as though] *all leave had been cancelled and they had been drafted in from everywhere. It was like West Ham didn't care, though. We would have been at their throats at the first opportunity.*

The police operation worked well, as we didn't get close enough to a Geordie to even verbal them. The Old Bill had devised a plan to hold us back in the ground until they had cleared the streets of Newcastle supporters. There were none in sight when we left the ground, and that's how it stayed, as we were marshalled in the heaviest police presence we had seen since we had played Millwall at home the previous year. Instead of letting us go to Newcastle Central station to catch the train back to London, the Old Bill had arranged to take us to this little local station, Manor's, where they would hold us all to allow enough time for Newcastle Central to clear of home supporters. They then thought they would take us back to Central station, to be met by only the police force, and put on a London-bound train specially arranged to take us out of Newcastle.

It was a well-thought-out plan that deserved to work, but once they had shepherded us all into this Manor's station, holding us on some platform while they got the rest of the trailing West Ham supporters in, they slipped up and made the mistake of relaxing their guard. With us tied up at Manor's and the Geordies way over at Central station they must have already begun congratulating themselves on their radios, but they hadn't reckoned on our resolve. Many of us have been involved in this football warfare since we were thirteen or fourteen years old. If we were really determined to slip an escort, we would somehow find a way, and we did. It only takes one determined lad to act before the rest start to follow and the escort collapses like a deck of cards. Believing that we couldn't get out of the station, the Old Bill started peeling off. One of the West Ham lads slipped the cordon and, before long, a good few of us began to follow. The Old Bill hadn't seen us go.

By the time the Old Bill had realised what was happening, more of us had jumped down off the platform... and began to cross the lines, with no thoughts as to whether they were live. We just knew the right faces had slipped and we were going with them. The Old Bill had to make a quick decision whether to come after us or hold the main mob back, as they were all trying to come too. They let us go, no doubt hoping that a radio alert to other police would thwart us. All we were doing was following the others. We didn't have a clue where we were heading, we just knew that we had to get clear of all the police attention if we were going to make the Geordies pay for the bomb.

We ran across the lines and on to another platform, joining others running along the same platform where a train was in the process of pulling out. With the doors swinging, we climbed into the train, which was packed with people. Someone I knew well was sitting in the train and with a big, wide grin informed me that the train was headed for Newcastle. As the train slowly pulled in to Newcastle, I couldn't believe our luck. The entire length of the platform was a sea of black and white.

We all dropped to the floor of the train, and some of the lads climbed under tables, to make it appear as if the train was empty. Then, before the train had come to a complete stop, the doors were all pushed open. All the Geordies were standing opened-mouthed on the platform. I've never seen looks on people's faces like the ones I saw on the West Ham faces at that moment. It was like we were all gone. Everyone just went mad. One minute the platform was like a sea of black-and-white Geordie scarves and the next, all you could see was a Cockney army wearing green bomber jackets going wild. We were running Geordies everywhere. I remember looking at the brothers Liddy and thinking that they had gone berserk, but we all had.

Once they had thrown the bomb, that was it. We were battering people, clearing the whole fucking platform and chasing them out into the street, up hills and into the city centre. There were enough Old Bill there but no one was bothered about getting nicked, we just didn't care. In the end the Old Bill just wanted us out of Newcastle.

Once we were out of Newcastle on the train back to

London, which if memory serves me correctly was the Flying Scotsman, the Geordie Old Bill on board got off at Durham. The mood was still there on the train. Nobody could switch off just like that.

Jimmy Smith remembers what went on during the journey back after the Old Bill got off the train:

Someone had gone and broken the lock on the drinks bar. We knew from one of our lot who had worked on the train that there were two bars, instead of the usual one. There must have been a few hundred West Ham on the train, all drinking bottles of champagne, wine, and anything else they could find. I remember saying to someone that the train had been deliberately delayed by about two hours, meaning that there would be hundreds of the Old Bill waiting when this train pulled back into Kings Cross. I said that they'd see us with all this booze and they'd start pointing us out. No one listened and everyone seemed too pissed to care. After we had drunk the first bar dry, the second bar got done. This was kind of funny, because if we had left it to the first bar then there may have been less trouble for us later.

When we were doing the second bar, we thought about getting the other passengers drunk as well, so that the Old Bill couldn't point the finger just at us. I remember this really old guy watching everything. I asked him if he wanted a beer and he said, 'Yes, alright.' Next thing, booze was being passed all around, no problem at all. We even had passengers joining in for a sing-song. There were also catering-size packs of ham going around, with people just taking a single bite before throwing the rest. However, like all things, you always get one... This particular man got all stroppy when someone ask him if he wanted a beer or a can of Guinness. He was giving it large in some authoritarian voice that could be heard above everyone, saying, 'I do not accept stolen property.' He got up as if to make a scene, but someone quickly gave him a right-hander.

We had the whole train in our control. I'd never experienced such a party atmosphere aboard a train home. There was one old girl who said, 'Excuse me love, couldn't get me a drop of gin could you?' I said, 'No problem' and came back from the bar with all these miniatures to give to the old girl. I even added a bit of lemon to it. I thought that at least when we got off the train none of the witnesses were going to go against us.

I remember getting myself up to the front of the train as it was pulling in to Kings Cross because I'd only been out [of prison] *a couple of weeks and didn't really fancy that nicking bollocks.*

As I feared, the Old Bill were out in force and wouldn't let us off the platform. There must have been about a hundred Old Bill at the station. We all got a little panicked and those in the rear of the train starting pushing hard from the back in a desperate attempt to force a way through. As people kept pushing and pushing, the ones in the front were getting crushed, myself included. In the end, the Old Bill began to let us all through for people's safety.

What a day. I recall that only one person got nicked,

poor old DC. In fact, I went to the court with him. He was fortunate because the court were going to give him a year when they heard that the damage caused on that train was £24,000 [worth], *but instead they gave him 180 hours' community service.*

QPR v Newcastle

The following week we had decided to seek further revenge on the Geordies at the first opportunity. However, the outcry following the bomb had seen the announcement that Newcastle fans were to be banned from the return game at West Ham the following season. We saw that Newcastle were playing at Queens Park Rangers the following Saturday, so we all met early that day and travelled across to the other side of London, to the QPR's ground.

There weren't as many West Ham on this occasion as there should have been, but there were enough of the right faces. There had been no prior liaison with QPR's little mob. No one really gave it a thought, as this was a thing between the superpower clubs. Just outside QPR's turnstiles is the Springbok boozer on South Africa Road. The pub couldn't have been open long before we staked out a spot inside and began drinking. As the pub began to fill with QPR supporters, they asked why we were here. When they found out, they bought us more drinks and said they understood. It was like we had suffered a terrorist attack.

While we were sitting in the pub, it was clear who we all were but we kept pretty low key so as not to attract the wrong kind of attention. Then one of the young 'uns ran in and told us that Newcastle had arrived.

Woolwich: *I remember that we were all running out to confront a Newcastle firm who were bowling down the road, giving it loads and singing. Well mob-handed in a big firm, which was taking liberties because it was only QPR. They came down the road looking like everyone did in the Seventies along the Wembley Way, with white butcher coats, bib and brace and bovver boots. There was even one big tattooed Geordie dressed head to toe like one of the dudes in Clockwork Orange. He even had a bowler hat on, painted with black-and-white stripes.*

The Geordies immediately started in front of us, in the middle of the street, thinking we were QPR. As soon as we told them we were West Ham, that was it. They just ran everywhere.

We were all Pringled-up and I was also sporting a pair of Stan Smith tennis shoes which were exclusive to Lilywhites. We had this Geordie lump, looking like a dinosaur, mouthing off that he wasn't going to run. He soon fled the other way, though, when Cass came running out of the bookie near the boozer to chase him. All I saw was him running down the road screaming that he wasn't the one that threw the bomb.

I recall another funny moment. QPR's manager at the time, Tommy Docherty, was standing in the street beside the ground, looking confused and saying, 'What the hell is happening? What's going on?' When someone told him that we were West Ham, he just stood there looking even more mystified, saying, 'But we're not even playing West Ham.'

Orient v Newcastle

Jono recalls another little match at which we sought vengeance on the Geordies in the months following the bomb attack, after a West Ham away game had been called off:

Jono: *A few of us decided to meet up over at Orient later on in the afternoon, as Newcastle were coming down. There were about fifty to seventy West Ham there. We got into the Newcastle end of the ground and ran them all out. The police arrived and threw about ten of us out. We had a few scraps outside the turnstiles with Geordie stragglers who were arriving just before kick-off.*

Just after kick-off about ten of us fucked off towards the station. As we turned into Leyton High Road to go back to the Underground, we saw another ten or so of West Ham being chased towards us by about forty Newcastle fans who had arrived late. We joined up and ran towards Newcastle, meeting them outside the hardware shop. They had reached there first, but being the thick northerners they were, they threw weapons at us. I picked up a broom and we steamed in. We chased them down a side street towards the ground. Then, out of the blue, Cass appeared in the middle of the road, trying to grab Geordies as they ran past.

When we were near the ground, we were rounded up by the police, put in a van and taken back to the hardware shop to be identified. Luckily, during the ID parade a West Ham fan out shopping with his girlfriend at the time [and who] *knew one of us, stepped forward to say that* [none of us had been involved]. *We were let go.*

Chapter 8

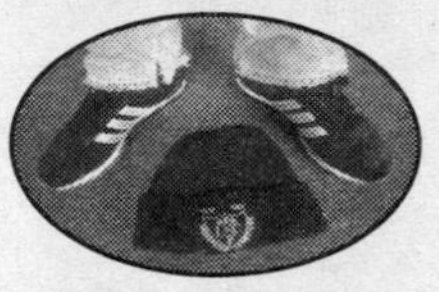

TAFF'S WORLD

I.C.F.

BEING RELEGATED into the old Second Division for the '78–'79 season meant we'd have a few rows with the Taffies. We would certainly be discovering the M4 for sure, with Wrexham, Swansea and Cardiff all in our division. It's never a just club thing with the Welsh. When you play them they always go over the top and make it Wales v England. When we looked closely at the division and saw so many teams with pathetic mobs, we reckoned at least the Taffs would give us a go.

We were quickly disappointed to find that Taff and his football club knew that if you came to West Ham you didn't play up. So we would have to see what happened at theirs.

The verdict: Cardiff have the bigger reputation, but the Swans put up the better show with us. Wrexham ain't worth the mention if you're comparing with the other two and you might as well put all of them on a par with the Midlands.

I went to Cardiff in April 1980. I remember it being the first time we realised they'd started to drag in plain-clothes detectives to combat football hooliganism.

We arrived in Cardiff at around 1 o'clock with a real good firm. We walked straight into the town centre, found their firm and ended up chasing them into what we believed was one of their boozers. To get into this pub you had to go down an alley, which led directly to the pub doors. It was so narrow you could only go down in single file. It was a stalemate: they fought to stop us getting inside the pub, but wouldn't fight to back us away from the boozer. Meanwhile we couldn't get all our firm all into the passageway. So we put in the pub windows then walked back to the top of the alleyway to bait them to come out and fight. It also meant we'd avoid being trapped in the alley when the Old Bill arrived.

We stood taunting them at the top of the alley, which led to their wrecked boozer, but they wouldn't come out. Out of frustration, and pure malice, one of us dragged over a motorbike that had been abandoned by one of their mob when we'd surprised them. Taffy the stunt rider just knocked over his own bike and ran into the pub with the rest of 'em.

Someone shouted that if he wanted his bike, he'd have to come out and get it. He didn't get the chance. One of the younger ones lit the fuel tank. As the bike blazed, the police arrived like a ton of bricks and everybody split. I ran into a nearby eatery, sat down and picked up a menu, quickly followed by Jono. He also picked up a menu, but that was more to hide his swollen nose and fat lip. Coast clear, we caught up with West Ham walking to the ground under heavy escort.

Now, it was during that escort walk that we noticed two or three unfamiliar faces giving us the evil eye. They stood out by their dress and by the fact they were older than the rest of us. We weren't having that, but we couldn't do anything with so many Old Bill close by. We sent word down the line: 'We're gonna sort the oddballs.' We got our chance when they slipped into a William Hill's. Seizing the moment, I went straight inside the betting shop to confront them. Jono, Liddy and Butler slipped in too.

As soon as they saw us come through that door, they knew they'd been rumbled. Two of them grabbed me while the third flashed his warrant card to everyone inside the shop, ordering all the punters out as he did so. It was a highly tense situation. They warned us that if we tried anything we were nicked, then warned us to try nothing on in this town.

The stakes had been raised a little too high for a poxy football match. We walked back out cursing them, but I think we were more shocked than anything at discovering that undercover police were now trained on us.

The following season we had an epic FA cup encounter with Wrexham. After drawing at home we played two replays that both went into extra time before finally we were bowled out 1-0.

We travelled down to Wrexham by train and stood with

most of the Brit lads and T.B.F. during the match. When the game was over, there was nothing but a miserable trip home to look forward to. And things were made worse by the fact that it was a mid-week night match.

Before we came out, I noticed a few Taffs had infiltrated the downstairs bar area in the away end. I thought I clocked about twenty of them drifting about and warned everyone that Wrexham were coming in. No one made a move, there was total disbelief from our lot. We'd seen enough of Wrexham not to waste our energy on them. As we moved out of the ground, I saw a blond-haired lad with another trying to kick off with these Taffs, so I steamed in with them. Once I made the first move, the rest of our lads woke up and did what they had to do – put the cheeky Taffs to flight. The blond Hammer who'd been prepared to take the Taffs on his own was Johnny Andrews, or Virge as he was known then. He was fuming all the way back to London about West Ham's slow reaction to what was a small Taffy raiding party. I'd noticed John before, but not really spoken to him. From that incident to the present day, however, we have remained great friends.

Who the fuck are they?

The fighting with the Wrexham Taffs was hardly worth noting, but it's the friendships born out of loyalty and helping out your own in the name of the team you support that will strike a chord with most of you out there. Those who follow football know it's a bond that never leaves you, and it's probably the only thing we ever gained out of it all.

I met many other pals the same way, through going to West Ham and fighting. Let Johnny Turner explain why we loved having the Hornchurch lads in any of our rucks; they were a solid part of the I.C.F.:

We're on our way to Swansea by coach; the coaches are leaving from Stratford Broadway. We all meet at my house – Shane, Morley, Motty, Stubbs, Pru and Tids. We're all from Hornchurch, Essex, and we have our own firm. On Saturdays and any match day we join up with the InterCity Firm to become one mob.

It's hard sometimes, because I'm really good mates with Andy Swallow, Grant, Cass and the rest. But some of our firm – Shane, Morley, Evans – like doing their own thing, causing havoc in the away team's end. On this occasion I've convinced everyone this trip to Swansea will be a classic. Two coaches of top boys are going and after the game we're stopping off at Newport for a night out.

We arrive at Stratford by Tube train just before nine. There's Andy Swallow with his book trying to collect people's money and separating them into the two coaches.

I see a few well-known Stratford boys and a few Canning Town snipers who fight each other regularly, except at West Ham games. I think, this could be fun, who's separating them?

There's a good firm of us: a few Under Fives, the Chads, Hornchurch, the Brit Plaistow, Townies, Stratford. This really is the I.C.F. All different firms coming together on match days to become one. We're off.

Everyone's sitting about on the coach talking about games and different rucks we've had so far. The Chads are holding court, telling how they'd all had a mass brawl up the Room At The Top nightclub in Ilford. They were explaining why three of their number weren't coming. They'd been nicked. But it wasn't in vain, because five of the other mob had been taken to hospital.

We pull into a service station on the M4. Andy reminds us there's to be no thieving or fighting, as we don't want to alert Old Bill that we're on our way. But the first thing our lot do is search the service station for other football supporters. There's no one on this side of the services, so we go over to check the other side. There's two vanloads of Cardiff. They spot us, gob us loads of Welsh abuse, then try to speed away. One of the vans stalls. Fancy that. We're now round the van, smashing on the windows. The engine revs up just as a paving slab goes straight through the back window, smashing down on the two Taffs in the back seat. The vans speed away, engines screaming while the eight of us give chase, shouting abuse. This is it, it's started already and it's only 11.30 in the morning. No police about, we go over to the services to load ourselves up with drinks, sandwiches, chocolate, anything we can nick for the journey. It's about 12 o'clock and we're on our way again, Swallow comes over: 'Turner, for fuck sake, low profile, you've got to keep a low profile.' Shane, who is next to me, gives Andy one of his stares then breaks out laughing. We all know Andy's only bothered because he missed it.

Everyone's drinking or playing cards but this journey to Swansea is taking forever. It's 2.15 p.m. when we eventually arrive. Everyone's off the coach. Only two Old Bill to meet us and all they can do is point us in the direction of the ground. We can't believe it: no fucking police escort. The pace is picking up from a stroll to a near run going towards the ground. We've already decided it's straight into their side. 'This is it,' I tell my mate Shane, 'I told you it's gonna be a classic.'

The ground looks a dump. We all gather near the middle, with no one saying a word. Then in the away end we hear the rest of West Ham chanting. All around where we're standing is a chilling silence. We're all getting edgy; it's nearly 3 o'clock. All of a sudden, the atmosphere changes. A few big fat Taffies are confronting the front row of us. They are now all around us; this really is it. One of the Stratford lads leans over the crowd barrier and smashes a steaming potato pie in the Taff's face, the Taff screams and as he lifts his head up, someone boots him straight in the face.

We charge down into the front of 'em. I see Shane's arms waving. I try and make my way to him when a big fat Taff grabs my coat, taking me off balance. He's now pulling me towards him, I'm struggling to get my balance back to break his hold. Next, I find myself on the floor, thinking that's it, but as I scramble up there's two chaps on top of the Taff. That's it I'm in, kicking, punching anything that moves. The whole side is in uproar as our two coaches are kicking it well off with all these Taffy lumps.

The Welsh Old Bill come running in. They don't touch the Taffs, only us, beating us back with their truncheons. Eventually they corner us and put us all back into the West Ham supporters' end.

Don't bother watching the game, everyone is so charged up. The Old Bill keep us locked in the ground for thirty minutes after the game's end. Then they tightly march us back to our corners – and they don't leave us. Using police vehicles, they escort us all the way to the motorway. They weren't going to get caught out again. We're still all buzzing, though, and we're now on our way to stop at Newport.

We pull into Newport and arrange to meet back at the coaches at 11.30 p.m. With time on our hands, everyone is charging around looking for trouble. But we soon realise that Newport is no London. It's very sleepy, but it does have girls. We all march down the chippie then move on to a local pub. It's about 8 o'clock, everything is just cool, we're just drinking and having a laugh. All the girls who come into the pub love it and stayed, but the blokes who come in leave very quickly. By 10 o'clock everyone is well drunk. A few of our lads came across a few locals wanting to know. They soon get chased off; nothing to mention.

The pub shuts, so everyone converges on another chippie. The shop gets abused, chips are being thrown around and the owner is trying to throw everyone out. The local police come and start pushing us around, Shane looks at me; it's a look I know all too well. I know exactly what he is thinking: now it's heated. The police back down and we march off to go and get back on the coach. No trouble in Newport, but we've had a blinding day. Now everyone looks mellow and fucked.

We pull into the first service station, as Andy explains this will be our only stop home. I'm dying for a piss. 'Hurry up', and we all bundle off. As we walk into the services we start going up stairs and notice it's packed – and it's gone midnight. My first reaction is: who is the firm? There must be at least 300 of 'em. I soon sober up and all our lot do the same. We join the queue, looking at them. They seem to be looking at us. It's definitely going to go off, right off, but who the fuck are they? I notice they seem to be big and older and there's a few girls with them. The rest of our mob come in. This is it. Come on Shane, it's going – Swallow and his firm are surrounded.

I steam straight over and smash one of 'em on the head with an ashtray. I immediately get hit with something. People are screaming, the whole place has gone wild, throwing everything they can get their hands on: cups, plates, trays, everything, with people just flying everywhere. I'm proud of my mob; we're right in the thick of it with the Brit boys. I'm being hit, pulled and punched, but we seem to be pushing them back. I'm lashing out at anyone.

There's now a stand-off and both sides are throwing things at each other. I sense one more charge and they'll go. We steam in again and, yeah, they turn, and then run down the stairs and out into the car park. I run back into the main hall. It's here I see some of them jump over the food counter, fleeing into the kitchens to escape. I then come back on to the stairs, where Andy, Danny Tiderman and a few of the others are pushing a pinball machine towards the stairs. There's a mob still at the bottom looking up when this pinball machine finally gets pushed off the edge of the stairs, crashing bumpety-bump smack bang into 'em. The other mob runs; that's enough for them. This was a victory against an unnamed mob. They were game, but who the fuck are they?

The Old Bill are now on the scene everywhere and rounding us all up. Some of our lads, who were covered in blood, run up the motorway and hide. Meanwhile, our two coach drivers have had enough. They tell the Old Bill they won't be letting any of us back on. After about twenty minutes we are put back on the coach and taken to the police station under police guard. They put us twenty to a cell then begin questioning the firm we had a ruck with. While this is happening, everyone is swapping clothes with each other, I'm finding it hard to swap mine, because emblazoned across the chest is 'Ready to ruck, Cockney Rejects'. In the end, someone swaps with me.

When the police get round to questioning us, the kid who I swapped shirts with is one of the first to be charged. The other mob recognised the shirt. Close one for me.

This questioning goes on all through the night and all day Sunday. The police aren't getting very far. Everyone they question either wasn't there or didn't see anything… The police tell us the coaches have gone and we'll all be kept here to appear in court on Monday. It's now late Sunday afternoon, we've had nothing to eat or drink; some of us have thumping headaches, I've had enough. People are banging the cell doors, all shouting and abusing the Old Bill. The window comes down in our cell. A copper puts his head through and tells us to stop this Cockney slang we are shouting. He says he knows what we are saying, because he's watched The Sweeney *on telly. This just cracks us all up and we roll around laughing.*

It's my turn to be interviewed. The only thing I want to know was who this other firm was. The police start with the good-cop-bad-cop routine, but are getting nowhere. Then it dropped: we had been fighting with 300 CB enthusiasts. They meet there every week. That's why they only nicked us, and that's why the CB enthusiasts were picking us out and identifying us. Still, I'd liked to have met them every week. The police need bodies, so in the end they make a deal, if we put up half a dozen people, we can all go. Now, trying to find six people with no police record amongst 100 I.C.F., you'd have more chance of meeting the Pope. So they had to arrest eight West Ham and let us all out, where, to our surprise, the two coaches are waiting. It's now 11 o'clock Sunday night. The police give us a police escort back to London. What a couple of days – a real classic.

Chapter 9

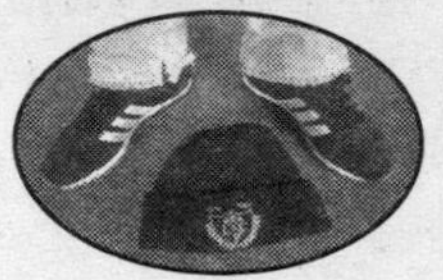

TOTTENHAM BOYS

I.C.F.

A LONDON derby in the early Eighties involving Tottenham was only of interest to us if it was an away game. At this time the I.C.F. were considered virtual untouchables in comparison to a Tottenham firm who were no longer the major players of North London. The Arsenal Gooners had now taken over there. From the early Seventies, Tottenham had their firm and we knew that they could also have their day, but as far as we were concerned it would never be with us.

Many of their main boys wouldn't even bother to show when they had to come to Upton Park. Why bother if their back-up was going to perform like they did the last time? They were probably wondering why it was that good lads went to pieces when they got West Ham and must have asked themselves whether all the front in the world was worth the slap they would get. If any did come, they always stayed glued to any police escort on offer.

The only Yid who offered himself turned out to be too brave for his own good. His name was Sammy Skys, or Skyesy as he later became known to us. Towards the end of his era he was no longer of interest to us and it was pitiful watching the Under Fives track him. This usually didn't amount to much, because the T.B.F. and Gardner had made it clear to everyone that Skivesy had their respect.

Skyesy was an older black guy from Barking, I heard. I had often wondered why he wasn't a Hammer, as it's a right West Ham area. Maybe that was why he had earned his reputation, because he felt that he had something to prove, having come from that area. But if Skyesy felt he had something to prove personally, Tottenham's mob had something even bigger to prove to West Ham.

Plenty of lads don't remember the times when West Ham would join with Vic Dorking's Tottenham against rival London mobs, or when Ronnie Parish stood alone with thirty good 'uns up our North Bank throughout an entire night match back in the early Seventies. Over time they had been reduced to nothing but a joke and I don't think they ever regained our respect after the season we went to take their end in another London derby. After each year that we took their end, they would switch to another end the following season, so we never knew which end was going to be theirs from one year to the next. For years it had always been the Park Lane end, which then switched to the Paxton Road end. They later proclaimed the Shelf as their popular end. It is not the done thing to keep changing your end and nobody could keep up with it, so one year West Ham's various mobs just went their different ways and into what each mob thought was the Tottenham mob's end.

I remember having it with Tottenham in the Paxton Road end and thinking that it was too easy. Then, looking across the pitch, I saw that West Ham had taken the Park Lane end as well. Another row was going on in the Shelf and ultimately West Ham claimed that end too. In those days, you could work your way from one part of the ground to another, so we began to walk around the ground. All we ended up doing, though, was bumping into more West Ham, as we had taken all their ends and whatever remained of the Tottenham mob had slipped out of their own ground altogether.

There was nothing after the game and everyone crammed on to the Tubes with big grins. We rocked the train all the way back to Mile End, singing 'Knees Up Mother Brown'. I think everyone realised at that point the advantages of not having an outright leader and more than one firm. Our army was getting bigger.

The '80–'81 season made a change. We were now in Division Two, though we made it all the way to the League Cup Final that season, only to be beaten by Liverpool in a replay at Villa Park. The quarter-final saw us drawn against the Yids at home for a mid-week night match. It was a full house, 36,000 people, and the Yids came in large numbers. They always think that any Cup run by them has their name on it. We weren't surprised to see that the Yids had brought plenty of old faces, whom we knew would be more than up for it if it was on.

It was on all right. It went off big-time in the South Bank – the papers the next day were full of it. One of the main daily papers carried a headline picture of the late Danny Tiderman bleeding across his face after being slashed with a Stanley knife. They said he was a young Tottenham supporter and made it seem to any rival mobs reading that the Yids got right savaged by West Ham on that South Bank. In fact, Danny was a major force in the West Ham Under Fives and had claimed to be a Tottenham fan upon finding himself ejected from the ground in the hope of avoiding getting nicked.

Tottenham weren't exactly savaged, but they sure got a big enough slap. It was going off everywhere and the Old Bill were finding it difficult to stop because West Ham's I.C.F. had fully infiltrated the South Bank end, which had been reserved for Tottenham's huge following.

Terry Sherrin can still recall the moment it first kicked off that night with the Yids:

We jibbed into the South Bank in ones and twos and firmed up in an area called the Cage. By now we had perfected the art of jibbing into the South Bank. The South Bank itself is a straight end behind the goal, but the entrance from the bar area, adjacent to the Chicken Run, has a landing above the stairs and steps from which you can watch the game. I reckon there were close to a couple of hundred in the vicinity of the Cage, including myself, Jono, Liddy, Swal Brett and Fellman, but there were none of the older, established faces like Gardner or the T.B.F.

We started to group up together up in the corner so that we had our backs against the wall when we were fighting. We'd heard rumours that Tottenham were going to be up for it this game, but they'd already enraged us anyway by being given the whole of the South Bank end, which holds 7,000. To us it appeared as if the club had given Tottenham fans licence to invade our ground and we were determined to make sure that they didn't gain our territory easily.

So there we were, gathering up in the far corner, facing across the length of the South Bank which was being filled with the Tottenham hordes. We knew this Tottenham mob, who were more North Essex than North London. We recognised the familiar faces of Buckhurst Hill, Walthamstow – Keithy Poleworth and Robbins. We knew the place that we had gathered in well, as we had been meeting up here all season, but this time Tottenham were all around us. They seemed to be everywhere. Some of the others from our lot that came to join us said that the former Green Jacket, Billy Gall, was gathered behind the goal, nearer to the front of the pitch, with Nat and a few others.

Our numbers in the South Bank were growing and Tottenham began to take notice and look up in our direction. We held our stare back at them as the big game atmosphere filled the night air. They'd realised who we were by then and I remember thinking that it was going to go any minute now... and, blimey, did it go!

I remember seeing the Yids' own Keith Poleworth who, in my book, has got to be the most game Tottenham cunt there's ever been. He should 'ave been a Hammer for his fearlessness. He stood out 'cause he was dressed in a light blue boiler suit. He looked over at us and we could see that he was fucking fuming. He was with Robbins and that little firm, and they were all fuming. They must have thought we were just boys in comparison, as they were about four to five years older than us, which is a big age gap.

They made the first move. A group of about one hundred started to walk over to us. I knew them and so was the first to spot them and I turned to warn the others. Everyone was there ready, like a proper unit, including Jono, Swal, Brett, Scully and Liddy. I remember saying to Jono, through gritted teeth, 'It's coming my way right now', and as I spoke, Poleworth just walked straight up and stood almost in my face. He said, 'You alright, Tel?' and as I answered, I clocked the geezer to Poleworth's right and became aware that Jono had stepped forward to my right. Without warning, Poleworth ran up and whacked poor ol' Jono in the chin. As Jono began to wobble, I bashed the Yid geezer who was standing beside Poleworth. That was it; it had gone right off.

The South Bank is the one place in the ground that anyone looking for a row is guaranteed to get one. Tottenham had the whole South Bank and it was like we'd disturbed a hornets' nest. All you could see was mob upon mob of Tottenham from the far side of the

South Bank, all making a move to get involved. We had the upper hand though, as they had to come up to us because we were on higher ground, and as they came closer we got into them.

By now we were all in it, doing the bouncing, flop, bosh, all sticking together. It's going off big-time. Poleworth was going mad, but 'cause we're mates he bypassed me and went steaming in the other direction. I remember thinking, crikey, he might not want to fight a mate, but he sure wants to fight the other 200. As our lot all come around from the top corner of the South Bank Cage, still holding the higher ground, everyone was giving the old chant of 'I.C.F.' Scuffles were breaking out and mobs of Tottenham were charging along from the top, middle and bottom of the South Bank in an attempt to get at the 200-strong I.C.F. steaming into them from the top of the Cage.

We started to come around and down as the Yids made their way up, everyone rowing. In the midst of all this, a fucking big gap opens right in the middle and it wasn't us who caused it. Make no bloody mistake, we were all doing the business. Then all of a sudden, who comes bursting through this bloody big gap on the terraces but Gally, our own Green Jacket. He had seen us up in the corner and when the Yids moved, Gally, Nat and a few others had snaked along from the front of the South Bank and into the affray, creating the massive gap on the terraces. We all saw Gally and began fighting a way towards him, as he did the same. The massive brawl between us and a firm of Yids must have been quite a spectacle for any observer. The game Poleworth was still fighting us all, but the Yids were split as Gally, Nat and several others came flying through.

Poleworth was eventually nicked and as he was getting dragged out of the ground, I watched the amazing sight of Tottenham's top boy shaking hands with our own Billy Gall, because they were mates. I would never forget the sight of Gally shaking hands with Poleworth.

Now that Gally had come through with the older lads we were all together, the old and the young, and it just went off again. This time the Old Bill were more evident and managed to get in quicker. They were really heavy handed with us and seemed like they were well pissed off. They broke everything up and ejected loads of us out of the South Bank altogether. However, there were about fifty of us, myself included, who had slipped into a section of the South Bank separated [off] *by a fence while all this was happening. It wasn't long before we kicked off again with Tottenham fans in this section, causing some to climb on to the pitch for their own safety. This time, Old Bill made sure all of us were coming out.*

We were pretty pleased with ourselves. It was brilliant, a night Cup quarter-final and Tottenham with a full firm turnout, all believing that they had the insurance of being given the whole South Bank to themselves, and then we show up. It was one of those rows you will always remember.

The South Bank Cage was popular with our lot that

year. We had been involved in a row in that end with Coventry and Villa, underneath the stand in the bar area. Villa had been a good battle. We had gone downstairs to the little bar where they had been gathering when one of our men whacked this Villa geezer over the head with a chair. It just bounced off the cunt. We all thought, oops, here we go, and we began fighting for our lives. After the game, we caught the same firm up by the station and chased 'em the length of Green Street.

Tottenham was the best, though, because we knew it was on the moment we got in to the South Bank. To this day, I bet Jono still remembers the punch he got off Poleworth. I remember him laughing about it afterwards. 'He can half hit', was all he would say.

Tottenham v Liverpool v West Ham

Sheffield Wednesday was supposed to be the big game that season and in the old Second Division they were described as a big club that had bit of a mob. However, after we arrived at Kings Cross we learned the game was off. When you're all keyed up to go somewhere, you can't just go home to read a paper, so we decided to go to Tottenham.

We got to Tottenham quite early, at around a quarter to eleven, and went walking down Tottenham High Road towards the Corner Pin public house. There were about 400 of us, with no escort. Tottenham were already there and came running at us, thinking we were Scouse, They screamed at us, 'Come on Liverpool.' Someone said, 'Fuck off, we're West Ham.' They just stopped in their tracks and then began to run everywhere.

The Scouse had a bigger mob there than us. There must have been about 1,000-odd Scousers, but we still managed to terrorise the life out of everyone. The Scouse didn't wanna know us because of who we were.

The Old Bill had now set aside the Park Lane end of the ground as the visiting supporters' section. Liverpool were all in the Park Lane end next to us, with a line of officers and fencing separating us. On the other side to us, the Shelf end, was all Tottenham. It was probably one of the quietest encounters between the Tottenham and Liverpool fans ever. The Old Bill looked uneasy about even letting us in, but in the end I think they'd rather have had us in a spot where they could contain us than let us free.

It was funny watching the reaction of the players from both teams. They looked totally bemused. Every time a corner was taken down our end, they had to endure West Ham chants of abuse.

I remember after the game the Scousers told us, through the railings, they would come back to the station with us. We told them to fuck off, that we were West Ham and didn't need anybody's help. We love to humiliate our rivals at any opportunity and the only reason we never got serious that day was because neither the Yids nor the Scouse really wanted to know. They no doubt thought that that every team gets a game called off at some stage, but neither of them would think of going over West Ham for a day out when they weren't even playing them.

'Chim-chiminey, chim-chiminey, chim-chim cheroo,
We hate them bastards in claret and blue.'

Yids Come East Ham

Someone once asked me if I remembered the time when the Yids got off at East Ham. While I wasn't there at the time, I do recall the incident. It only involved a few of the favourites, but it was a big story and was all the talk that day. I remember thinking when I heard the story that we should have realised it was on, because Tottenham could be a proud lot, even back in the early Eighties.

Tottenham were having it with Chelsea and Arsenal at the time, and we had destroyed their reputation. We turned up for their own meet after finding out that they had distributed leaflets with a call-to-arms for all Tottenham fans to stand against West Ham. We looked on these matches as the usual piss-take of taming the Yids. To further rub in our superiority over them, we raised the humiliation stakes by turning up mob-handed to their Liverpool game when we weren't even playing them. You could take it for granted, then, that Tottenham would have some right faces just itching to restore hurt pride.

The following is an account of the clash between the Yids and West Ham in the '83–'84 season, which clearly demonstrates the risks you took by clashing outside grounds in the Eighties:

I was standing outside the Queens at Upton Park market at about 10.30 a.m. on Saturday morning. We had heard that the Yids were coming at about 12 o'clock, so I arrived early.

There weren't many West Ham about. I saw Grisso, Carlton, Swallow, Tiderman, Sherrin, Hodges and a few others arrive from the Pie & Mash Café. There were about twenty of us in all.

At about 11.30 a.m., a young Under Five came running out of the station, looking worried, shouting a lot and not making much sense. He was trying to tell us that 400 Spurs had been on his train and were heading for East Ham station. Looking back, this would be a very different story if they had got off at Upton Park, as there were only a few of us there at the time.

About thirty of us gathered together and started to run towards the Boleyn, the pub at the other end of Green Street. Everyone seemed excited. I don't think they believed the Under Five about how many Spurs he had seen on the train. Even so, nobody questioned the decision to take the firm on. All that mattered was the Yids were on our turf and it was up to us thirty to stop 'em.

We turned left at the Boleyn pub and headed along the Barking Road towards East Ham Town Hall, checking every side road we ran past. We knew the only way they could come was down Wakefield Street, which meant that we were running parallel to them.

All of a sudden a shout went up: 'They're here.' A mob was turning the corner into the road leading into ours. A big noise was coming from that end of the street. I saw Swallow and Kerry turn into the side road, and start to head towards them. A few of us stopped. My heart was beating and I was excited but nervous. One half of me was telling me to run, the other was warning me not to let West Ham down. My legs seemed heavy, but I knew I couldn't stop now. I turned to catch Swallow and Kerry up. There could only have been ten of us at that stage.

The Yids got to about thirty yards from us when they stopped. Swallow and Kerry were facing them and we were ten yards behind them. I then saw two West Ham fans pull out blades and I thought that Swallow had something in his coat. There was this big stand-off and I couldn't believe the amount of Yids on show. The Under Five's guess of 400 would have been about right. The Yids seemed nervous.

All of a sudden, a big shout went up and the rest of our mob, about twenty, came running around the corner. They were screaming all sorts and waving pickaxe handles, brooms, Stanley knives, you name it. Someone had two big plastic buckets and was swinging 'em round his head and another had armed himself with an armful of roof slates, which he began hurling at the Yids. I later learned the lads had hit a nearby hardware store.

The Yids backed off. I swear they thought it was an ambush. They turned and ran, falling over each other in the process. The West Ham mob steamed into them. The Yids were being hit with pickaxe handles, bricks, brooms and anything else the lads could get their hands on.

It was reported in the News of the World *the next day that six Spurs fans were treated for stab wounds. The street was in total mayhem. The Spurs mob were only saved by the arrival of three vans of the Old Bill. They gathered up all the Yids and lined them up against a long wall. The Spurs mob seemed relieved but angry as well. They had met some of the most active I.C.F. and I reckon it was lucky for them there had only been thirty of us that day.*

After the Old Bill arrived we all split up, ditching the tools, and left the scene pretty much the same way we came, but this time we were skipping back down all the side roads on our way back to Upton Park.

Later that day there was a buzz of excitement and total ecstasy around the ground. Four hundred Yids, thirty West Ham, our ground, our turf, keep off... enough said.

Chapter 10

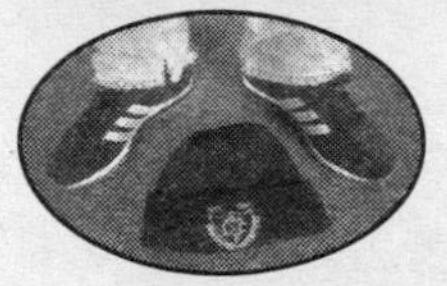

CHELSEA SINGERS

I.C.F.

I LOVED the Chelsea years. They had a firm renowned throughout the country. A fighting army as big as Man U's, and a reputation to match. They played the numbers game, invading the opposition in hordes, always proud to wear the colours and confident their army was too big to have a go at. But when the real hard men got among the Stamford Bridge mob and put it about, they dismissed Chelsea as singers, fucking singers.

Singers was how I best remember them – vociferously goading you about how great they were and how shit you were. They had the support and the numbers. Outside London they were given enough respect. But the way we saw it, they were only good at smashing everything up. Football Specials, Brighton seafront – you name it, they smashed it. The Chelsea singers grabbed front-page headlines wherever they went, from the pink Saturday evening northern papers to the Sunday papers. Them and Man U's Red Army were in the news all the time. We were pig-sick of the way they grabbed all the headlines like they were the hardest fuckers in the land... as far as they were concerned, no firms would ever take the Shed. And that included those miserable bastards, West Ham. Chelsea were the kings of hype; the Osgood years had gone to their heads.

My first recollection of going to Chelsea to take the Shed was in '73, when West Ham's famous black player Clyde Best banged in two goals to give us a 4-2 win. I went with the King twins and we met up with the Woolwich lot. Everyone was so much older than me and working in their first jobs. We were a collection of odds and sods, but made a fair turnout nevertheless. We were West Ham's representatives from South of the River Thames. There were lads from Dartford, Belvedere, Erith, Woolwich, Plumstead and Thamesmead.

We were greeted warmly by a packed train full of the West Ham mob thundering to a stop at Embankment Tube station. We piled on, pushing for a footing as everyone sang, *'She wheels her wheel barrow through the streets broad and narrow'*.

This was West Ham's mob: singing, jostling, heaving and sweating, smiling urchin faces, grown men with beards and beer guts laughing with long-haired youths who didn't give a fuck about school and hated work. We were a procession of Doc Martens. Everybody used to look lovingly down at their bovver boots, admiring the polish, discussing the pros and cons of steel toe-cappers. The nutters swore by them, but most lads didn't like the way they caused your boot to lose that classic look. As the train thundered nearer, you'd start pulling your laces tighter still. Everything had to feel right for when you stuck the boot in.

Earls Court and the doors open. What's going on? Everyone's getting off. You pile out too, because everyone else has, but what about Fulham Broadway, your designated stop for Chelsea? Your head is twitching and searching over the bodies all around. The chant of 'Mile End, Mile End' rings out, echoing along the platform... You're charging up the platform towards the way out, your mates are there one minute, split up in the crowd the next. It's a stampede, then a panic as gaps appear. Your own mob turns, pushing back through you. 'Back on! Everyone back on!' yells leper Wardy, a popular, scruffy-looking West Ham character of the 70s. Everyone's piling back on to the Tube and you push through the carriage, smiling at being reunited with the mates you first set out with. Bodies crash into you, everybody's getting squashed, some accidentally slump over the ones sitting down and you're all treading on feet. It's the Old Bill, they're getting on. 'Cass, you fucking missed it all,' pipes up one of the Bagnells. Chelsea had been all over the platform and the first carriage piled out straight away followed by the second. By the time all the others had got out, Chelsea had run back up through the exits.

The Old Bill have piled down, but not before we nick a few silk scarves off some of the Chelsea mob who'd stuffed them up their Slazenger jumpers. We all grab for the scarves, trying to nick them off each other. Trophies of war – your bedroom walls would be covered in them, and whenever you told the stories to your mates supporting other teams, you'd always pull the scarves out to emphasise how fresh the tale was and that you were there in the annals of terrace history.

Pile out at Fulham Broadway, leaving the transport police behind. It's up to the Met now. Everything goes quiet when you first come out of the station. Careful when choosing which ticket collectors to dodge through. Old Bill nick one or two, clearing the way for the rest of us to pile through. Like sewer rats surfacing from underground, the sunlight hits you. You're out and on their manor, but there's a ring of Chelsea Old Bill all around the entrance. They're there to break up the mob, to stop them spreading out the width of the road and looking unruly. You make sure you've no colours on show as you pass quickly by the away supporters' entrance to Chelsea's North Stand. Looking back, you glimpse the sight of police removing fans' bootlaces, and, if they're lucky, a steel comb – they were popular back then. For these West Ham fans, the day is already over; they can only hope for some action after the game.

You're walking alone to avoid attracting any unwanted attention, but with everyone in front and behind you all doing the same, we're still altogether. Now we're behind Chelsea lines. We've passed all the Chelsea pubs, giving them the once-over... No good nobody in them except Chelsea fans who don't want to know. The older fans know it rarely goes off in the street beforehand. Chelsea would be waiting in the Shed for us, or in the courtyard entrance to the Shed. The courtyard is like a big playground – if they're up for it, they'll want to see us off there. There's also a small pub almost opposite that their boys would pile out from. But more often than not, their spotters would have warned them that they'd seen a good mob of us coming – maybe the same Chelsea guys we'd jumped out on back on the Tube. It's the only way I can explain why they all go from milling around the courtyard to waiting for us in the Shed.

They won't be disappointed. Never mind all that bollocks about 'No one takes the Shed.' West Ham didn't just take the Shed, we used it as our meeting place for years. So much so that whenever we get round to recalling the days when we took the Shed, it's very hard to work out what season is actually being talked about. Most regard the best-ever taking of the Shed end by West Ham as the mounted horse year. We took the Shed, got put out then ran across the pitch to do it all again. It was Boxing Day '77–'78 season, as Mouthy Bill recalls:

We came in the other way to the Shed, near where the toilets were situated, opposite the main entrances into the Chelsea home end. As we looked up, all the Chelsea were waiting at the top of the stairs. We realised it was a bit early, so we shot into the toilets for about ten minutes.

When we'd come out they'd gone, so we went up into the Shed end. I bought a program and decided to sit down and read it right by the stairs we'd come up; there were about eight or nine of us. As we were sitting or standing around, all of a sudden I was punched. I heard, 'It ain't Christmas now', and they flew into me; they'd tumbled us and knew who we were. So we shot up the back, where we got pushed in against the fence. I remember Dickle and them were on the other side of this fence. They were leaning over, trying to bash the geezers coming into us. The Old Bill came up to rescue the situation. They said, 'Look lads, you can go through there and sit in the seats, this is the Chelsea end so it's advisable you don't remain.'

So I said, 'No we're going to hold on here mate, it won't last like this for too long.' Then we all heard this roar, we could see it because the Shed end was built in a sort of half-circle and you could look across and watch West Ham come over the top, fighting and bashing their way up the stairs. I watched Chelsea all run back. Then they appeared to turn and run across. Then you could see the whole Shed run – every part of the end was running.

Now myself and the guys with me started bashing Chelsea supporters from the other side. We grabbed them and said, 'What's happening?'

They'd reply, 'It's West Ham... they're coming in!'

Soon as they said that... bash!... 'cause they must be a Chelsea supporter. So we were steaming 'em and we were getting right away through, until we flew into a load of West Ham geezers. That was it, we'd all linked. We'd taken their Shed.

It was bedlam as the Old Bill got involved and Chelsea tried to regroup. The Old Bill weren't taking prisoners and West Ham got pushed all out on to the pitch.

As we were pushed out on to the pitch… do you remember them big, long advertising boards they would have behind the goal? Well, this particular board was propped up by a chair. A load of geezers jumped out from behind it and came on to the pitch going, 'C'mon… we're Millwall!' So I picked the chair up. The board was gone and… bash… I hit a geezer with the chair then threw it. A copper on a horse had seen me and started chasing me… he grabbed me by the hair, but I managed to dive in and out through the goal and get away by mixing in with all the other West Ham supporters going across the pitch to the other end as a line of mounted police sealed off the Shed behind us with a row of horses.

When we got to the other end and stood in the North Stand, we watched another sizeable West Ham mob kick it off in the Shed end. That was it, everyone in our end was trying to get on the pitch again. Many did and started running back across the pitch, only to be thwarted by a line of police horses advancing to the halfway line.

As for the other lot of West Ham running amok in the Shed, the Old Bill could only get them out by running them on to the pitch. That day was something. We had pure mob superiority on the biggest bovver boy army in London.

Woolwich also remembers the occasion as the best-ever

taking of the Shed. He describes that attack on the Shed through the main entrance:

Chelsea had just come back up. The season before they'd been playing all stupid teams. I remember them going to places like Norwich and doing all sorts of silly things, like smashing a few trains up. That year was my last year at school and the Chelsea lads I knew would go on and on about how hard their firm was. When we finally got Chelsea away I told them, 'Look we're gonna walk in your Shed.' They just didn't stop giving it to me that we wouldn't get in the Shed.

We met in a pub called The Palmerston on the corner of the Kings Road. Obviously there were no colours among us and we came out together in a mob of 200. When you think about it, who goes to their own home game in a mob of 200? It just don't happen. Well, we all came walking down the road and someone had the sense to have a Chelsea scarf on and bowl along up front with us all singing 'Chelsea!' outside the Shed. Nowadays, the Old Bill would be straight on to yer, but in those days the Old Bill didn't seem to care.

You paid at the turnstiles and entered the Shed by these really steep stairs. Although I wasn't right at the front, I was part of the first group through. We were walking up the stairs as everyone was coming in. We all got to the top of the stairs, where we all mingled about. It was obvious they knew who we were and they all came around us. I remember a geezer going, 'You ain't Chelsea.' Someone said, 'Fucking right we ain't, mug.'

Bang. It all went off. Someone hit that geezer and we ran into the middle of the Shed. As we did, all the other West Ham plotted up in there already stopped making out they were Joe Public reading their programmes. They turned round and came in with us, everyone steaming the Shed together.

We took the middle of the Shed, with Chelsea pushed either side of us at the front and behind. Then the Old Bill tried to get us out. We were at the barrier with most of the West Ham forced back out on the pitch, Chelsea tried to hit the few of us left in the Shed from behind. The West Ham guys down the front saw this, turned around and came running back up again, with those on the pitch jumping back in too.

With all these idiots saying, 'We're going to do ya', it was absolutely superb to take the Shed. I have respect for certain teams, but not them. I've never really rated Chelsea, because every time we came up against them they'd have it away as far as I was concerned.

Although this was the season the I.C.F. started, we weren't as organised as we were to become later. In those days it was all about waiting for the right faces to come along and follow on. But when it came to Chelsea's Shed, we all used it as a West Ham meeting point.

Jimmy Smith's account of the first real group of West Ham in that end, and events after the game, reinforces the buzz we felt at taking the Shed that time. It's pure classic: two firms, two reputations, one of which ends up in tatters:

I was at Mile End from ten in the morning; there were

hundreds of West Ham arriving. Left about 11.30, train completely full. Half the train got off at Sloane Square while the rest of the mob stayed on to Earls Court, then Stamford Bridge. Met Nat up there and we had a few skirmishes because some muppet pointed us all out. About 1 o'clock a mob of fifty of us got in the Shed, in no organisation whatsoever – unlike the Chelsea, who were all in there well early. By 1.45, the Chelsea mob came storming around and I just stood there looking at the sky, admiring the poxy rainy weather. The fifty West Ham in there got run on to the pitch. I was still in there keeping myself to myself. I'm thinking, it's getting to about 2.15. I'm thinking, fuck this, I'll give it another twenty minutes and if West Ham don't come in, I'm getting out of this place.

Out on to the street in that courtyard entrance to the Shed were all the Chelsea and there among them I could see Ted, Bill and Scoeby. It was the mob of West Ham that had got off at Sloane Square. Oddly, they were singing Chelsea songs. One of them said to me afterwards, 'We were singing Chelsea songs walking along the Fulham Broadway. The Old Bill turned round and one of them said, "Fuck me, isn't it a good job that's not West Ham supporters coming in here."' After two minutes, West Ham got in. I remember seeing big Ted on the way up the stairs. At the top I said, 'Fuck's sake Ted, we've just got run out of here.'

Ted's deadpan reply was, 'They won't be running this lot out of here.'

A couple of hundred West Ham had come up those

stairs and Chelsea had now twigged the enemy were in. A few fists flew and all you could hear was 'West Ham!' I remember Kerry Tidman, Vic Dark and Chingy all being at the top of the stairs and it kicked off all around us. We ran underneath all the barriers, kicking the fuck out of all the Chelsea in the way. We stopped at each barrier, mobbed up, then went through to the next one. By the time we got right to the back of the Shed all you could hear was, 'We took the Chelsea Shed, Stamford Bridge again', clap... clap... clap...

Everyone was congratulating themselves. With 400 or 500 West Ham all at the back of Chelsea's end, we couldn't help but give it large, singing, 'C'mon, get your end back.' The Chelsea supporters looked absolutely gutted that they couldn't get their end back.

There was a black Chelsea fan who was hyperactive, running around like a headless chicken trying to have a pop at everyone. I nodded over to him, giving him a wink as if to say, 'Come here mate, we're with you – we're Chelsea.' His arms came up and he pulled himself into my part of the Shed. As he did so, I booted him right underneath the chin with my steel cappers. He went flying, bounced backwards, only to come back all hyper again – a real loon. I thought, this is fucking brilliant, we'll stay in here, but the Old Bill had other ideas. They got all their reinforcements in and started to have us out of the Shed.

As they took us around the pitch, I remember seeing Tony Barker dangling himself along the crossbar of the goal. I thought Fatty was trying to break the crossbar so we could get the match postponed. West Ham were all over the pitch, kicking up lumps out of it. I thought, lovely, get this postponed and we could do it all over again in a night match. But unfortunately, the game was played. West Ham's keeper Mervyn Day let in two of the softest goals and we lost 2-1.

We were out of the Shed and in the North Stand when the game ended. Word went about, 'Nobody go yet, nobody go yet.' Then, fifteen minutes after the final whistle, Gardner finally decided to make a move. Swiftly, everybody around me moved out of the North Stand exit. A few West Ham supporters that had gone early got run outside. But these were yer North Bank boys, idiots who just made a lot of noise. The firm was moving now, all knowing the feeling that you're fucking untouchable.

We came out and all the Chelsea mob were waiting outside the pub opposite the North Stand entrance. But we just casually bowled out, no scarves, no noise, no nothing. We just got tore fucking into 'em and proceeded to kick the fuck out of 'em. They ran off in the direction of the North End Road. Our mob of about 300 to 400 just carried on walking past Fulham Broadway station, where queues of supporters were heading into the Underground.

Half an hour to forty-five minutes after the game, Chelsea's Babs showed – the one-armed, half-caste man with the big reputation. He came out of the streets somewhere with all the front in the world. No problem, we've got everybody here, we'll rip his mob apart.

Nobody gave a fuck about the rumour that the one arm had a meat hook attached. The road hushed with anticipated excitement. Both mobs shaped to go. We were all itching, scanning One-Arm Babs, thinking the first one in on him could be a new name to talk about when the time came to recite the story of the day.

You've got to give One-Arm Babs his front, because he called it on: 'Where's Bill Gardner? I want Gardner!' He was seriously fronting us all, taking one step forward then fucking eight backwards as Gardner came out of the crowd. The next thing, they'd fucked off – the Old Bill pushed them away.

With Old Bill heavy on the scene we thinned out but still continued down the road. One-Arm Babs came back, 'Where's Gardner?' Gardner wasn't there, but he recognised Natley and said, 'If Gardner ain't here, you'll do.' Nat came out, there was a bit of a stand off, we ran at them but the Old Bill got in the middle and that was it. The end of a happy day for West Ham.

The only way a Chelsea fixture could be interesting was if they showed up at ours to make a point. Going over Chelsea was even bringing all our scarfers out for a day out. A scarfer was a run-of-the-mill fan who fancied himself as a hooligan, but was more mouth than action. For a while Chelsea turned their North Stand into the equivalent of our South Bank, by getting a decent firm in there and giving it to all the visiting supporters, except when they played us. They knew the Shed wasn't safe, so for a bit of style they took to the seats in the sides. Word went about that they were going to Gate 13. The I.C.F. were on the rise at the time; we did the old one-two with the touts, some of us printed our own tickets and Swallow and co. took over Gate 13.

The Shed had been taken by us more than once. In fact, it had got beyond a joke. The only saving grace left open to Chelsea was for them to come to Upton Park.

So Chelsea came to ours. Three-quarters of an hour before kick-off, crowd disturbances broke out in the South Bank resulting in hundreds of Chelsea fans spilling out on to the pitch. Further fights on the pitch brought in police reinforcements. Fifty-seven people were arrested, leading to calls for the club to erect fencing at Upton Park. It was the '80–'81 season, a year we all fought tooth and nail to keep our hold on the South Bank to ensure our intimidation made Upton Park a no-go area for visiting supporters.

Mark Woolwich was there on the South Bank for that game. He remembers that that season, the club had gotten wise to our South Bank capers and had started to make it all-ticket for the away supporters. But we got in there somehow, like we did with Tottenham that season:

After tickets became available to us we managed some old caper to get enough of us in. For quite a few of the boys it was nothing more than a straight swap with the touts outside the main club gates. It went off towards the middle of the South Bank. We had some characters like mad Dicky, who could kick it off any where on his own. For years he was a regular sight being escorted around the pitch with his arm forced up his back, whether we were at home or away. Dicky was getting himself the first of a series of Monday morning fines.

A big gap opened up, as it always used to in these situations. We all started throwing haymakers left, right and centre. Loads of the Chelsea mob were jumping on the pitch just to get out of that end. It was pathetic. Some of them were fifty yards away, nowhere near any incident, just jumping on the pitch to get away. We ended up having to go on the pitch with 'em.

I never found Chelsea stiff opposition, 'cause every time we ever came up against them, we always severely embarrassed them.

Chapter 11

ABERDEEN AGGRO

I.C.F.

The I.C.F. didn't restrict itself just to action south of the border. Mark Woolwich recalls a pre-season crack West Ham were involved in during a tournament in Aberdeen:

A friendly pre-season tournament had been organised to take place in Aberdeen before the '81-'82 season. It involved four clubs: West Ham, Man United, Aberdeen and, surprisingly, Southampton. It must have been some kind of a joke including Southampton in such a prestige event. Then again, I don't really know what we were doing in it either!

We went up on a night train on a Friday night. The turnout wasn't great, maybe 200 in all, because we weren't sure if Aberdeen had a firm and we knew that Southampton definitely didn't. We looked to Man

United as our main target, with whom we shared a mutual feeling of absolute hatred.

Our crowd on the train were the familiar faces you knew you could rely on to perform. Gardner was there. So were Scully, Swallow and a good few Under Fives, Durridge and Woody. There was a fair mob of up-and-coming youngish lads. We must have looked an oddball collection compared to a lot of football mobs at the time. You couldn't get a greater difference in character between the lads: the T.B.F. with their hair growth and dress sense firmly set in the Seventies, compared with the smooth, sharp operators among the Under Fives. Despite the difference, when it came to fighting and West Ham, we'd all come together as one. [In those] days, as the InterCity Firm, all the various firms had come together and were determined that they wouldn't let local differences split the mob.

One thing I recall about this period was that everyone seemed to have plenty of money to hand. Thirty quid is nothing now, but back then it was a lot and yet that would be the cost of the new trainers everybody was into, or a nice pair of Lois jeans or Farahs. Thirty quid also got you a Diamond Pringle jumper to slip on over a slim roll-neck. We called our style casual, and we were into designer labels in a big way. Ignoring T.B.F. and its Scoeby fashions, the InterCity were at the forefront in the football casual scene.[Scoeby was a large member of the older West Ham TBF firm. The casual Under Fives considered the 70s clothes of the TBF old fashioned.] If you take in the cost of our clothing, along with the cost of our travelling, you had to wonder how we all afforded to go to any away matches.

The InterCity wasn't short of lively characters. The East End was full of them, and we had our fair share of artful dodgers. This was where the Under Fives, and maybe the Towners, came into their own.

They had plenty of scams going. One such scam doing the rounds at that time, and one that lasted us well, was the train ticket scam. Everybody knew about it. British Rail had the bright idea of providing inspectors with ticket pads to write out on-the-spot tickets when passengers got caught travelling without one. We soon discovered that one East London station was an easy touch, and it was continually getting broken into for its pads. Once you had the pads, you could write out a destination to anywhere in the country.

This scam seemed pretty obvious to us all, because the starting destination was always the station from which the pads had come. However, because it was assumed that the tickets could only be obtained from a legitimate ticket inspector, they were accepted as bona fide. We had an amazing run with that scam and I think it only came to an end when someone got nicked at a game with a load in his back pocket.

Brett Tidman explains what it was like to travel with the lads up to Scotland for that tournament – travelling inter-city with the InterCity:

On the trip to Aberdeen, I remember one Under Five, a

young blond geezer, being a right pest. Being young, he was up and down the whole way and wouldn't let anyone sleep, even letting off a fire extinguisher. While you were slumped in your seat with your head on your arm, trying to kip, you would be woken up by him again and again. He was everyone's worst nightmare, a proper fucking pest.

We decided that this kid was going to get it. We knew he had to sleep some time, and when we found him sleeping with his mouth open, we thought, right, we've got him now. Someone rolled up some paper and gently propped it on his lips, then set it alight... bang! There you are, you little bastard, have some of that!

We got to Aberdeen at about 10 o'clock on Saturday morning. As soon as we got out we saw Man United, just standing there waiting for us. They must have checked the arrival times to find out when our train was due in. There was a bit of a fracas and we chased them out on to the street. After we'd chased them we came back and started to think about where we were going to stay.

The official travelling West Ham supporters had already booked rooms in advance in the local hotels, so we asked them if we could leave our bags in their rooms, which is what we usually did when we went on England trips. Once we'd stored our bags, we went to the first game.

After we returned from the game, we met up with four Southampton lads. They told us that they'd all spent the previous night in a car park, sleeping in the mini that they'd driven up in. If you're familiar with the weather in Scotland, then it didn't bear thinking about.

During our game against Aberdeen we were backwards and forwards, fighting with the Aberdeen supporters. We later learned they were Aberdeen casuals. Behind their end was a big hill which overlooked the ground. I'll always remember being at the top of that hill, chucking things down at the Aberdeen lads as they ran up towards us. I also recall four West Ham guys pissing on them as they were running past them.

After the fracas had subsided and the Old Bill had pushed us on, we all went back to the hotel. While we were there we learned that one of the four West Ham guys had been nicked. Immediately, we were all struck by the same thought... a spare room! Sure enough, the next morning when we woke up there were twenty-odd people squashed into his room. Imagine five in the bed, a few in the bathroom and loads of other bodies spread around on the floor. Not only had they nicked his room, later that morning they went down and nicked his breakfast as well. I'll never forget the sight of the waitresses serving about twenty-eight breakfasts for a twin-bed room!

The action behind the scenes during these pre-season friendlies often turned out to be just as interesting to the supporters as the action on the pitch. Take a night with unknown opposition on unknown territory, throw in a few scores to settle with known rivals and a few dodgy alliances, and you've got all the potential for a mad beano weekend. Aberdeen was not to disappoint!

Recalling the brawls that occurred after the first games of the tournament had been played, Woolwich maintains that he was not impressed with either the Mancs or the Jocks:

There were about 200 of us lot in total at Aberdeen, while Man United had the usual thousand people or thereabouts. Aberdeen, being the home club, wouldn't be short on numbers, and yet they decided to join with Man United to have a pop at us. How ridiculous is that?

I seem to recall that Man United played Southampton and we played Aberdeen. After the games the Mancs and the Jocks came back to the town centre, where we were drinking at the hotel. I was there with a small group, including Scully and several others. We started to have it with the Mancs and Jocks as they came in to the pub, but there were just too many of them, so we run back to the hotel we were staying at to warn the others that it was all on top.

It was still early, around evening tea time, and most of our boys were in their rooms having showers. They weren't expecting it and so we really had to convince 'em that Man United were here and up for it. I saw Bill Gardner come out wearing nothing but a towel, but it didn't stop him chasing 'em. There were several hundred of them and there were our boys, coming after them wearing shaving foam and pants! We did alright though, chasing them and their Aberdeen mates up the road.

A large group of Texans had been staying in the hotel at the time because of the nearby oil refinery. When the Mancs had tried to gate-crash the hotel, the Americans just stood over to one side, watching the two sets of fans running up and down the road, the Man United supporters throwing everything they could lay their hands on... everything but their fists! I recall the Texans saying that it had been like watching a cow stampede back in America.

The next day, Sunday, we had to play Man United. I think we were beaten with a ridiculous score of five or six to nil. That was the last game of the tournament and we all headed back to the station. We knew that we couldn't fuck about because the train was leaving at about 6 o'clock and the next one wasn't leaving until midnight.

While we were all hovering around at the station, waiting for the train, a Man United mob arrived wanting to catch the same train. We start bashing 'em and chasing 'em up the road again. They reached a place where they had nowhere else to run, so they turned and started chasing us back. It had now become a full-scale fight. Some of the Mancs started jumping into gardens in an attempt to escape, as we were absolutely terrorising 'em.

Even though the Mancs outnumbered us three to one, they were now too scared to even come back down to the station. We wouldn't let them on the train and they

As we are now. Old faces from the firm outside the gates at West Ham. (*left to right*) Bunter, Bill Gardner, Brett Tidman and me, Cass Pennant.

Top: Upton Park station. 'Will you come?' Was the I.C.F. question.

Bottom: Pictures from times when the hair was longer and the trousers wider. The TBF (Teddy Bunter Firm) in Frankfurt in 1976.

The pubs around the ground were always ideal meeting places for the firm.
Top: Me outside the Brit in Plaistow, which we used as an HQ and meeting place.

Bottom: The Queens, next door to the station and market, served us as a staging post.

Inset: The Prince of Wales is still used as a meeting place for West Ham fans.

Bernabeu Stadium, Madrid 1980, the Cup Winners Cup first round. The Second Leg was ordered to be played behind closed doors, after a night of shame.

Fans and police clash at West Ham v Milwall, October 1978. West Ham's South Bank became a no-go area for away fans.

How it all began…

Top: Andy Swallow.

Bottom left: Mickey Ramsgate.

Bottom right: Big Ted, one half of the rock we all stood on.

’Ello ’ello… the Old Bill have a word back in the days when trouble was never far away on a match day.

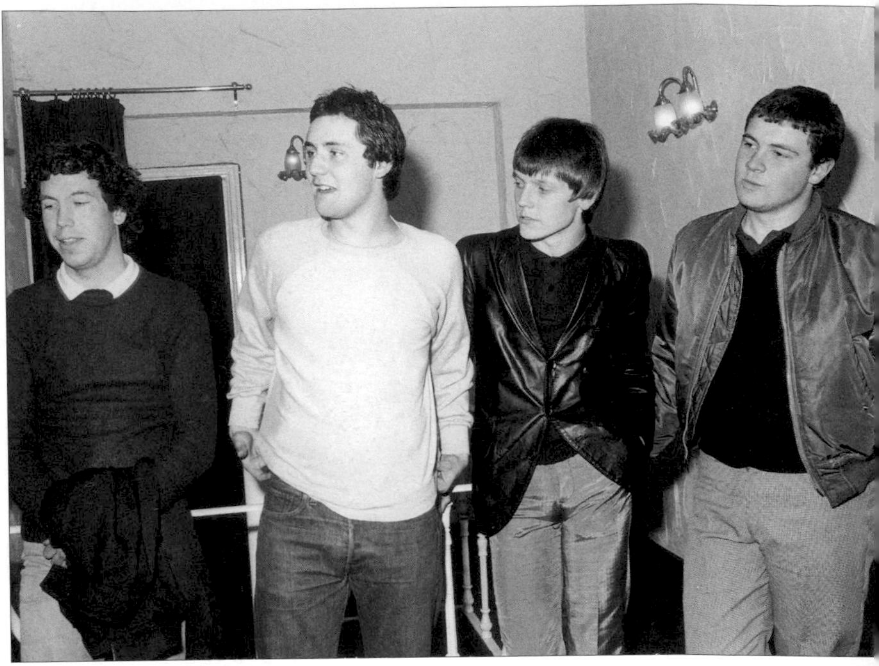

Top: The I.C.F. casual look, as perfected by the lads.

Bottom: Some of the old faces today.

didn't want to get on it with us. It was at this point that the Old Bill stepped in to put an end to things, cordoning off the station, which well and truly blocked the Mancs out. We left them pleading with the Old Bill that they were going to miss their train.

Meanwhile, while our train was pulled in at Edinburgh station, someone looked over at the screens on the other platform to see an announcement for the fast train from Edinburgh to Euston. We all thought that will do us, and we all ran out and across to the other platform, heading for home. It had been a mad weekend.

Chapter 12

WE ARE LEEDS!

I.C.F.

IF THERE were such a thing as an elite or premier league of football thugs, then it would probably include ourselves, Millwall, Man United, Liverpool, Chelsea and Newcastle. You would also have to add Leeds to that list, because they did a lot of damage over the seasons.

In the Seventies we never had the numbers to go anywhere far and Leeds was one of those fixtures that was either a mid-week night match or a postponement rearranged to a night match. As for Leeds at ours, they were guaranteed a hammering either on the South Bank or outside the ground. But at least they showed up.

I remember one season, which could have been the first I.C.F. season of '77–'78, when they took to coming down in an invasion of coaches. As soon as the coaches had been found by our lads, they smashed them all, whether they were parked or still moving. The Leeds fans were getting picked off in the street. It turned into an orgy of destruction on the level of a Chelsea or Man United turnout. It wasn't like West Ham's usual behaviour, but Leeds was the sort of club that got you really worked up. Think of Revie's dirty niggling, wind-up of a Leeds team, and how arrogant the likes of Giles and Bremner were on the pitch, and that's how we looked upon their fans... dirty northern bastards.

With West Ham in the Second Division and Leeds in the first, it wouldn't be until the '81–'82 season that the notorious sets of thugs from both clubs could get a proper meet. There had been one match though, where we thought it might be on. It was the night we had to go Elland Road for an FA Cup semi-final with Everton. That was a great night. None of us will ever forget how delirious we were when Frankie Lamp went up to score the winning goal in the dying minutes of the game and did a mad jig in celebration around the corner flag at our end.

The mobs were even-numbered, but the Everton lads, who had our respect, never tried hard enough to breach the police cordons to get something going with us. We never even saw them. They just went their way. However, Leeds had been making noises about joining up with Everton and doing us in the city centre. After the game, loads of West Ham went into Leeds town centre, partly to celebrate and partly to oblige, but it all amounted to nothing. There was the odd skirmish, but Leeds largely stayed on the outskirts that night, just looking on as

West Ham walked around their city, not even bothering to mob up.

Two seasons later we were back in Leeds again, but this time they were out in force for it and it made for an interesting day.

Leeds Away '81–'82

Terry Sherrin remembers the crack everyone had at Leeds:

I'd missed the first train to Leeds, which carried the main mob, and had to catch the second train. This train was filled with all the stragglers that had missed the main mob on the fast train, plus all the young 'uns, mainly Under Fives. There were about 150 West Ham in all.

When we stepped out of the station at Leeds we began to group up. There were about thirty of our own lot, including Bruce, Micky Bowers and Liddy. We were all gathered outside the station when a few lumps from Leeds came by. One Leeds geezer gave some verbal abuse and the kids gave some back about Leeds being wankers. When the Leeds started taunting us with, 'Come on then', everyone ran across the road at them. We chased them into the shopping centre, where a few more Leeds had gathered. I looked around at our firm. It was mainly odds and sods that had missed our main mob, and young 'uns. We knew that we had to go in there and that our first target had to be this small firm of twenty lairy Leeds, so we thought, right, let's go. Let's have it and don't worry about these mugs. We went straight into the shopping centre, all together as a group.

It was a set-up. The whole centre was full of Leeds and they were all there waiting for us. What we didn't know was that the first train had been through and given it to them. Leeds had the hump, so they were all on it for the second train in from London. They came running in at us from all directions, filling the air with screams of 'Leeds, Leeds, Leeds!' Our young 'uns were up for it, yelling, 'C'mon then, we're West Ham!' The old 'uns were standing together and when I looked around to see that the rest of the young 'uns were standing together as a firm, it felt fantastic. It was like a scene from the film Gladiator as the older ones held the line, wait... wait... wait. Timing was everything. The Leeds geezers were running for us, screaming 'United, we are Leeds!' As the screams were almost on us, the only thought racing through my mind was, 'Fucking hell, there's a lot of these cunts.'

Whenever we met with other firms, it was usually the same old story, just the same twenty to thirty lads standing. That day was different. We were all there standing strong, the stragglers and the young 'uns. Little Crapka from Custom House was right next to me. He was only fourteen but he stood in line with the rest of us. I said to him, 'Whatever you do, just stand there and follow me.' I knew that it was going to be a proper turnout.

The moment had arrived. The mobs were about fifteen feet apart and we started running towards 'em, full pelt. There was a huge collision as we ran right into 'em. The row was unbelievable. It was all spank, spank, spank and there were a few of us getting upped, but I couldn't believe all the young kids. As you looked around you'd see a big fucking Yorkshire geezer with about four kids on him.

The row wasn't going Leeds' way. They could see they weren't winning and they seemed to be thinking, 'Running up and down the street is the way you fight, not this "Stand there and just have it."' They started parting off and as we steamed towards them we were yelling, 'Don't be screaming this and that, just come over here. C'mon Leeds, stand here and fight.'

Then, bang on cue, the Old Bill arrived. They surrounded us and pulled us out, pushing all 150 of our lot back to the station. Leeds had started regrouping and they seemed to be everywhere. It didn't stop us, and we starting chanting 'I.C.F., I.C.F.' You could actually feel the complete hostility in the atmosphere around us.

I realised that we had taken Leeds by surprise in the shopping centre and that we'd faced only part of a Leeds mob who were, in fact, under strength. They'd tried to be too game by taking us on before the bulk of their mob had joined up with 'em. We knew we'd had a result so far, but we still had to get to the ground. As far as Leeds were concerned though, we'd had a few right-handers but we hadn't been done. Meanwhile, with all that had gone on, we were all wondering where everybody was and what had happened to the boys from the first train.

The Old Bill were bang-on up there, they really knew the score. They escorted us down underneath a big, dark bridge, rather like the one at the back of Millwall's Cold Blow Lane. The Old Bill told us that our first train came through here and caused havoc. Blinding, that was our main firm! The coppers then warned us that we were going to pay the price. He told us that the Leeds fans outside the ground were going mad and that they had crowds all along the route to the ground.

The Old Bill held us all under this big bridge, saying, 'Stay here boys while we sort this one out.' That's when we saw what the cops were going on about. On the other side of the bridge they were all waiting for us. There were hundreds of them. They were armed with bricks, bottles, everything, just standing there waiting for us to pass under the bridge. You can just imagine what would have happened if we hadn't been diverted to the shopping centre, bringing a ton of Old Bill on to us. We would have passed through that bridge unescorted and copped it big. But the Old Bill were on to it and cleared all the Leeds boys, giving us a passage right to the ground.

Outside the ground, we met the other lads from the first train. We asked them where they were going and what they had planned. One of the boys said they'd found out that the Leeds main boys went to the seats behind the goal opposite their Kop end. Everyone was up for going to their section and jibbing into their seats. As we bought tickets for the Leeds' end, I couldn't help chuckling with anticipation. Just think about it, big tough butch Leeds and all West Ham in their seats. Fucking liberty, out-and-out liberty, and we were up for it.

Brett, who was with West Ham's main mob that day, recalls what went on at the ground:

A good 500 of us went to Leeds on that rainy day. We got to Leeds quite early, about quarter to twelve, and went straight around to their ticket office and bought all the seats to their brand new end. It was a proper firm that day. Bubbles's mate Hampton was there. He'd been going for years. The G.L.F. firm were all there too, with Butler, Carlton, Dickie and Dorsett. McCarthy was also there. After we'd walked around the ground we went and found a pub down the road.

There weren't any dramas until we took our seats in their end. Back then, Leeds had both ends behind the goal, the main end being the Kop. The away supporters were always put on the right, in the West Stand. As soon as we took over the seats in their South Stand, Leeds fans were on us with their thick Yorkshire accents, telling us we were in their seats. We said, 'Fuck off, we've all got tickets', but we knew it was going to go because the Leeds firm was coming up to us.

I remember Monkey Woods redeemed himself that day, after having once bottled out of a straightener with Babsy, Chelsea's main man. This massive lump of a Leeds geezer was putting himself about like he was their top man. Woods dropped him with one peach of a punch and it was all off from there.

A massive off in the seats ended with us holding our seats throughout the game. After the game, it went off everywhere. As we came out steaming, the West Ham who'd been sitting on the side all came out and joined with us. Leeds were all outside, just waiting. It was toe-to-toe fighting, running up and down streets, bottles and bricks flying. People were getting nicked, but we all thought, fuck the risk of a nicking, let's go for it. So we did, straight into 'em. This time we proper bashed 'em. This time they were gone.

The Old Bill came round and gave us quite a long escort. I was walking at the back of the escort with Carlton when three Leeds geezers infiltrated our escort. I remember turning round and cracking a punch on the biggest of them, causing him to spit teeth. I was steaming in when Carlton dragged me away to prevent me getting nicked. The Old Bill rushed over and tried to nick me and the Leeds bloke I hit. The big Leeds bloke immediately squealed on me, but Carlton reminded the officer of our size difference, because I'm on the small side. The Old Bill quickly lost interest in the squealer, holding his mouth still, and told us to get on our way.

It was a long walk back from the Leeds ground. You have to walk through part of a motorway, past an estate and then through a field with trees. It looked like Leeds were hidden in 'em, but nothing kicked off. The Old Bill were on it.

It was a good day 'cause Leeds ain't a bad firm.

Leeds Home '81–'82

Mouthy Bill can recall another run-in with Leeds:

Leeds used to bring a big mob down. I remember Ron

Greenwood was the manager of England at the time. Quite late in the year, a mob of Leeds headed down to Upton Park. We had a big mob of ours go looking for them on the Tube while the rest of us were tucked into the little wine bar, RJ's, in the corner of the square adjacent to Queen's Market and Green Street. The plan was for all of us to get into the square just before they come out of the station. They wouldn't be able to see us because there was a wall blocking their view.

We were all hiding in the square when suddenly the plan went to pot as four West Ham supporters, who didn't know we were there, came across the road and bash, they're steaming these Leeds fans. Now it's off and instead of having all their mob go past us so we could come up in the middle of 'em, we had to go in from around the corner. There we were, diving into this Leeds mob. Someone had even taken a broom off a road sweeper and lobbed it into the Leeds mob and it went flying back and forth between both sets of supporters.

The Leeds mob tried to run back into the station just as the West Ham mob that had gone looking for them on the Tube came up behind them. That was it. Leeds were sandwiched and we absolutely slaughtered 'em.

Now Leeds still had to come down Green Street and they'd still got to get past The Queens; this time it would be with the tightest of escorts. So we would follow them down with more lads coming in from the Barking Road, knowing the Leeds fans would be led into Castle Street to be put on the South Bank.

The Old Bill used forceful measures to keep the rest of us contained on the pavement on the station side of Queens Market. So we slipped the police lines in ones and twos to infiltrate the front and back of the Leeds escort. It was easy enough and we'd practised infiltrating police escorts season after season; Green Street belonged to us. You soon recognised the familiar faces mingled in, all assuming a low profile until the right moment arrives. Sometimes you'd get half a dozen leery West Ham doing the backward walk at the very front of the escort. In the process, they'd end up getting tugged by the Old Bill. This would slow the escort up enough for the rest of us to get on the back. Sooner or later it would go off again. Thump – it's off as some gobby Leeds fan gets a clump just as we near the entrance to the ground…

It's off now and it's sheer bedlam as the escort opens up and collapses. There's more Old Bill than ever. There's absolute chaos among Leeds, as they all realise what's about to happen. You see the away fans get twisted neck syndrome as they point out the West Ham faces, picking them out from across the road. You feel their apprehension as they recognise the snipers that had travelled on the Tube with them and are now declaring who they really are. No sanctuary when they see the Old Bill move a dozen or so West Ham from the street corner on the left, only to see the gang reappear on the right. Their shiftiness tells you they're tooled. Now someone's whispering, 'The Cockneys have got in behind and it's their firm.' That means twenty to thirty of our game boys, but Leeds don't want to hear that because they've clocked even more faces they've never seen before in front and alongside. Before the Leeds thug can turn to warn his mate, BOSH!... it ain't his mate.

Chapter 13

CITY 'TIL I DIE

– Cool Cats

I.C.F.

'I'm City 'til I die' is the popular chant from the fans of any team called City these days, but it is regarded in the football world as Man City's copyright. It's a meaningful chant that will echo on for decades and will always be associated with the Maine Road faithful, the supporters regarded by themselves – and us – as being true Manchester, in a dig at the worldwide support of their neighbours, United.

However, my real interest in City fans dates back to the time they had a firm, known first as the Guv'nors, then the Cool Cats. The City boys suffered the same problem as their team… they always lived in the shadow of Manchester United. They were nowhere near as notorious as their hated counterparts, Man United's Red Army. Even though the team got the gates, they didn't always get an interested mob. It may have been that they just didn't travel to certain places, because in my time I never saw them make a point with mobs at either our ground or the other main London clubs.

They were always quick to make their point up there with numbers, like any big northern club in the Doc Marten-wearing days of the early Seventies. It was always dodgy going to Maine Road, but that was also true for all the other grounds if you didn't have the numbers. Moss Side was a fearful place to put on a show of heroics if you didn't have a good bunch with you, but as a kid I remember that it was a lot easier going City than United. Being true Manchester with a truly local support, you were only going to bump into them at one place and face one mob somewhere along the route of row upon row of terraced housing.

There was one year in the early Seventies when we even got in their Kippax side, which had been claimed by their boys as the City end. At that time we had just the one coach made up of Gardner, Hampton and Steve Morgan's crew. We held the Kippax throughout the game. They tried all sorts to repair their dented pride, but even the West Ham supporters that don't usually get involved stuck with us.

That was the day I first saw the blond-haired Bill Gardner. He was down the front in his donkey jacket, whacking City yobs trying to creep up from the front with a cleverly folded newspaper. It had been folded in such a way that, when used in the right way, it had the force of an iron bar. In fact, the City fans were squealing to the police about him, but whenever a seemingly disinterested Old Bill went over to confront him, Gardner would just unfold his paper and start reading. It was amusing to watch.

I was standing nearer the back and was absolutely buzzing. My lasting memory of that day was waiting for what seemed like an eternity for the final whistle to go so we could completely claim their end. Things had hotted up like crazy in there and I can still recall the sound of a bike chain being wrapped against the corrugated back end stanchion by four West Ham lads who always went together: H, Page, Hodges and Binsey. Clank-a-dang, clank-a-dang, the sound rang throughout the entire game.

Once we got out on the streets of Moss Side, our numbers gave the game away. I was still with the same game guys who had stood up to everything City's lads could throw at them in the Kippax, and who were still just as game in the streets outside. The City hordes came around out of every exit in the ground. Pockets of us spread out across the road in an effort to make the firm appear bigger than it actually was. Both sides started bouncing around a bit, then you're in, toe to toe.

The fact that we had come from London made the northerners wary of us, and I thought it was going our way. I didn't realise how badly I had misjudged this bitter street fight until we were forced to back off a bit. I had no fear for my own safety, because I'd seen the way the older West Ham always looked after you in those situations. They'd tell you when it was time to run, so I fought on. However, while we were regrouping I caught sight of the two tallest, biggest West Ham lads stampede past me. They were Mick and Martin, two big lumps out of SE18 who always travelled on away trips. I couldn't believe these two. They were men, far older than me, and I knew them well. In fact, I would often follow them if it looked like it was going to go off on our travels. I thought, if they're running like they've spread wings, what are my chances?

My concerns were too late. City were all around us.

I turned towards the fleeting backsides of Mick and Martin and yelled the biggest 'Oi!' you've ever heard. They actually stopped in their tracks and looked at me rather sheepishly as if to say, 'Sorry, we didn't know if any West Ham were still around.' Pissed off, I yelled, 'Stand you cunts!' as I took a big kick up the arse and blocked a beer-bellied swinger by putting my arms up. To their credit, Mick and Martin came back to rejoin the fight. My shouts had got the attention of the others still around fighting for their lives, and I think guilt got the better of them.

We had been overrun and were split in all directions but, as so often happens, just when you think the worst is about to happen, the Old Bill make a show. They nicked a few of us and rounded us up. They would pick on one group of lads and hold them to the side of the road. On this occasion we didn't see the Old Bill as our enemy because we were looking for a breather, so we willingly went along with them. In fact, it's at times like this that you're glad of the Old Bill – London had begun to seem a very long way away.

This interruption gave us the chance to regroup and see familiar faces and we were soon raring to go again. We knew that no one had left and that City were still there as we were being escorted in the direction of Manchester Piccadilly station. Both sides continued to verbal each other out of sheer hate, desperate not to give an inch. With both sides steaming, manic northerners tried to get through the escort to have a pop at us. We knew that if we let them get to us they would break through no matter how many of the Old Bill were around, so we all stuck together and stayed in our escort all the way back to the station.

It wasn't until we were at the station that we told the Old Bill we'd actually come by coach. We had the Old Bill at it now, because they had to call up the vans and cars just to escort our small party all the way back to the coach.

I guess one reason why City's firm never became notorious was because the spotlight was always on United's fans. City had a firm that was never going to make any national headlines and you just had to find out about them for yourselves when you went up there.

My clearest memories of City were during the bovver boy years. During the Eighties I had spells of missed matches as a result of my reputation catching up with me. I had become a little too well known with the Old Bill and if I wasn't doing bird I was liable to be on bail for football-related offences. However, I was smitten by the football drug and it wasn't long before I was right up front with the lads on the terraces again, only now everyone was the I.C.F.

By this time the terraces had gone casual and we fought

a different style of warfare. Most of the old geezers that had been names in the past had been replaced by a dangerous group of young fly-by-nights. It was no longer fashionable to go under the team's name. Everyone was now a firm of some sort and everybody was desperate for their own firm's name to be known. Seeing your firm's name splashed across the headlines after an event became as big a buzz as the event itself. The firms no longer relied on a single leader. Everyone wanted to be a face on the football scene, so instead of leaders and lieutenants you had a large group of top boys, all jostling to put their firm on the map.

When we first started chanting 'I.C.F.' across the terraces after Villa in '78, it was like a secret, sinister code. Even our own players looked puzzled about what the initials stood for and were shocked at the violent way it was chanted. The press soon latched on to us, and began to romance the name 'I.C.F.', always adding the word 'notorious' to every headline we made. Eventually people began to cotton on to the fact that 'I.C.F.' stood for InterCity Firm and everyone who didn't already have a name was suddenly rushing to think of a name for their mob. They soon began to come thick and fast.

Portsmouth's Pompey lads became the 657 Crew, travelling up to London to get themselves all the latest Aquascutum gear. The deerstalker hat and Pringle-wearing boys of Millwall became the Bushwhackers, while Chelsea must have employed a PR company to dream up Head-hunters. This from the firm that said we were too serious!

My favourite name was Naughty Forty Stoke City Boys.

They were pretty late on the scene, but not as late as Snorty Forty, which was pure Scouse wit by the Evertonians. Established names stayed, particularly if they had already gained notoriety, such as the Red Army, Cockney or London Reds, Toon Army, and not forgetting the Yorkshire mobs who liked to be known as crews – Leeds Service Crew or Blades Business Crew.

The names were taken pretty seriously by the firms but there was one that I couldn't take seriously when I first heard it – Cool Cats. This was the name for City's firm and it instantly reminded me of the cartoons *Top Cat* and *Fritz the Cat*. The firm was led by some young upstarts whom I never thought would be of any concern. The last time I had stood in City's ground we had been under the control of the police and no real effort had been made by the City lads, but the younger element of our firm were going potty about a group swapping verbal through the fences. Word had also spread that their firm had our photos. This was a new one to us, and we weren't sure of the relevance. Being the gentlemen we were, we would introduce ourselves before steaming in anyway, if not leave a little calling card afterwards. It was as baffling as it was irritating.

We discussed it on the train on the way home. We wondered what this forerunner to the criminal intelligence unit was. Mickey Ramsgate said that the members of City's firm nearer to our age had introduced themselves as the Cool Cats.

A season or so later, things were destined to go off big-time with the Cool Cats. Ramsgate recalls the events that led up to it:

I think it was the first away game of the season that had any hope of a row and was the first time we had a run-in with City's Cool Cats. It was a sunny September's day and we'd gone up there firm-handed, which was another sign that it was early season. Everyone was into wearing or taking mad things. We all had these party streamers. It was silly season.

All of a sudden we heard this clicking noise coming in our direction from across the bridge near the ground. Everyone was scattered around a car park at the time, some of us lying down, sunning ourselves. This clicking racket, which we were to later learn was the Cool Cats' signature tune, alerted us all. The police stepped back and let 'em through. Our lot started blowing the streamers we had as if they were bugles, just like a scene from The Fox and the Hounds. *Suddenly we jumped up and they ran like lightning, like they had roller blades on.*

Later that day, inside the ground, Donald Francis and his little Cool Cat firm were mouthing it off at us. They said they had taken photos of us standing at Crewe station while others were gesturing to us by drawing a line across their throats. We spent the match gathered along the side, so they had come around from the back of their end and were leaning over the fenced-off sections, giving loads of verbal. We had never been into verbal, unless you were prepared to back it up. We told 'em they were mugs and asked them why they were taking pictures of us. It was pathetic, we couldn't see any point to it. In fact, the whole day turned out to be pathetic, with no major rows between the firms.

There was only one time that I can recall when we had a major row with the Cool Cats. It happened when City were at home. I think we were playing Oldham and we were actually coming back from the match. That morning, we had all left the train at Manchester Piccadilly to walk across the city to Manchester's Victoria station. There must have been about 300 of us. As we strolled across Manchester we weren't confronted by a single soul. We couldn't believe it.

After we had watched the game we made our way back via the same route. When we arrived at the station I remember seeing a local youngster hanging about the station like he was a spotter or something. I asked him where his chaps were today. The kid told us that they had been watching us through the station windows and thought we were all proper geezers, well older than them. They couldn't get over the number of men we had.

It looked to us like City no longer had a firm, so we decided to catch the train because we all wanted to be in the Brit by nine. However, as we went to get on the train we were stopped by the Old Bill. They told us that Watford were here first and were going back on that train. We all argued that we had paid for inter-city travel and this was an inter-city train, so by rights we were public passengers and couldn't be stopped from getting on. They stood firm though, and things turned heated. Someone said, 'If you don't let us on, we'll all go and smash up the city centre.' They weren't amused by this remark, but gave us an indifferent look as if to daring us to do it. They then allowed us to all walk off, as if to call our bluff.

Loads of us started to make our way out of the station, heading down the hill leading to the square. It was about a quarter to six by now and we were all feeling a bit hungry, so we stopped for chips, mushy peas and gravy, a real northern delicacy. Food sorted, we walked around the corner of the Piccadilly Centre where all the taxis park, with a big green nearby, when we suddenly spotted the Cool Cats all in the Wimpy. We went into them but they sort of backed off us a bit, so we didn't have it all our own way, it was a bit fifty-fifty.

I'll give that Donald Francis his due, he came out holding his hands up, but I think he was carrying a big machete or something. They were trying to creep up on us. They had tried to creep up on Danny Harrison but he had a hold on one of them – no one anybody knew – and was slamming this no one's head into a bus shelter. Suddenly it went right off. It was just like a free-for-all. Local cab drivers were jumping out and wading into the fight with long torches, spanners, car jacks, anything they could lay their hands on. A wrong move on their part. We all went proper mental and, true to our word, we more or less smashed up Piccadilly. The Old Bill couldn't wait to get us back up to the station and get us out. As for the Cool Cats' main face, Donald Francis, the story has it that he got served up so severely in the fight that he was later to get around £14,000 in compensation. He had gone through the Wimpy window.

Mark Woolwich backs up Ramsgate's account of that day, and highlights one Hammer that wouldn't forget it in a hurry:

> *To be honest, they're not a bad firm. The fighting between us was going on around the whole square. As the Old Bill tried to force us up a ramp to separate us and herd us up to the station, some policewomen let the dog go. On my life, this dog took a chunk out of Andy Lewisham's arse, ripping his strides. My mate Lewisham was a familiar face who didn't miss many games and we'd seen him in a right few scrapes, but the pain of the dog bite he was to suffer was unbelievable.*
>
> *Back on the train on the way home you could hear him sobbing in pain and sniffing his words about how he was going to have the policewomen's fucking numbers. He moaned that we were out of order for laughing. Swallow was rolling around the carriage in stitches, as Lewisham was wandering around asking if anyone would be a witness, but none of them had seen anything. All he could say was 'Look at me strides.' They were completely bloodied because he couldn't put a plaster or bandage on the wound. You had to feel sorry for him because of the pain he was in, but sometimes you couldn't keep yourself from laughing.*

Chapter 14

SMOKE GETS IN YOUR EYES

– Gooners '82

I.C.F.

OF ALL the times West Ham had taken or run the North Bank at Highbury, the most spectacular was during the '82 season, when a smoke bomb was let off. It also turned out to be the most tragic clash that took place between the two rival groups, after the death of an Arsenal fan as a result of a skirmish at Finsbury Park Tube station. The press went overboard in their reports on the clash, claiming that West Ham's I.C.F. had left calling cards on their victims – which had never been proved. As a result of these reports, it seemed that every football firm in the country were now renaming themselves and printing out their own calling cards.

The tragedy that occurred that day certainly made quite a few of us think for a moment about the risks we were all taking and realise that what we were all involved in was no game. However, we couldn't let it cloud the fact that the Arsenal lads had been up for it that day and were just as game as West Ham. The taking of the North Bank and the carnage that followed it was the work of just two small firms: Andy Swallow's crowd and the Towners.

Andy's own version of events was that he had headed for the Gunners pub, which was the Arsenal firm's boozer during the Seventies, before going to the North Bank. For many West Ham fans who remember, the pub had traditionally marked the first row of the day, but by the Eighties it was no more than a claret-and-blue watering hole that we stopped off at before going on the Arsenal North Bank end. The following is Swallow's account of the last-ever taking of the North Bank Highbury:

A dozen of us decided to leave the pub and get in to the ground early, as the Old Bill were getting strict on preventing West Ham supporters from getting in the North Bank end. Among the group were Grant, Danny Harrison, myself and a few others. We got in to the ground at about 12.30. Once we were in, we proceeded to set about Arsenal fans drifting in and coming up the stairs. Looking back now it was a pretty crazy thing to do. This went on for about an hour or so and then we sat down in the middle of the Arsenal North Bank and just waited.

We knew the main firm of West Ham were going to come in soon, because there were so many boozing in the Gunners pub that they had spilled out on to the street. We noticed familiar faces starting to come in and sit down on the floor.

All of a sudden, as it drew closer to kick-off, a Gooner crept up on us. He was known to us because he was the brother of Alfie Barker, one of the B.G.F. and staunch West Ham. Barker's brother appeared with an Arsenal firm which was full of all the older faces. This was their firm. All the West Ham in the North Bank stood up. Barker's brother walked over and stood toe to toe with us. He used to wear these gloves and the moment he pulled his gloves up we steamed straight into 'em. It all went off. This was Arsenal's firm and we knew that they had been putting a decent firm together.

What happened from there can be best described by Terry Sherrin, who had entered the North Bank that day with the Towners. The Towners were always a firm within a firm and were so called because they came from in and around East London's Canning Town. Terry describes the way events unfolded:

Just before 3 p.m. all the Townies, about thirty of us in total, left the Gunners pub. The group included Churchy, Dawkes, Feldman, Tallman, Jed, Weasel and myself. West Ham were already in the North Bank getting sorted and there seemed to be loads of them. They made at least two attempts to take the North Bank, but couldn't do it.

By two minutes past three we had run the North Bank and they had stopped the game. It was that quick.

We'd come through the usual entrance of the North Bank, coming from the direction of the pub, past all the

Victorian terraces leading into Avenell Road. The West Ham mob already in there were hemmed in on the far side of the North Bank, towards the front of the open, uncovered area. Quite a few people were being dragged out by the police to be escorted up to the Clock end, the south end of the ground.

The Arsenal support had all the covered end of the North Bank, so we plotted ourselves halfway up the back and alongside them. Just in front of us was a long gangway that runs through the middle of the North Bank. We noticed Swallow with a good seventy lads situated below us, towards the middle. A few more had followed us or found us from the pub and we had grown to about fifty or sixty strong.

We clocked an Arsenal firm with all their boys. They hadn't noticed us but they'd clocked Swallow's outfit and started heading across in their direction. They walked past us in ones and twos, but still moving as a unit. Some of them looked us up and down but, like them, we were watching Swallow and company, so they probably thought we must be more Arsenal plotted up.

One of ours whispered, 'There's Denton.' Arsenal's face was standing right there at the front, with only a barrier separating us. We waited a minute but we were all just itching to go. These Gooners were that close to us. They were all walking past us when all of a sudden someone threw a right-hander. Bosh! It was all off. All fifty of us erupted and were up in the middle of them before they even knew what had hit 'em. They had nowhere to go.

We knew exactly who we were fighting. We'd watched them attempt to move in on Swallow's lot. We were now toe to toe with Arsenal's top firm, but we'd got in the first blows. We were also very much together as a unit, while they were more a mob of individuals. Most of us were right tanked up, as we'd been drinking in the pub for three hours. I remember thinking that geezer Weasel could really punch a bit, but I later found out that he had a bottle of vodka in a carrier bag and was smashing Arsenal heads with it.

The Gooners knew that West Ham had been trying to take the North Bank all afternoon but had been out-manoeuvred. Arsenal had held their end and done it with pride. By now they were probably thinking that they were the bollocks and that West Ham had had their go. Then they saw Swallow's firm and were probably asking themselves, 'What the fuck they were doing in there?' You can imagine what they were thinking – yeah, we'll flush them out as well. They made their move and we were just behind 'em, ready.

As is often the way in these clashes, a gap opened where we were fighting. When the gap opened, you had Gooners running down on to the pitch. We just ran down after them to make them all get on the pitch. To our side, Denton's boys were fighting, moving backwards, not out of any real fear but because we were forcing Arsenal back out of the North Bank. Swallow's lot were now steaming through the same gap to join up with us.

Things were getting really chaotic and confused. The Arsenal fans on the pitch didn't know what the hell was

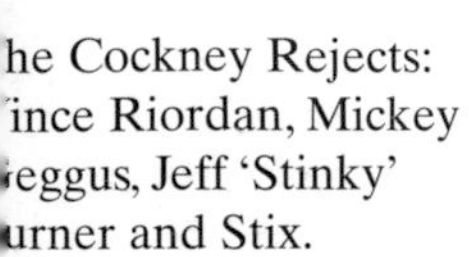

he Cockney Rejects:
ince Riordan, Mickey
eggus, Jeff 'Stinky'
urner and Stix.

IT'S EITHER HIT AN ICEBERG OR THE WEST HAM FANS ARE ABOARD!

Notorious and always attracting media attention from all angles.
'op: Swallow gives it some.

ttom: This cartoon appeared in the *Sun* after West Ham fans clashed with nchester United fans on board a ferry.

CONGRATULATIONS !

you've just met West Hams

ELITE UNDER FIVES

POSSE

Surprise! Surprise!

You've Seen The Programme

Now Meet The Stars

I. C. F.

(WHEN THE GOING GETS TOU

THE TOUGH GET GOING

The Under Fives had their own calling card.

Inset: This calling card was a 'tongue in cheek' response to the attention we received after the documentary *Hooligan*.

CHAMPIONS
LYALL STYLE

TORCH

but crazy times with the West Ham
Army.

News of the World, February 19, 1984

HAMMERS FACE FA 'COURT' OVER FAN INVASION

BIRCH 'EM!

Saunders lashes hooligans

REG DRURY reporting

BIRMINGHAM manager Ron Saunders last night blasted the hooligans who twice held up the closing stages of the club's 3—0 FA Cup victory over West Ham.

And his solution? "Give 'em a taste of the birch. A deterrent is clearly needed. I believe that's the answer. What else can you do? If you have a wild dog you don't stroke it, do you?

"The pity is that these people are not football hooligans — they're just hooligans. If they weren't causing trouble at games, they would be out on the streets doing it.

"Unfortunately, it's a social problem of this day and age, but clearly something has got to be done to put it right."

Birmingham were coasting to victory with eight minutes to go when several hundred West Ham fans raced across the pitch, jostling the home players. Birmingham's Kevan Broadhurst was pushed to the ground, but was unhurt and soon regained his feet.

At that stage, the situation looked ugly as a number of Birmingham supporters came on to the pitch from the opposite end as though determined to do battle. But within four minutes the pitch was cleared without any major casualties and the game re-started.

But just three minutes later, more trouble. We had a second pitch invasion and this time referee George Courtney led both teams off to the safety of the tunnel for a spell of eight minutes while police again coped—helped by three mounted colleagues who patrolled one touchline on their horses to prevent any more troublemakers getting into the act.

FA secretary Ted Croker immediately left his seat in the stand to go down to help try to calm the situation.

Croker said afterwards:

Birmingham City 3 West Ham United 0

"Clearly, we will look into the matter to try to find out exactly what happened and see if there is a case to answer by either or both clubs.

"I thought the referee handled it extremely well. However long it had taken, we were determined that the full 90 minutes would be played."

Saunders also praised the referee, and the players of both teams, for the way they conducted themselves in a difficult moment and added: "It was such a marvellous match for us that I only hope that the spot of bother doesn't take the gloss off it."

West Ham boss John Lyall said: "It seems a lot of people got frustrated. Perhaps they will feel that was understandable, but it hardly helps the game and it doesn't help either club."

It's difficult to see what action can be taken. The old solution of closing a ground would obviously be unfair in this instance, when there was no need for any Birmingham fans to get involved.

The biggest crowd of the season at the ground—nearly 30,000—were happy to see their club on the way to the Cup quarter-finals.

Referee Courtney refused to comment afterwards, but will be making a detailed report which—as Croker admits—will be the basis of any official investigation.

The game itself was as good as over by the 14th minute. By then, former Aston Villa players Robert Hopkins and Tony Rees had put Birmingham 2—0 ahead.

West Ham, with seven first-team players missing, never produced their league form and were buried in the 78th minute when Billy Wright thundered home a penalty after Ray Stewart fouled Rees.

"We must look into this and see if the clubs have a case to answer — football's the loser"

Ted Croker, FA secretary

FIRST AID . . . this ambulanceman risks injury wrestling a corner flag from pitch invaders while (above left) the thugs run wild

WHISKY GALORE! GET ON OUR GRAND NATIONAL WINNER—PAGE 20

ore trouble as West Ham clash with Birmingham City at an FA Cup match.

Top: Ian 'Butch' Stuttard, the man behind the documentary *Hooligan*. He was th
only outsider ever to have been allowed inside the I.C.F.

Middle left: ICF faces – Big Ted and Haystacks.

Bottom right: Vaughny and Bill Gardner.

he I.C.F. reunion at the Theatre of Dreams, Old Trafford, in 2001.

op: The black Hammers.

ottom left: Carlton Leach and Jon O'Brien.

ottom right: Terry Sherrin.

Top: Timmy Mac reflects on days gone by.

Bottom: Nat and Brett, and Johnny Hampton.

going on behind them. They'd just jumped on the pitch in order to look round. The West Ham fans at the Clock end thought Arsenal had run and we could hear them singing and clapping a chant of 'We took the North Bank Highbury again'. Arsenal's firm hadn't run, though. They had just been caught by surprise and were trying to regroup.

Another gap opened up and I went under another barrier to steam in. Arsenal steamed back and we were all fighting again. I was hit and had claret over me from a cut. I looked around to see what was happening. They were coming for us – a fucking big firm. For those who aren't familiar with the ground, North Bank is a big, big end and – forget all the bollocks – Arsenal's got a tasty firm. We were still going toe to toe, right in the middle of North Bank. We were a bit spread out with all the skirmishes, but it was West Ham all together, maybe 200 to 300 of us.

Another big gap opened where the regrouped Arsenal were coming back at us. Just then someone let off a smoke bomb right in front of the Gooners. I'm telling you, it was like fucking Vietnam, a cloud of orange smoke choking the whole North Bank. Luckily, where we were was clear. The Old Bill couldn't see us and the Gooners were coming through the smoke blind. To us, it was like Christmas. Arsenal were all coming through in spluttering groups, not knowing where the fuck they were. They just got battered as we picked them off at will. We ran them right out of the North Bank, with loads more of them opting to go on the pitch again.

Once more you could hear the Clock end erupting with, 'Hello, hello, West Ham aggro' *and* 'What's it like, what's it like to run at home?'

Arsenal were gutted, the whole ground witness to the carnage. It wasn't that we were better than them, but we'd caught them with yet another surprise. The Old Bill couldn't see what was going on, so we could get laid in real sweet.

When the smoke cleared and the Old Bill had cleared the pitch, we had the whole back of the North Bank. Our numbers had been strengthened further by other mates that had been ejected out of the ground only to pay to come back in again. We were all rightly full of ourselves and taunted Arsenal rotten.

The Old Bill came to us first. Loads of them were going berserk, but we just took to whistling this inane tune that the older West Ham lads used to whistle in the Shed in the early Seventies. The Old Bill were fucked, as any attempt to take us out would mean they'd have to take us through all the Arsenal, who were on all sides of us. Arsenal at that stage were going mental as we conducted our own musical, singing the 'I.C.F., I.C.F.' chant and winding them up with, 'Thank you very much for the North Bank Highbury, thank you very, much, thank you very, very, very, much.'

One Arsenal fan had to be held back by the Old Bill, his face enraged and blood vessels popping. He was the next to get it as we sang, 'Does your mum, does your mum, does your mummy know you're here?' *followed by* 'Jeremiah, the sugar puff fairy, has got some boots and cropped his hair and now he's gone to join the North Bank Highbury.' *Everyone was just buzzing and full of it.*

The Old Bill feared that by escorting us out they might lose control and would find themselves in the middle of it. In the end they thought it would be safer to accept that we were in the North Bank to stay and to completely surround us with a ring of officers. We didn't care. As far as we were concerned it was business as usual and we just wanted to rub it in. We continued to give it to Arsenal with more adapted pop ditties or children's songs, such as 'We took the North Bank in half a minute/We took the North Bank with Arsenal in it/With hatchets and hammers, ratchets and spanners, you don't dilly dally on the way.'

We had taken it away from Arsenal and they couldn't get their heads around it. To any casual observer it would have seemed that most of West Ham had run the North Bank. In truth, however, it was a hardcore of only about 150 West Ham in the thick of it all, but it showed Arsenal that we were more than just one mob. In fact, we had taken three mobs into the North Bank that day.

What was left now was the nucleus of two mobs, Swallow's and the Towners, with Arsenal's geezers all around us. Alfie Barker's brother kept popping up to have a go at West Ham. I also remember Monkey Woods fronting out their man Jenkins and giving it to him about his red V-neck jumper because he never changed it. What Arsenal were in fact trying to do was to get behind us in order to steam us into the Arsenal crowd in front of us. The momentum would take us down, causing the Old Bill to split, leaving way for an Arsenal pincer movement to get us from either side... No way were we prepared to fall for Arsenal's move, we just turned around and steamed in on them. When the Old Bill saw what was going on they ran around the back of the stand to fuck the Arsenal off, which left us in the back of the North Bank again for the remainder of the game.

It was after the game, in a separate incident at Finsbury Park Tube station, that the real tragedy occurred. During a fight, an Arsenal fan was killed. This would have hit home to everyone. No football match is worth dying for.

The first anyone really knew of the incident was when the Old Bill came up and took photos of everyone. We all thought we were getting nicked. This was during the early years of what later became known as the Criminal Intelligence Unit and the result was that West Ham were never allowed in the North Bank after that day. They put spotters from K Division (West Ham Old Bill) on the North Bank entrances and asked questions only an Arsenal fan would know the answer to.

Some years later, while I was on a train hurtling up North, I overheard the North Bank smoke bomber talking about the events of that day. I heard him say that he had been in the Army at the time, but had gone to the Hammers whenever he could. He said that he had an orange smoke grenade his pocket, as they didn't search everyone coming through the turnstiles in those days. He knew that as soon as the bomb went off there would be large amounts of confusion. He said that after he pulled the pin and dropped it on the floor 'the fucking North Bank just filled up with smoke and they didn't know what him 'em. And I thought they were called the Gunners!'

Chapter 15

ENGLAND HAMMERS

I.C.F.

FOR WEST HAM lads, going to England matches was not always considered worthwhile. In fact, it was often more of a problem.

In the Seventies the West Ham mob were ready to fight any other club's firm at any time, particularly their London rivals. They were obsessed with earning a reputation as the hardest firm in the land and went about it with some consistency. It created a real resentment with our rivals throughout the country. Such was the reputation of West Ham that our opponents had difficulty in mustering their regular lads to turn out when they knew they would be facing West Ham.

The West Ham support knew that part of their strength lay in the tightness of their following – keeping it all East London-based with no outsiders.

They trusted no one outside their community, an attitude more commonly associated with the East End underworld. They had recognised the loose following of rival mobs as a weakness, and believed that the tightness of their own mob would always give them an edge.

Their point had been proven in past clashes, at the time when the northern clubs dominated all the cup final appearances. On their regular trips to Wembley each season, the northern clubs thought nothing of forming easy alliances with rival northern clubs to take on the Cockneys. These alliances were made the night before a match or on the morning of Cup Final day. When the Cockneys found themselves on the run they would level up with alliances of their own. This would nearly always be a combination of five London clubs: Arsenal, Chelsea, Tottenham, Millwall and West Ham.

The problem was that these London alliances wouldn't hold together, particularly where West Ham were concerned. West Ham viewed themselves as the top mob out there, and they didn't like the idea of going up front, fighting everyone else's battles for them and carrying mugs from other firms that they didn't rate. A lot of resentment had built up against West Ham among the other London clubs, based on pure jealousy. Millwall believed that they were the hardest mob around and resented the idea of joining up with West Ham. With this mutual feeling of loathing rife between the clubs, the London Super Club gang could never really be sustained.

It did happen for a couple of seasons, mainly because

the Chelsea and Arsenal lads would mix with the Millwall lads at times, but when it came to West Ham it would always end up with the London firms turning on each other before the day was over. The arrogant West Ham members would either find some excuse to kick off with our allies, or the other London clubs would take the first opportunity to settle old scores and turn on West Ham when the numbers were in their favour. The latter happened enough times to confirm that West Ham couldn't trust the other London clubs. The unwritten rule for West Ham was to go with no one, because there was no one we could trust. London United had established that and besides, we didn't rate anyone except our own mob. On the few occasions that we did join up with other clubs, we only went with the Tottenham lads because we knew Tottenham couldn't trust their rivals Arsenal, Chelsea and Millwall either.

This was the first time that the London rivals began to realise they could form temporary alliances, albeit not as easily or on the scale of the northerners. It was at this point that the possibility of getting it together and taking the troubles on the terraces over to the England scene first began to dawn on people.

The possibility was exciting, but it raised a problems for West Ham: what were we to do when it seemed like all the action was with going England abroad and we weren't there because we couldn't stomach going along with all the England following? We didn't know who the boys on the England scene would be. In the late

Seventies, Man United had the biggest England following. By the Eighties, Chelsea had become the influence. West Ham and England was never on. In the Eighties, West Ham's I.C.F. had several new firms and some new faces on the scene. These were younger men looking for new challenges and they began looking to the England scene. The Cup Winners' Cup campaign had given everyone the taste for having a crack abroad.

Swallow – England Hammer

Andy Swallow was one Hammer who was keen in getting involved on the international front. He remembers when West Ham decided to add their name and reputation to the cross of St George. They chose Scotland v England in '82. It was time the Jocks were taken to task for ripping down our goalposts at Wembley...

About a hundred of us met at Euston, which was a big firm from one club all in a mob. We were probably the biggest single following going with England from any club, second only to Chelsea or Manchester. Even though Chelsea and Man U dominated the England scene with their numbers, it would be the West Ham lads who dominated the sequence of events abroad.

We had all decided to go up and have a pop in Jock land as West Ham, not England. It was mainly a young West Ham, with a few Towners, a few Under Fives and a good bunch of lads you could rely on.

When we got on the train there were quite a few other London clubs on the train. I remember Chelsea's Hickey got on wearing a shirt with 'Bomb Argentina' on it. Chelsea had a good firm of about fifty to seventy lads. On the train, he came up to us to see if we were joining up with them. We said, 'Bollocks, we're West Ham' and told him to fuck off, even though we knew him from previous England trips. We weren't having it. Hickey wasn't put off and suggested that everyone stay together when we got to Scotland. Our lot said, 'You lot go with England, we'll go on our own.'

By the time the train reached Scotland it was full of England who had got on at various stops en-route. There were a few Jocks on board the same train and they got a slap as they got off at Glasgow. They couldn't believe they were in Glasgow and were getting slapped by the English!

Glasgow was a massive station. As the England were getting out of the train they saw a few Scotland fans around and everyone ran at them until they ran off. But West Ham weren't having any. We just stood back and looked on. The Chelsea lot and the other England came up and said, 'Come on West Ham, England together.' We told them that West Ham went with no one, so the two firms walked towards the ground separately, England on one side of the road and us on the other.

On the way to the ground it kicked off here and there, becoming more frequent as we got nearer to the ground. It was nothing major though, as the Jocks didn't seem to believe that we could ever bring a decent firm up, [one that could actually be] walking around their patch looking for a row. There were little mobs of Jocks who came up to have a look at us, saying, 'C'mon then, England', but we told them to fuck off because we were West Ham.

We didn't have tickets, so when we got to the ground we just hung around. The Hampden Park stadium was phenomenal. There were plenty of minor skirmishes with the Jocks. They seemed bemused that we had come to fight and seemed to prefer abusing us verbally [rather] than fighting.

The game had started and the doors of the ground had closed, leaving us outside without tickets. There were about one hundred of us left and a load of Jocks. We had already fucked all the England off, so, between us and the Jocks, we managed to smash the doors down and run in. It must have looked like we were running the Jocks in the ground because a big gap opened up, but it was only us bunking in. We were all segregated, about thirty to forty of us in with about one hundred Jock and English in this side.

When the game ended, we became separated as we came out of the ground and ended up in silly groups. You just couldn't see anyone in the crowd of that size. I seem to remember coming back after the game in a group of about six people. We went and had a beer in the Gorbals and eventually met up with the rest of our West Ham lot there later when we walked to Glasgow Central. The train wasn't due until later that night, so we decided to go to a bar across the road from the station.

By now the Jocks were making their way home and as we were standing at the station all the Jocks started coming around us. A geezer who was literally covered in loads of scarves came up to me and started giving it that he was Scotland. I said, 'Fuck off, you Christmas tree' and the Jock retorted with 'England are wankers.' We steamed into him and his mates and it started from there. Word quickly spread around the pubs and streets that England were at the station.

By the time we got on the train it was filled with half England, half Scotland, with a lot of Jocks that had just piled on with no intention of going anywhere. The train was packed but nearly all West Ham were together. We were about one hundred strong. I remember being up the front of the group when I noticed that half a dozen Chelsea had slipped in with us, which became quite noticeable when it kicked off with the Jocks again. Everyone was squashed up in the tiny train compartments when we steamed into the Jocks. It got quite fierce. We were actually smashing them backwards, forcing them along the carriage.

At one point a Jock grabbed me by the hair and England had me by the arm, pulling me back. I'd already had an arm bandaged up, so when the lads pulled me out of it I said that it was someone else's turn to go in front. The rest of our lot got in front. Some had handle-like things which they were using as weapons, so we broke them up and started smashing them over their heads. I was lying across the top of the West Ham fans, leaning down with a pole, whacking [the Scots] on the head. Then I decided to get back down again, so I was right in the middle of them.

This must have been going on twenty to thirty minutes and in the end I just lay down on the floor. I'd had enough and thought it was someone else's turn, but when I got back up it was still going, both sides fighting non-stop in the carriage. Finally, we had the Jocks on the run. They retreated to some glass compartments, shutting all the doors after them. That wasn't going to stop anyone, and the windows were soon kicked through. By this time the Jocks were terrified, as the train was in the middle of nowhere.

One of the Jocks got stabbed in all the fighting and the rumour going around was that the geezer that had done it had pulled the emergency cord and run off, never to be seen again. Someone said that he was Chelsea.

The police were waiting for us at the next station and they pulled all the England fans off the train. The train had been a half-hour into its journey. At the station, the Old Bill interviewed all the Jocks, including the Jock who had been stabbed and his mates. They lined us all up but the Jocks deliberately failed to identify us, which meant that the Old Bill had to let us get back on the train.

When we were back on the train, we started talking to the Jock geezers that we had just had the big fight with. They asked who the fuck we were. We told them that we were the I.C.F., West Ham. They said that they were mainly Rangers fans and that they came from all the towns a few stops down the line. They told us that it had been the best fight they'd ever had and that they'd like to meet us every week.

Taffy – England Hammer

In one of their books, the Chelsea lads claim that they gave I.C.F.'s Taffy a bit of a hard time on England's trip to Luxembourg and at another match in Romania. Taffy was always up for a bit of England in-house fighting. Andy Swallow comes to his defence. He was there when Chelsea had a run-in with Taffy at a France v England match:

There were about fifty to sixty West Ham on the French Underground, all the Under Fives. I was one of the eldest. At Gare de L'or station a whole trainload of Chelsea got on, so Taffy, myself and a few others had sent Nazi Mick and one of the others to have a little scout. Chelsea were saying, 'We'll do West Ham' as we were getting ready to get off the train. What they didn't realise was that all the West Ham fans had iron bars, choppers and axes. As the doors opened, we jumped off and opened our coats and said, 'Alright Chelsea.' They backed off when they saw that and asked us where we were going. I told them, 'Never mind about where we're fucking going' and Taffy turned around and said, 'Well come on then, I'm Wales.' They all immediately said, 'No, no, no. We've got no trouble with you Taffy, we've got no trouble with you,' but Taffy just went on offering them out, shouting, 'Come on Chelsea, I'm Wales, West

Ham Wales. What are you going to do about it?' All the West Ham were laughing and we just walked off. They went off as well. They had the hump.

The story going around was that they fucked him off. No way. The confrontation with Chelsea went on for about five to ten minutes and all that time he was going up to them, offering them out to try to get into a fight.

You could always feel the animosity between Chelsea and West Ham and it continued on the England trips. Chelsea were always wannabes. They'd found their little niche on the England scene when along came those spoilers, West Ham. Many an England fan has said that they can feel that uneasy atmosphere whenever both sets of supporters are around. One England Villa fan summed it up by saying, 'Most England fans just ignore West Ham because you never know how they are going to take you. We all go to be England but the West Ham like to let you know they are just West Ham.'

Animal – England Hammer

West Ham all met around Mile End for the France v England match. There was a big mob of us having a drink in the Horn of Plenty. I'd never seen a turnout like this for an England game and I don't even know why everyone decided to go. You knew everyone was in good spirits because someone said that they were having bets on who they were going to have it off with first. They just knew this was going to be the day.

When everyone was ready, we moved on to Victoria. The train for Calais wasn't going yet so we decided to drink in the Shakespeare, because we had a good twenty minutes to kill. We went in there with every intention of just having a drink, but all I could hear was, 'Oi, you Chelsea bastards' and 'C'mon Chelsea.' It was Taffy having it, so it's gone off. The Old Bill came in and tried to split it and they had to take Chelsea out because there were so many West Ham. Chelsea then left while we stayed on drinking.

After a while, everyone started to get bored so we began making a move for the train. We walked into the station and who do we see but loads of Chelsea, all sort of penned-in in a section of the station. We just ripped straight into 'em and done 'em and then got through on to the train. The police clued on to the situation and again got hold of Chelsea, herding them on to the first three carriages of the train. Then a ticket geezer got on and locked all the doors between the carriages and made sure that there was one empty carriage between the three Chelsea carriages at the front and the four packed West Ham carriages behind.

When the train got to Dover, the doors opened and it all kicked off again. The Old Bill on the train had to get off to split us all up.

Then we started thinking that if we were behind Chelsea, they were going to get the first boat out, which wasn't right. We went in front so that Chelsea were behind us and we all watched ourselves. By this time, the Old Bill had had enough because they wanted to go, so they put us on the boat but put Chelsea on as well. The captain came over and said that if there was any trouble then the boat wouldn't leave.

We were all sitting there at the bar with a beer, the boat about half an hour out to sea, when World War Three erupted. Before we knew it we've got a mini riot going on, with glasses and bottles flying and chairs being ripped out. The captain announced that he was sending in the British police and about seven, maybe eight coppers came in. The place looked wrecked, but everyone was sitting there in the plastic seats drinking and it looked as if everything had calmed down. The coppers realised they had both Chelsea and West Ham sitting there, but what could they do? It looked as if there was no problem at all. They must have thought that little gap between us was an invisible brick wall.

The captain came back and he was having none of it. He told us that if it didn't stop, he'd turn the boat around. That sort of ended it because we'd done Chelsea but for once they'd put up a good show, they'd had quite a go. Anyway, we were now ready for the French.

Our firm was mainly Under Fives. I think all the Under Fives were there with Swallow and BJ, but there was also Shakesy and all that lot and I was in another mob of Goldtooth, Swede, Gary Long, Stevie. When we got off the boat, we were all ready for partying and for another go with Chelsea. It didn't happen though, because they ended up making us laugh. They'd got off first and, along with a few Scouse and other England fans, were nicking motors and driving them into the sea. There were forty, fifty or more cars all lined up on the dock waiting to be shipped, with all the keys left in the ignition.

The French police came and we stayed together, letting the first train go. We all got on the next train to head into France.

Gardner – England Hammer

I went to the World Cup in Spain for two weeks in '82. That was an interesting situation, getting shot at by Argentineans. We stayed in a place called Zarautz. I took a coachload of supporters with Trans Euro Travel. They were a mixture of Southampton and Tottenham fans with some Man U and Chelsea fans there as well.

It was in the pub that night that I first met Hickey. He introduced me to all his Chelsea mates, all sitting round the wall. I had to give them all a hard handshake, 'cause there was about thirty of them. I thought to myself, 'I'd better do something here to keep them under.'

A couple of our boys went down to the nightclub and paid some brasses some dough, but when it came to getting the leg-over, the brasses said, 'No, piss off English.' I kept out of the way and used to go out on my own with one or two of the quieter ones. Anyway, the boys came back to the bar and said that they'd been tucked up at this music bar. A group of about six of us went down to the disco with them to sort it out, myself included.

Right in the corner of the bar were these two

Argentinean pimps with two old brasses. I said to this geezer, 'What's the score, like?' and he gave it the large one. This was just after the Argentineans had surrendered in the Falklands. I looked around the room and they were all around, standing around with lumps of wood and metal, you name it they had everything.

I told the boys that we'd better make a hasty retreat. We made for the door, but just as we got there, somebody whacked me over the leg with a lump of wood and done my ankle. Luckily, it didn't break anything. I had another England supporter on my back who'd been done as well, so I just dived through the shutters with him. We went back into the hotel, which was just around the corner, and these two Argentineans came up and ran through the window of the hotel. They just went straight through the window, like they were on something. One of them had a gun and shot at us. He missed, but he had shot the light out and shot a bullet through the television.

He may have been upset over losing the war, but he was even more pissed off when I hit him with a bar stool! That quietened him down a wee bit!

By this time all the Old Bill had arrived and it was mayhem, absolute mayhem. The hotel was getting bricked 'cause all the English fans were in there. It was the ETA, those Basque Separatists. They're two bob an' all. While they were throwing things at the hotel, I was on top of the roof garden, trying to calm it all down a bit. Someone threw something at me from below, which just fucking missed me. That was it. Everything that I could lay my hands on went over the top at them, plant pots, garden furniture, you name it. These Tottenham fans were also giving me cans of beer out the fridge, which I chucked down like grenades. It was unbelievable.

After it had all calmed down a bit, we went up the hospital because some of the English lads had cuts and needed some stitches. Obviously we had had to give in our names, so the next morning the police came and arrested all the lads that had given their names at the hospital. I was one of them.

As for the man with the gun, he got away with it. We asked to see the British Ambassador from Madrid. When he came up I told him I was just a courier and had tried to stop it, and that I was in the hospital for the lads while they was getting stitched. He said ,'I'm going to get you all out of here but you mustn't make any press comments. This is the first incident after the Falklands where guns have been used between Argentineans and England and we want to calm the situation down.'

The Ambassador was true to his word and we eventually got out. I've actually kept a Spanish newspaper describing what happened that night, but we didn't hear any more about it after the incident.

There were two lads that helped me on the balcony that night. One was a Chelsea lad from Bookham, whose name I've forgotten, and the other was a Man U supporter. He'd jumped two floors to help me and he'd badly done his ankle in, but he still came down to have a go. I had a lot of time for those two. They were good lads and I never forget things like that.

When it comes to England games, I'd rather go and watch West Ham than England, simple as that. If I only ever had the money for one match, it would always be West Ham over England.

Chapter 16

SCOUSE WARS

I.C.F.

THERE HAVE been a lot of changes to Liverpool over the years, with the development of its dock area and a decent nightlife. The only downside has been the loss of its championship trophies to a cabinet in Old Trafford.

The image of Liverpool I'll always carry from my football days was one of miserable living conditions, like those we thought we'd left behind us with the war. The slums and wastelands you encountered on the long walk from Lime Street station left you positively crowing about your own backwaters – like the East End was something to gloat about. As far as we were concerned, the only thing they could crow about was that they gave the world The Beatles, unless the Under Fives want to put up their borrowed Scouse wedge-haircut look!

All said and done though, there was a hint of

admiration for those Mickey Mousers, who gave us a game battle nearly every time we met. The pride of being a Liverpudlian was plain to see in all of them.

Rucking with the Scousers was like fighting Red Indians: they always had the numbers, no matter how many you took up, and you need the numbers up there to be able to do anything. The Scouse reminded us of olden times, when you wouldn't find anyone on a Sunday because they'd all gone to church. The only difference now was that they'd changed the day to Saturday and replaced the church with the football team.

The Scouse had huge away support. They showed at Upton Park, but that would be it from them. The only show of a fight was when they were ready to board the return train back at Euston.

If we were the best, as we thought we were, then we knew we had to prove it in Mickey Mouse land. They were a different story on their own patch.

We had many an off with the Scousers on away games, and none more so than during the '76–'77 season. It was the last away game of the season and we needed the points to stay up. Loads of Hammers fans had been locked out and couldn't get into the Liverpool ground. They walked mob-handed over to the nearby Everton ground, whose reserves were playing at home to Leeds reserves. My mate Brett said that hundreds of us had managed to get into Everton's ground and they all clapped both teams coming out. Apparently the look on the players' faces that day was a sight to remember.

This game with Liverpool was vital and we drew 0-0. It

was about the only time that we should have beaten them. Pop Robson was put clean through and missed. Micky Ramsgate recalls that game:

I'd gone to the game by car. After we'd parked we started walking to the ground when a little kid with LFC tattooed on his knuckles in Indian ink latched on to us. He couldn't have been older than thirteen. He just looked at us and said, 'You're going to get fucked.' I thought, fucking hell, this is a rough place.

All of a sudden, as we got to the corner of the Anfield Road end we saw a firm of West Ham marching along with a great big Union Jack up front, so we slipped through the main gates of the Kop. I'll never forget that day. As we all steamed in to the seating above the tunnel at the Anfield Road end, I remember Scoeby punching this horse. The horse reared up on two legs, neighing like mad, and the cozzer on the back of the horse panicked. I'd even lost a shoe in the skirmish to get into the ground.

These Scousers kept coming up to us and saying that we were in their seats and that we couldn't sit there. I said, 'All right, we're Cockneys. We've got manners, so 'ave your seat back.' Suddenly the Old Bill were back with those big sticks they used to have in those days. Luckily, at about the same time the Liverpool manager, Bob Paisley, came out to receive some end-of-season award, so we all pretended to be Scousers, standing up and clapping. It worked, 'cause it covered the fact that we didn't have seats. The Old Bill were fooled and we started watching the game.

Some of the West Ham lads that had gone over to Goodison Park stayed until the second half and then decided to come back. Even though the official away support stood in Kemlyn corner, they started climbing the spiral staircase to get into the Anfield Road end. I've never seen the Kop empty so quick. You had West Ham coming up into the Anni Road and they were doing the firm of Scousers in that end, but coming up behind them was the incensed Kop end. Our lads, forty-odd strong, also come out from the side to join in. It was mayhem. You've never seen so many Scousers out for blood. Then some of our lot got stuck in the cage and got real busted-up, fighting for their lives.

Then after the game came the long march back down Scotland Road. Another nightmare.

Most of us had learned our lesson by then... Never wear your best clothes there, stick to donkey jackets and boots. If asked for the time don't reply.

The worst scenario was if you got yourself split up, which was often unavoidable – the Scousers knew how to take all the advantages. The famous 'fairest fans in the land', the mighty Kop, would taunt Londoners with a song which started with the line, 'He's only a poor little Cockney... His face is all tattered and torn... 'cause I hit him with a brick... and now he don't sing any more.' *This would always provoke an immediate response. We had a reply chant that would be considered outrageously politically incorrect these days but back then caused the Kop to briefly sulk, and some to have a bit of a chuckle: 'I'd rather be a Paki than a Scouse'.*

Oh yeah, the Scousers were always up for it on their own patch, but I remember doing them good and proper when two full coachloads of us from the Brit sneaked into their back yard for the fifth round of the League Cup.

Scouse blood was spilled on the snow-covered streets that night. We never took as much as a backward step all night. By the time we had come to play them in the league that year, they were all out for our blood.

A past veteran and serious campaigner in all the battles we had with those Mickey Mousers was West Ham's Steve Vaughan. Wickedly nicknamed Captain Vaughan by some of the lads, he was often backed up by two other campaigners, Light & Bitter and Haystacks. No one remembers those encounters as well as Vaughan, Here he recalls two such incidents with Liverpool and Everton. One was the encounter we had with Liverpool when we went back again in the league that same year. The second is a short tale of our encounter with Everton the following year.

Liverpool and Everton, two teams from the one city. Yet any Londoners who had been up there for an away game would know that on those occasions, they would face a combined foe... all Scousers together.

Liverpool

Steve Vaughan: *Seven weeks later we were back at Liverpool for the league match. We had a good firm up again, this time by inter-city train.*

We were down 3-0 and at around 4.30 p.m. we all upped and left, with ten to fifteen minutes left of the match. As we were leaving the ground, a row started underneath the stand with the Scouse Old Bill who were pulling out these fucking long truncheons as everyone was steaming into them. The truncheons were a favourite of the Scouse Old Bill, and we'd never seen the Old Bill elsewhere with 'em. They were banging our lads right left and centre with 'em.

We've now come out of the ground with the right hump and all filed along an alleyway that leads in the direction of the Kop, the Liverpool end. As we came around the corner, we could see Scousers coming out of the gates at the Kop end. Several Scousers walked right past us in the alley, but we didn't do anything until we reached the Kop entrance stairs. Once we'd reached the stairs, we didn't hold back. We just went 'Yeah!' and ran the Scousers coming down the stairs back up into the Kop.

We never made it fully into the Kop; the fighting reaching to about halfway. The steps to the back of the Kop end are huge and always packed with Scousers. It's just too big a job to try and take the Kop and we've never known any team's fans to be successful in trying. We came close to giving it a go on this occasion, though, and the West Ham fans at the opposite end of the ground said that such was the Scouser's panic and confusion that it looked like the Kop was getting taken. Several Evertonians there that day later confirmed this and talked of seeing the whole Kop go pushing down.

In all honesty, the Scousers were actually heading for the side exits to come out to us, streams of Scousers pouring down on us like fucking ants.

It was time for us to go, but there were still more West Ham leaving the ground and coming out through the alleyway. It was going off in pockets all around the Kop entrances. The Old Bill charged and split us up, pushing us all back down the road. The running battles continued, but everyone was now well split up; we were no longer a mob.

I remember some massive rucks going on as we were heading down the road and it was starting to get evil, really evil. One minute they were on the other side of the road, the next they were behind us, pulling blades out. I was with Swallow, Bill Gardner and several others at the time and all we could see was that we were all getting run everywhere.

I'll never forget our big fat mate who was with us right in a middle of a ruck, when all of a sudden he decided to go into a sweet shop to feed his face. I couldn't believe it, he'd slipped into a sweet shop bang in the middle of all this! When he came out, the Scouse turned on him, ready to steam into him. Bill reacted quickly, wincing a bubblegum machine straight out of the pavement. He stuck his back against a wall and fought to hold a few off. I joined in and got stuck into a couple of them as well. When that Lone Bone geezer [so-called because he was the only skinhead amongst the ICF casuals] *started to run, I got hold of him and dragged him back. I continued trying to drag several of them back, but they were all running past me and it was like trying to stop a tide.*

As for the Scouse, they were out for revenge after that League cup game. This was their top firm and they were all around us, charging us. This was the worst situation I'd ever been in. I looked over the road and heard one of them shout out 'Hey Gardner, where's your fucking firm now?' When I looked back around to see who was standing, I saw that there was only myself, Gardner, Swallow and the fat one left. I replied with, 'We're still here, you Scouse cunts', but we knew the threat was thin. We were game enough, but the odds were no longer with us.

Bill, realising just how bad the situation was, told me to run. I said, 'Bollocks, I ain't running', but you could see flashes of silver as they were pulling out blades. The Scouse loved a Stanley knife. Bill shouted that we had to run, now, so we took off. Swallow got knocked down in the rush and was immediately set on by a load of Scouse, so we all grabbed hold of him and managed to get him up. Then we fucking ran.

We soon saw Big Ted with about twenty other geezers run past us, with all the Scousers chasing hard on their heels. Don't ask me how, but we all managed to run through them, including the fat one, who managed to keep up with us. We ran about 300 yards when a large force of Old Bill stepped in. They managed to stop the ruck with their sheer numbers and herd everyone up.

I stood there for about five minutes trying to catch my breath and wondering how we'd managed to escape such a close call with the Scousers. I looked back and saw a few notable West Ham faces starting to firm up on the other side of the road, having slipped out of the police escort. There was Giant, Light & Bitter ('Light'), Big Ted and the Harrises). A few more of our lads started to slip the police escort and it looked like all the right lads were going across the road. Bill, Swallow and I decided to join, and by this time we were about forty in all. We weren't strong in numbers, but this was our top firm. The Old Bill hadn't noticed us all slip from their escort and so we started walking back up the road.

The Scousers all followed us, but nothing happened for about quarter of a mile as there were too many Old Bill. However, when a double-decker bus, cream and green (because they couldn't afford the red paint) got caught in the traffic, the Scousers made their move. The bus driver began to make noises that everyone running about in the road was preventing his bus from getting through. He was right, there was a ruck going on around his fucking bus, but this didn't stop Haystacks from losing the plot. Haystacks tried to get hold of the bus driver and drag him through the bus window because he'd had the audacity to complain.

Everybody moved to the right of the bus except me, Haystacks and Light, who all went to the left. Five Scousers immediately came at us, one flashing a Stanley knife. Going to football as long as I have, [I believe] the dirtiest thing another fan can do is pull a blade... It didn't matter though, as Light and Haystacks were big seventeen-stone lumps and as soon as we ran at them, they turned on their heels and fled. The blade merchant wasn't quick enough, and paid the price for pulling the blade on us. Light and Giant caught him and beat the crap out of him. I couldn't get a toe in at any angle, for the pair were pummelling him so much that they left him lying unconscious.

The Scouse were really coming in for us now, the street was full of them, as far as you could see. This time, they were led by a bloke in his mid-thirties, with long grey hair and wearing a grey sweatshirt. I later found out he was their top man, Peter Kelly, whom we'd had a number of run-ins with over the years. Their firm had undergone some big changes over the years. They no longer had grown men wearing donkey jackets fronting their ranks, like they did in the early Seventies. Their firm was now really young, and most of those being led by Kelly that day were about half his age. They were almost girlish, with this stupid wedge haircut look they were all into. Kelly looked out of place, like an old dinosaur, and must have thought he was with the wrong firm. In contrast, we were no spring chickens, most of our forty being geezers.

As they followed us, the running battles stated again and the fighting started to stretch our small group. Big Ted whizzed past us, chasing some geezer, but conscious of the need to stick together as a mob, someone yelled, 'Get back, Ted. We need everyone here.' We headed in their direction on the other side of the crossroads and they steamed at us again. The rucking was going on full swing.

There was one copper at the scene, an old boy trying to stop the row at the crossroads, but he had no chance. He pulled out his truncheon, but no one took any notice. We were all too fired up and just kept steaming in at each other. Slowly, we were starting to get the better of them, even though there were only forty of us. We were confident and kept going forward all the time, but our run was quickly cut short. Another Scouse firm came over from the waste land in front of us, throwing bricks and bottles. We all ducked behind some nearby cars. All the windscreens were getting smashed, but we started to collect the bricks and throw them back at the Scousers with a charge of our own.

As we started to retaliate, all these angry Scousers came running out of their houses, grabbing anything they could lay their hands on, to protect their damaged motors. Of course, it was us they were going for. A shout went up among us to get 'em, so we started bricking the ones coming across the green. We were all still fairly together at this stage, but with only forty to fight all the Scousers, we were soon getting stretched again.

We were doing 'em, but another blow came when I looked around and saw Kelly coming up behind us with hundreds of Scousers. I shouted a quick warning to Light and a few others. Light was about ten yards in front of everybody else and he was unwittingly going to run straight into the lot of them. I quickly followed him but it was too late, Light and Kelly had met head-on. Light whacked Kelly and as Kelly's head went down from the punch, Light drop-kicked him and carried on booting him all over the place. A young Scouser with a wedge haircut shouted out, 'Run. It's Herman and he's just done Kelly.' We then charged them back up the road. The Scousers knew Light & Bitter by another name, Herman the Munster. They thought he was a real nutter, and they weren't far wrong. He was steaming the lot of them on his own and doing 'em.

This was the turning point of the battle. When Light did Kelly, the Scousers' bottle went. The row went on for about fifteen minutes, the Scousers continually backing off as we ran at them. I saw a signpost saying half a mile to Toxteth. We had driven them back well into their own back yard.

We saw no more of Kelly, who seemed to have just disappeared. I reckon he'd gone away to lick his wounds, probably thinking that his firm wasn't good enough for him.

All the time that we had been fighting, we had seen little of the Old Bill until we got further up the road, about a quarter of a mile from Toxteth. The Old Bill finally caught up with us and just descended on us. Surrounded by mounted horses, we were rounded up and herded towards the station. There were police vans patrolling alongside us, plus mounted police and loads of the Old Bill on foot.

We got to the station at 6.40 p.m. It had taken two hours ten minutes to get there, a journey which normally takes half an hour. That remains one of the longest street battles we were ever involved in, longer than the often-talked-of epic with 'Boro in the Seventies.

When we got back to the station, the copper who had tried to stop the fighting at the crossroads came up to me, pointing an accusing finger, and told me that I was lucky to be heading back to London. Light asked what I'd done. He said, 'You're lucky too. You're madder than he is. Both of you ought to be locked up in a mental asylum.'

Everton

It wasn't all Liverpool back then. Vaughny recalls the events at Everton the following year:

A year later we went back to Everton. The police had organised buses to take us from Lime Street station to the ground, but no one used them. We all decided to walk. While we were walking we saw Peter Kelly... On the way to the ground there were a few minor skirmishes and Kelly seemed to be at the front of most of them.

After the game ended we came out in a big firm, a really big firm. There could've been more than a thousand of us. Soon as were out, a row started and there were a few nickings straight away. I was with a group of about forty to fifty lads and we broke away from our main mob, getting so far in front that we had lost the Old Bill escort. Perfect. We were now having non-stop battles with 'em and a particularly huge row was going on back along the notorious Scottie Road, which lasted for as long as half an hour.

We were thinking, this is good. The Scousers are game.

As we turned the corner near the roundabout on Scotland Road, we looked at the hill ahead to see that it was covered in Scousers. It was our worst nightmare, like something out of the Apache. What happened next was like Custer's Last Stand.

Everyone stood their ground. We had to, or we risked being sliced to ribbons, as we knew they would be tooled up. I just don't know where our courage came from, as we were outnumbered almost twenty to one.

They started to throw rocks at us and we were forced to duck behind cars to avoid getting hit… there was one funny incident in the middle of all this chaos that sticks in my mind. Big Ted, Cliff and Meatball ducked behind a big box van to avoid the flying rocks, but the van slowly drew away and there they were, still ducking down but now totally exposed. The fun soon ended though, when they couldn't draw the Scousers off them. We knew we now had to get into 'em and Gardner and me did just that.

However, I was suddenly grabbed by a motorcycle copper, who had been positioned in the middle of the roundabout trying to stop it all. He was really agitated, saying he'd had enough of our mob coming here, and then whacked me in the guts with his truncheon. He hit me three times, and after each hit I've gone, 'Yeah, yeah, alright.' After the third hit he let me go, telling me to fuck off. Undeterred, I steamed straight back into the fight, whacking up the Scousers.

Hampton was right bang there with us. It was a good

firm – Bill, Ted, Hampton, Brett and company. We gave them a right caning and there was a good 700 of them getting run by forty of us in the middle of this roundabout. They realised then that all of us were prepared to stand. The Scousers had no bottle, no bottle whatsoever, but the place was always a dangerous place to go to.

Chapter 17

GETTING THE BLUES

– Brum riot '84

I.C.F.

ON FEBRUARY 18, 1984, West Ham met Birmingham in the fifth round of the FA Cup. The game would decide who would go on to the quarter-final of what I call 'the fans' cup'. We were humiliated. Birmingham, under the management of Ron Saunders, hammered us 3-0. Frustration wasn't the word. We did our bit in the effort to keep the team in the FA Cup by invading the pitch twice, attempting to get the match abandoned. There are some who would say that the team and its supporters deserve each other. At least the supporters could argue that they'd performed on the day, which is more than our team could say.

As a result of our efforts, Birmingham was declared an official riot, resulting in the usual public and media outcry. Ron Saunders made his feelings well known: 'Give 'em a taste of the birch, a real deterrent is the answer. If you have a wild dog you don't stroke it,' he fumed. There was also the usual stuff about it all being a social problem, in an attempt to deflect the blame from football. Football pundits argued that if the firms weren't doing it at football, they would be doing it out on the streets. John Lyall, West Ham's manager, tried to avoid overreacting and pleaded for people to consider every aspect of the situation. He said, 'It seems a lot of people got frustrated. Perhaps they will feel that was understandable. But it hardly helps the game and it doesn't help either club.'

As for us, everyone kept all the cuttings about their exploits and laughed as we read that it had all been supposedly planned and organised. That was a load of bollocks, but when we hit the train station that morning and saw the West Ham turnout, we just knew that something would be on. The firm was so big that we had to follow in separate trains. Every firm and nutter from Tilbury to Canning Town and Mile End turned up. We were sure that Birmingham would also have their firm out for the day. That was the magic pulling power of the FA Cup.

The West Ham fans didn't really rate any of the Midland clubs, but when pressed we would always put the Blues above the likes of Coventry, Leicester, Wolves, Derby, Villa and Brom. The Birmingham boys liked to think that they were up there and had made enough headlines in the past, though they had never been a real problem for us.

Some clubs talked up their Zulus, which was a gang

that had quite a few notable blacks. We had fought the Brum over the years and it had never been black. Villa had a few more. It was the original Birmingham Zulus that we had to respect. They never went to a Blues game, preferring to prey around the Bull Ring complex, picking off and robbing the away fans. These gangs were mainly black and we quickly learnt not to go through the Bull Ring unless we were firm handed, or tooled up, after one of our three notorious ex-Green Jackets – Benny – nearly lost his life in a stabbing incident in '75.

When the day came we all set out looking forward to a West Ham win, and maybe a bit of the usual on the way. With a mob that size, it would have been impossible to have any plans – there would be too many firms doing their own thing. And in the end that's what happened.

Ramsgate recalls the fifth-round riot:

We travelled by coach to Birmingham with all the Townies. I didn't have a ticket for the game, so I ended up outside the ground behind the area where all the Birmingham supporters were seated.

As a cover, I made out that I was on leave from the Army and was waiting for some W.R.A.C.S. from Sutton Coldfield who were meeting me there. In fact, I was actually trying to jib into the ground. As I was waiting underneath the stands, just before kick off, a fellow said to me, 'Hey Cockney.' As I turned, this fellow banged me straight on the chin. All of a sudden a steward has grabbed me and slung me in to the side stand, next to Birmingham's Kop end. As it happened, this was the side where all the boys from the Brit had tickets, but it had also been set aside for Birmingham fans. West Ham had been given the main stand behind the goal opposite the Kop.

There were about eighty Brit in this side, but there weren't any dramas, as the supporters in this section of the ground were quite low key. The game wasn't much of a distraction, though. West Ham weren't getting a look in, to the point where you were wondering whether they were really trying.

As we were seated on the side, we weren't fenced in like the lads behind the two goals. The West Ham behind the goal all looked proper caged in.

Things didn't start to happen until well into the game. Taffy was with us and, as we all know, Taffy was one of those lads that wasn't happy unless there was some rucking and abuse going on. He lived and breathed West Ham, twenty-four seven. At this stage, the rest of us were resigned to just seeing out the game, but Taffy was bored, so he'd taken to playing the joker. He started to amuse everyone by putting on an orange bib, which was a jacket he'd managed to swipe off a railway staff employee on the train on the way up. He also started bluffing that he was a steward. In his Welsh 'I've learnt a bit of Manc' accent, he managed to fool all the stewards, who also happened to be wearing orange security coats. He had us in stitches with his antics.

Although we were all on the same side, we weren't all seated together. We decided to use Taffy, mistaken as a steward, to our own advantage by getting him to legally move us so that we were all seated together. We were all squashed into the one section, sharing seats, but at least we were together. We had now become a more visible as a mob. Our mates caged behind the goal recognised us and saw that, unlike them, we didn't have a police cordon around us.

Taffy had decided to test his luck by walking further along the edge of the pitch to where the Old Bill were standing. The West Ham fans positioned near that area began calling to him to get them out so that they could join us on the side. Taffy was already on it and was winking at them to stop them from giving the game away. He began talking to the stewards through the gate in the fence to distract them. Slowly but surely, in ones and twos, he began moving the rest of our firm out and over to join us along the unfenced side. A steady stream of people came over and there were soon so many of us that we started to spill out of the seats and into the gangways. They all had big grins on their faces, but none bigger than Taffy's. We were sure he'd get sussed soon.

Meanwhile, the mood had slowly started changing as we started to become increasingly frustrated with the game. The score was 2-0 and time was quickly slipping away. We were all more or less near the barrier to the dugout when an incident occurred on the pitch. Birmingham's Robert Hopkins slung the ball and hit midfielder Paul Allen in the nuts. Paul immediately went down. We all erupted, outraged that this had happened to one of our popular players. We hurled all kinds of abuse and obscenities at Hopkins and his team, but it didn't stop there. In hindsight, I went that little step too far and jumped on to the pitch. Lampard, who recognised some of us, looked at us as if to say, 'No, don't.' Too late.

With the crowd behind the goal egging us on, we steamed on to the pitch after Birmingham's black centre-half, Noel Blake. A few of the lads were right going for him, to the point where he had to pick up the corner flag to protect himself. Chaos reigned as more West Ham scaled the fences to join in. The Birmingham fans threw coins and the referee, Courtney, had to quickly take all the players off the pitch.

As the skirmishes continued, Lampard came back out and made a desperate appeal to the lads to leave it all out, saying it wasn't helping the players. We all returned to the side or moved back to stand off the pitch and along the touchline. A touch of normality returned, but it wasn't to last long. Five minutes later we were back on the pitch doing it all again.

The second pitch invasion demonstrated how slack the authorities and security were that day. It caught them all out, regardless of the fact that our crowd had all been chanting 'On the pitch. On the pitch.' Lads who were still trying to come off the pitch from the first invasion were now joined by a stream of others surging back on to the pitch.

The Old Bill finally got on it and sent in mounted police to tackle the crowds. I dived back in to the seating just as a steward went to make a grab for me. I managed to escape by taking me jacket off and sliding underneath the seats like a snake. I got away with it.

Listening to Terry's recollection of events brings back the day as though it was only yesterday:

I don't remember much before the game. I think we just had a mooch round. At the ground, we were all sitting in the side and towards the front. Over in West Ham's end behind the goal, they had already begun fighting the Old Bill over a big Basildon Hammers flag, which they'd tried to pull down.

After the third goal went in, it all turned a bit nasty. Before we knew it, it had all gone off in the corner of Birmingham's Kop end. I later found out that the situation had been caused by West Ham leaving the ground and going around to their end. As a result, Birmingham were coming on to the pitch from their end, some to escape what they thought was a full-scale attack. We looked across at them and thought, right, this is our time, and we all now ran on to the pitch.

I'll never forget it. Everyone was just charging and bouncing around like lunatics. I recall watching Gary Weatherman, a lad out of Poplar who I recently saw on the 'Three Lions' video, cop a dig off Birmingham player Noel Blake in the centre circle. That was something you just don't do, have a pop at the very people who pay your wages. Players shouldn't get involved. Quite a few people saw this and it was no surprise to see someone run up and kick him right up the bollocks. He legged it in the direction of the far corner, just as Birmingham was ripping up the corner flag. West Ham then steamed straight into their firm.

Lol Pearman worked for a central-heating firm and the director of the company had invited them all up for the game. He was supposed to be watching the game from his exclusive seating in the upper tier but, true to West Ham, our Lol had climbed down from the upper tier and run the length of the pitch to join the row. There he was on the pitch, wearing cream trousers and a cream shirt. He later said, 'I couldn't stand and just watch you all, but I daren't think what my guv'nor will make of it. He's up there with all the people I work with, plus a few clients.'

It was quite funny to watch all the Old Bill trying to nick everybody on the pitch and get us off. Everyone was getting chased all over the pitch or being blocked off by the Old Bill's horses. Danny Harrison played a cute one: he went and sat on the players' bench. John Lyall, West Ham's manager, went in there to count his players and make sure everyone was all right. When they had all assembled in the dugout, Lyall said to Harrison, 'Who are you?' Dan replied, 'Danny Harrison's the name. Pleased to meet yer, John.' This was your typical hilarious Harrison move to get out of being nicked. You can just picture Lyall wondering who his twelfth player was.

The pitch invasion was only pulled off because a load of us from the Brit had managed to get into the side stand, which was basically un-policed. Taffy's stunt got our numbers up to over 200, but we had already doubled in number when Swallow and about forty to fifty others joined us at the start of the game. It was one of those days when we had a lot of firms all doing their own thing.

Andy Swallow told us that at the start of that day, he and about fifty others went into Birmingham's end and sat amongst the Birmingham fans. He'd soon clocked two Brummies coming up behind them, so he went up to them and smashed their heads together, saying to them, 'Yeah, we're West Ham. Now fuck off.' The Old Bill came over to give Swallow an ultimatum: 'Get your firm and fuck off or I'll turn my back, these Birmingham can do you, and then I'll nick you. So what's your choice, then?' Andy said 'We'll have the second, please.' Looking none too pleased, the Old Bill just yelled at them to get out of there or they'd nick them all and started to throw them out. That was when we moved along and got into the side. Andy was later nicked that game and got a £500 fine.

Vaughny recalls that he and his mates had remained with the thousands of West Ham away supporters until that third goal went in:

We were behind the goal but when we went 3-0 down, we left the ground and went around and steamed into their end while the game was still going on. I was with Cliff, Light & Bitter and all those lads. Light was pissed out of his head at the time.

Everyone was steaming into Birmingham and really having it. A copper grabbed Light & Bitter, but couldn't hold him. They said, 'You've had your chance, now clear off out of it', but Light said, 'No, you've had your chance and blew it', and ran steaming straight back into their end, chasing them on to the pitch again. He had an absolute mental.

The Old Bill were steaming us out of the ground, so we didn't know that Birmingham were on the pitch. When we came out, about thirty to forty of us were crossing a bridge by the ground when all these Birmingham started coming up behind us and throwing rocks. The Old Bill were still steaming into us, but we had decided to make a stand on the corner. We started bashing 'em in a ruck that seemed to go on forever and we couldn't understand why the other West Ham hadn't come out to join us.

It was about 5 o'clock by now, but the game was still being played, so we decided to walk back around the ground to see what was going on. Someone said there had been a pitch invasion. We had no way of knowing then what was going on. We just thought, fucking hell, we've missed out again.

I recall that after the game, a line of police motorbikes blocked the road that led to all the Birmingham supporters. They told us that we couldn't go down there, but that was never going to stop us. Someone ran up and drop-kicked one of the motorcycles. That was our cue. Everyone ran in and started further skirmishes, just looking for a row.

The following day, Sunday, Ramsgate turned out for the Brit football team playing over on Wanstead Flats. For us, the Brit was the in-place to go. We would meet there on Friday nights to talk about the game. At that time we were still in the era when the mark of a successful football player was to have a pub. The Britannia was Frank Lampard's.

Ramsgate recalls Lampard turned up on Wanstead Flats later that day and asked how the boys were doing. They told him they were losing 2-0. His reply was as sharp and sarcastic as you can get: 'Don't worry, if they get the next goal to make it 3-0 we'll have it on the pitch.'

The lads today still talk about that funny old set-up we had with the players and the awkward situation it created when we all went on the pitch at Birmingham. The Brit was a little backstreet boozer on the borders of Plaistow and Stratford that had only been of interest to locals until news spread that a footballer had it. It practically became a HQ for the I.C.F. Other players would often pop in from time so some of the regular lads were well familiar to the players.

This familiarity led to some embarrassing confrontations on the pitch on the day of the riot. To many the fighting was all it was about, but we were still fans. Here are two snippets of conversations between player and fan that were exchanged in the height of it all to show their different viewpoints, both of which contain an element of truth:

Frank Lampard's appeal to Andy Swallow:
Frank: 'Andy, why don't you do everyone a favour and get off the pitch?'

Andy: 'Bollocks. I'm doing a fucking better job than you.'

Tony Cottee appealing to Bill Gardner:
Tony: 'What's up with you? What is it with all of you?'
Bill: 'I'll tell you. All these lads want to win more than your lot do.'

And if you followed West Ham everywhere, as we did, there were plenty of times you'd find yourself echoing Bill Gardner's words at the Birmingham Cup riot!

Chapter 18

C'MON MILLWALL

I.C.F.

MILLWALL VERSUS West Ham, West Ham versus Millwall. Whatever way you looked at it, it spells serious trouble. Football is fortunate these two teams very rarely meet in the league, but many fans puzzle over the mystery of why they have never met in one of the cup competitions.

The bad blood has always been there between east and south of the river. You can go back to your forefathers and then just take in the areas that would be London's toughest, whether you looked at the activities of the Krays and the Richardsons or as far back as the early Victorian slums of London. But the set-to and showdown between the supporters of the two football teams began in May 1972, when Millwall crowd favourite Harry Cripps had his football testimonial at the Old Den against

West Ham. That was when the blood was really spilt. Hooligans from both sides treated it as their own Cup Final, because at the time both laid claim to being the guv'nors of London. It was one of those games – if you went, you went tooled up, simply because you knew the other side would be too. If you didn't take a tool, you didn't go. Simple.

The story of this legendary confrontation is best told through two eye-witness accounts, from Mouthy Bill and Simo, though I'll also throw others in. I've heard the story so many times over many years. The events of that day may well constitute the worst instances of football violence I've ever heard of. Just listening to the accounts of what went down brings out the hairs on the back of the neck.

As a kid – I was just fourteen – I went to that match, got chased off the bus and split up from my mates when the bus pulled in along New Cross. I'd hoped to find sanctuary in the ground by meeting up with my fellow supporters in the away fans' end, a safe haven from where I could watch the older ones take Millwall up the other end. The atmosphere of that cold night was tinged with a touch of pure evil, something I had not yet encountered as a football fan. It was not down to the butterflies you experience through the excitement of a bit of bovver happening. The sanctuary I hoped to find in the ground was non-existent. I managed to have the wind put up me by both Millwall and my own supporters, who were searching each other out in a supposedly neutral part of the ground.

No coppers in sight, no evidence of club colours on either supporter; furthermore, no sign of my pals. I felt no shame in leaving the ground. I decided that whatever went down would be a personal matter for the boys off some very mean streets in the east and south.

Mouthy Bill remembers that particular testimonial as Mile End's day. The myth and legend of the Mile End boiled down to this one game:

The Mile End mob had some real powerful individuals, names like the Williams brothers were out of the top drawer, you'd want them on your side every game. Joe Williams was once a top amateur boxer, well respected. They were the first mob up West Ham's South Bank. They went up there to originally get away from all the aggro with kids up the North Bank every week. They went up the South Bank to be within their own little mob. Altogether they were a mob that nobody over West Ham could mess with.

That night they left Mile End, jumped on the train, went straight to the ground and walked into their Cold Blow Lane end. Nobody wanted it to kick off outside the ground and attract any unwanted police attention. We wanted to make sure we took their end, that's all we had in mind, because people kept saying, 'No one can take Millwall's end.' So we were determined to take their end and that's what we did. You should 'ave seen it when it went off, we cleared their end out, we'd taken Millwall and it's all before the game. Meanwhile, outside the ground Millwall were looking for us, word went round we were already in there. They all came in and as they came in, the ground just swelled up full. We were banged up solid but we stood our ground, though we were pushed up to the back of their end where we had a big ruck with them, then another big row on the stairs leading to the back of their end. They were pushing us from pillar to post trying to retake their immortal end. But we were holding our own.

Then I saw the late Steve Morgan and [some others] having that big row down by the corner flag. He'd jumped up and started whacking a few with the corner flag.

Next, that little mob that's supposed to be hard who gather in the side, they called themselves The Treatment. They... came across from where they were standing in the halfway line, forcing all West Ham's mob to be fighting back together again.

Don't ask me about the game. I never watched any of it. Before you knew it, it was over anyway. So it's all outside now and we just couldn't go nowhere. You had to keep standing your ground. The Old Bill and what you call police protection, or escort for away fans, was non-existent in those early years. Certainly nothing like today. You had no choice but to stay together, stand and fight.

Simo from the T.B.F. describes the violence that evening as the worst he'd ever encountered:

I remember me and Bunter travelling down with Mile End from Mile End station after meeting them there. You had to change at Whitechapel; it was here the Mile End raided the work boxes belonging to the railway. They'd taken all the tools out of the big boxes on this station. Now, tooled right up, we came straight in behind the goal, West Ham was already in there, mobbed up towards the side. Now, with all West Ham and Mile End together, we just mullared them. Throughout the game it was going off continuously, stuck up the back of this Cold Blow Lane. I remember six-inch bolts were getting thrown back and forth, but that was nothing to what went on after the game.

When we came out at the end of the game we came out early with all the Mile End, and we stood. There were two gate exits, they only had two gates to get out. And we stood at both gates, then the Millwall started coming out.

Then I witnessed something I wouldn't like to see again, especially if [I was] on the wrong end. Out came these biggest… fucking hell, well… Do you know those great big spanners you use on railway lines? They must have been… something like the size of your arm. Then they just battered these cunts as they came out of these gates. They didn't care who they fucking were, they just battered everybody that came. It was worse because the crowd following out behind were forcing those in front out; they would batter 'em mercilessly. The fucking first lot would go down then the next lot would be forced straight on to them, bash, fall down, then the next one, bash, and they would… well, it was just like the fucking Zulu film.

It wasn't so much fear I felt, but it was frightening to watch, purely because I wasn't really into that level of violence or that class of violence, certainly not at that age I would have been – sixteen.

All of a sudden the non-existent police came charging in on horses. They just steamed and scattered everyone with their horses, everyone was getting knocked all over the place. I got knocked over this fence, falling behind it, so now I'm pinned up by this fence by this big horse's arse. The copper on it has tried to grab hold of me and I sort of legged it up the road. It was a bad, bad, scene I left.

Even today I can still see the image of that Millwall crowd. They tried to back up but the force of the crowd coming out was pushing them forward. Half that crowd had not taken part in any of the violence, but those with the tool box selection just didn't care. Like I say, it was pure evil.

The man after whom the T.B.F. was named can back up the claim that a West Ham–Millwall derby is like no other derby in the country. Big Ted recalls the night of that Harry Cripps testimonial:

I remember before the game we were getting mullared. I was in there early with West Ham and before the Mile End came in, we were getting forced out to the side, then the Mile End came in pulling out hammers, axes, all sorts. Then West Ham got on top and [were] winning. Then the Millwall came back with more... They kept rallying their own up to try and get us out of their end. The Cold Blow Lane. But we took them that night... it was a long night, though.

Bill Gardner says simply:

I've never seen nothing like that. I think that's the worst I've ever seen any trouble at football. West Ham waited at the bottom of the stairs and eleven times they came out and eleven times they got run back in, and it was just unbelievable... you've never seen anything like it, it was really bad that night.

Old Bill dispersed all the West Ham attacking the exit gates, but it still didn't end. Mouthy Bill recalls the Old Bill marching them away from the ground to the station, with a continuous brick-chucking barrage between rival sets of supporters amidst a hostile atmosphere. The West Ham contingent that included the Mile End mob were now all on the train again.

There have been various accounts of what happened later, at Watney Street's Shadwell station. Mouthy Bill describes the incident as he remembers it, in the following grim account:

> *We were on the train and we'd come back to Shadwell station. At the station before that one, an unknown mob got on. Just as we got to Shadwell station, a geezer said something to Terry Adams, something along the lines of, 'I fucking hate West Ham supporters.' Terry's hit him, bash, it's gone. A big battle [has] gone off on the train.*
>
> *They've chased us down the station, where we've picked up the metal fire buckets and old-fashioned fire*

extinguishers. We've run at them and we're throwing all this gear at them. Now we're having another massive ruck, so the train pulls out. But as the train pulls out there's live exposed wires there. Now this station is only three or four foot wide and you're thinking to yourself if this ruck goes the wrong way, you're dead.

So there's this massive battle going on. The Old Bill's turned up now. Everything gets broken up, a load of people get bashed on both sides. A good few end up in hospital with heads split open and that.

We slip Old Bill by running upstairs out of the station and into Watney Street, splitting for home.

Now that was a night that just went on and on, a fucking long night, I'll tell yer.

The infamous night of the Harry Cripps testimonial decided two things: who ruled London and who were the hardest fans. It also set the seal of a lasting vendetta and grudge between the supporters. The hatred aroused that night never left the fans of either team.

The thing with Millwall is that they are good at the fear of the unknown. Both the fans and that Old Den ground are pure intimidation, believe me. One of ours stated that they're the only other team that if you ain't one hundred per cent, you know you might come unstuck. They used to love a tool and are just about the only club with supporters that have no respect whatsoever for the Old Bill. Something unique that, among football supporters.

I would say Millwall have played the fear factor well over the years. Rival firms shit out without ever coming face to face with 'em. And that's why I admire the West Ham lot. They've never succumbed to this. Millwall know only one team has ever come looking for them, whether we are playing them or not. The other three big London clubs with firms don't even enter into this equation. In the past, we've suspected that certain Arsenal and Chelsea lads also swell the Millwall ranks when it suits. We wondered where Millwall got a firm like the one they had that infamous year when they terrorised Luton.

One season, Millwall had Dagenham in a Cup round. We turned up something major, terrorising many all along the Tube route before the game. During the match we knocked down part of a concrete perimeter wall attempting to invade the pitch to get at Millwall. They had the numbers to respond in kind, but to everyone it appeared as though they didn't want to know. Someone said had they been at Southend, they would have been going barmy.

Expectations were high of a full firm turnout when we played Millwall in the league during the season of '78–'79. This was a first official encounter between the clubs. So the call went out to show your face at this game, even if you never cared for another. Because this time Millwall were coming to ours, they had to come to Upton Park. It was the day of reckoning, there was a dead fan and vendettas to avenge. In 1976, a Millwall fan died after an incident involving West Ham fans at New Cross station. And just in case we forgot, they put out leaflets billing it as Judgement Day, though the only one seen was in the press. It was like a big, unwanted advert days before the game. The result was the biggest-ever police operation to be manned in London, the highlight of which was the sight of the first use of a police helicopter in the war on football violence.

Massive police power on a previously unknown scale ensured the forces of law and order won the day. They knew what could happen and weren't taking chances. They came out on top by containing each encounter so that the violence was limited to a series of skirmishes. It didn't help Millwall that in what was a short trip across the water for them, they could only muster up 800 to 1,000 of their finest to come on our South Bank. Maybe the leaflet wasn't such a dumb idea, considering numbers.

Even so, their piss-poor turnout still managed to create an atmosphere of pure nastiness. Everyone was looking forward to seeing how the return at their place would go.

I guess a Millwall–West Ham derby will always be a big thing as far as violence is concerned. It's always going to be about who the true guv'nors of London are. It wouldn't be wrong to say that a kind of begrudging mutual respect has grown up between the two sets of supporters over the years. From our point of view, we reckon we have proved it by now. But it's something Millwall are never going to concede, and so it goes on. What was the F-troop and Treatment versus Mile End later became the aptly named Bushwhackers doing battle with the I.C.F.

Bushwhacked at Bank

Brett Tidman, as game as they come, recalls the day

when fifty of some of the I.C.F.'s top boys were bushwhacked by Millwall:

I'll never forget it, that horrible day. We were playing Villa away and a good few of us met at the Brit in Plaistow. Among them was Terry Liddy and his brother Micky, Bernie, Dickle, Butler, Lol Pearman, Dorset, Carlton and several others.

We all caught the train to Mile End, where we met quite a few more of us on the platform. There were about sixty of us in all and we packed two carriages on our next train to Euston. For reasons that I can't recall, we then got off the train and walked to Moorgate, where we caught another train which passed through Bank station.

When we pulled into Bank we spotted a big mob spread all along the platform. It was Millwall, bloody Millwall Bushwhackers. The mob must have been about 200 strong, some of them right meaty lumps. As the train stopped and the doors opened, in came our nightmare.

As soon as they got on the train, the fighting began. I could hear commuters crying. Only moments earlier we'd been having a laugh and joke and now we were fighting for our lives. One lad had escaped through the carriage doors and out on to the platform full of them. I thought, 'Fucking hell, I'm going to have to go out that way.' I saw another lad, Butler, punch and kick his way through everyone and get out the other door, so I tried it myself. I couldn't make it.

Lol was still there punching, kicking, screaming and

shouting, doing his utmost to fight a way out. It was total mayhem. They were up for doing a real number on us.

I'll always remember the innocent people around us that were caught up amongst the fighting and couldn't get out the way. I remember helping two American birds to get off the train. I had blood pouring down the side of my face and was in real pain, but I remember grabbing hold of these two shocked birds, thinking, right love, c'mon, I'll get you out of here.

I was off the train and walking to the escalators when I realised that they were everywhere. We had bumped into their entire firm. A group of us began gathering at the top of the escalators, including Lol Pearman and Fellman. We were all wounded and bloodied, so we decided to get out of there and made Euston our next meeting place.

When we got to Euston we heard that one of our lot at Bank station had been stabbed. We didn't know any details or how badly he was hurt, so we left it as late as we could before eventually getting on the train to Birmingham. On the train, we were all talking about the fight and Black Roger recounted to us that when he was getting bottled, they were calling him Cass.

Villa turned out to be uneventful and, as you can imagine, everybody was on a downer after the incident we had just been through at Bank. But that's how it always seemed to go with us. All the time we would go out looking for 'em, we could never find 'em. Then, unexpectedly, they found us with their full firm and bashed us.

We kept making calls to find out how our lad was doing. The news reaching us was that he was bad, really bad, and that he'd been stabbed near the heart with a knitting needle. We all feared the worst. Everyone said, 'Right, that's it. It's Millwall on the way back. As soon as we got back to Euston we're going after them.' We knew that Millwall had to return to Kings Cross, down the road from Euston and that was where we'd get 'em.

When we got off at Euston, the Old Bill in plain clothes were waiting. This was something you didn't often see when going to football games, and certainly not so visibly. They were there for a particular purpose and knew who they were looking for amongst us from photos they had. They made themselves known to both the brother and brother-in-law of our mate who had been stabbed, now lying at death's door. They were informed they would be taken to Kings Cross, where Millwall were being held. The Old Bill down there had been given instructions not to let any of them go until they had been identified.

All of us standing around in earshot of this conversation immediately spread the word that the Millwall firm were all being held at Kings Cross station. We were off.

We started walking to Kings Cross, which is literally a four-minute journey along Euston Road. As we neared the station we spotted about fifteen to twenty Millwall walking towards us, suspecting nothing. We had similar numbers, as the main mob was a couple of hundred yards behind us, but we didn't wait. We flew straight into them, driven by rage and desire for revenge. Some of them started running off and when I looked back, I saw that the rest of the West Ham mob had just hit Kings Cross station.

We were 400 strong and all the favourites were there, all the lads you wanted in the thick of things. I remember running in to the middle of the road, ignoring the traffic, so that I could take position to spot any Millwall. The Old Bill had let Millwall go and they all started heading out into the streets. Their mob had all regrouped while being held at the station and there were a good 500 to 600 of them. One Millwall geezer came running out with his mates and jumped the metal safety barriers that formed a fence between the taxis and the front station entrances. He gave it the usual, 'C'mon, we'll have it.' I just went up and bashed him, 'Have that', and he went flying straight into the fence with a crash. His mates were quickly on the scene and our lot started running in between all the cars, upping Millwall in front of the Old Bill's blind side. Onlookers simply carried on driving by.

No doubt Millwall could see the mood was ugly and knew why. They tried to escape by running on to buses or back down the Underground. No one now gave a fuck about the Old Bill any more and Millwall were just getting upped. It was their mob against ours and the numbers were more even, but we were fuelled by our fury. I'd never seen West Ham like that before.

The Old Bill just seemed to stand back and let it happen. Probably in the hope we'd destroy each other and do their job for them. The lads that had been bushwhacked at Bank were hunting down every Millwall in sight. There were later stories of Millwall running on to moving buses and trying to blend in with Joe Public, pretending to read the papers. Some had been caught by West Ham lads who had followed them on to the bus. They were easily recognisable with their red faces, sweating their heads off and out of breath, panting like a mule. Someone would saddle up to one and make out they were also Millwall, saying things such as, 'Those bastards nearly had me.' As soon as the cunt gave himself up by replying with, 'Yeah, nearly got me too', bang, smack, the boot goes in. I even heard that a few had been slashed with blades while trying to flee on the buses.

* * * * *

Walsall wash-out

Natley was a powerful 6 foot 3 inch-tall black man, originally from the Barnsbury Estate in North London; he took some stick for his Arsenal background. Although he was a bit of a loner, everyone knew him on the football scene. He'd been around since the early Mile End days and had a long reputation. Wherever West Ham were involved, Nat would appear in the thick of it. The way he could give out the stick meant he was popular with us lot.

I liked Nat. He was a character you could learn a bit from on the football front. He was as shrewd as he was powerful. Later, when we worked the doors on the club circuit, I nicknamed him the Fox. We were pretty effective when we were together over West Ham. But I wasn't there when the I.C.F. scored a lasting result on Millwall at Walsall. Remarkably, it never actually went off. In the end a row that never was is still looked upon today as a result for West Ham in the history of our vendettas with Millwall.

For the West Ham lads it was never enough just to run firms, do firms, or take ends. We liked to add a bit of humiliation. It was a West Ham trademark we honed over the years, just to add something to what we call having a result.

The Walsall–Millwall game could count as such. It was all about how far one would go, mentally transferring a threat so real your opponents would back out and bottle it without putting you to the test. Everyone came back from the Walsall v Millwall game full of it and everyone told it more or less the same way. They'd scored big-time for the I.C.F. and afterwards you felt gutted that it wasn't you telling the story. You'd just missed out on a little bit of history being made.

Matters were made worse when Nat told me, 'You should have been there.' Villa's firm were shit, why risk the nick? I was pissed off with going to Villa, but Swallow and company went and so did Nat. This is Nat's memory of that day:

That '83 season we were playing Aston Villa at theirs and Millwall, who were in the Third Division, had another Midlands club, Walsall, away. On the way to Birmingham, someone suggested going to Walsall to do Millwall. When the train pulled into New Street station, we scattered a few Brummie boys on the platform then, ignoring the few Old Bill that were about, we switched on to a little shunter train that took us to Walsall.

You came out of the little station at Walsall and their ground was just a short walk away. We were quickly outside the Old Fellows Park ground. Millwall were at the turnstiles and inside the ground. They just didn't seem to notice another team coming. There was a good hundred-plus of us. This is what a close-knit firm we were. There was no advance plan and we should have been at Villa. A few voices confirmed everyone was in. That's all we wanted to know. For a good half-hour the Walsall Old Bill didn't click what was happening. They thought it was Londoners arguing with Londoners. They didn't work out it was West Ham and Millwall.

That day showed everyone who rates Millwall what we would do to get at them. Millwall spotters alerted their mob that we were coming in. Those Millwall stuck outside quickly put themselves into the ground. We looked up to see Millwall creating a hive of activity all along that top bank of terracing. They were finger-pointing and gesticulating. Swallow and our mob went 'Shhhhh', silently mouthing to them that we were coming in and to play the game, as Old Bill had mistaken us for Millwall late arrivals. If you weren't there, you'd never believe what happened next. They went and grassed us up to the Old Bill. A Bushwhacker who'd made himself busy in the past couple of seasons – known to us as McSomething – was screaming to the Old Bill that we were West Ham and not to let us in.

I couldn't believe this act coming from Millwall. They knew we weren't there to shake hands. We were there because we wanted blood.

After the Old Bill had sorted us out and we were all coming back from Walsall, we all thought it was a good day's job done. Nobody could now say the best firm was either West Ham or Millwall – there was no Millwall.

No disrespect to Millwall, but they could not touch us. That day at Walsall confirmed it. Looking back, it was a dangerous move. Millwall had all their away firm with them that day when we showed up with our firm and we could have been totally exposed if it hadn't gone right for us.

I think we really proved something the first time we had to officially play them in the '78–'79 season, in the old Second Division. After a piss-poor turnout at ours we had to go to them for the last game of the season with fuck-all to play for.

That was the day West Ham turned out the biggest firm I've ever seen. I remember turning round to my mate, telling him to look back down the long road we were all walking along. The view was full of West Ham still coming everywhere. It was all West Ham, with Millwall nowhere in sight. When some of them did manage to make themselves known, Gally, one of the legends over West Ham, launched one of the Millwall mob through the window of the White Hart pub.

I felt proud of West Ham that night. We were in our

twenties but that night some real older faces came out. I'd never seen it like this, it was pure ruckers. We showed who the guv'nors were. It was their turf and their manor but we were the guv'nors – east had come south.

Everywhere in the ground it was all West Ham. Until then we'd always been in the First Division and Millwall had never come up. Now we'd gone down it was shame on us, but we weren't going to let the boys across the river down – we'd all be there.

To me it's always been that way with West Ham, we would always turn up because we always go looking for it.

I don't like [the way people used] the words thuggery and hooligan [about us] because we loved a fight. In fact, I feel we were like gladiators. I'd go further and say we were sporting gladiators, because we liked to test ourselves. I think I'm good and can throw a fair right and he thinks he can throw a right, let's just see who's the hardest.

It's no different from two boxers in a ring, except we didn't have a referee. The only ref for us was the Old Bill trying to stop it, but we would have it and the time we would have it most was always off our patch. Nobody would come to ours.

* * * * *

Caught out at New Cross

It was January 28, 1984, and we were going to Palace for the fourth round of the FA Cup. Millwall were at home to Hull.

The train to Norwood Junction goes through New Cross and we thought that if we got out at New Cross, we could take our most hated rivals by surprise. We all relished the thought, and in the excitement the idea began to grow. Rather than just jumping out at New Cross to have Millwall, we were now considering continuing on to take their fucking ground. There had been no prior planning. We had a fucking good firm and it was purely what came to mind when we all met up that morning. We thought it would be a great surprise. Little did we know that the surprise would be on us.

Millwall knew. Fuck knows how, but they knew. What they hadn't anticipated though, was how big our firm would be. We had all the right faces, too. You only had to look around. Everyone was creaming themselves... the big liberty was on.

As we got off at New Cross station late that morning, almost everyone was so bloody casual that they were just strolling out. Most of the older ones were in no hurry at all, their attitude sending out a clear message to Millwall: 'We've been here before. There's nothing you can show us.' As always though, the Under Fives and a few nutters were far too excited to be that calm and were already out on the bridge, scattering anything that looked like a South Londoner.

It was on as soon as we left the station. We started running at a mob of thirty to forty Millwall that had formed a line right across the New Cross Road. A Millwall mob on show. None of the lads in front were gonna wait for the rest of us to catch up. They knew the strength behind them. Driven by pure hatred towards Millwall, there was only one thing on our minds: run Millwall. This is what we came here for. Run these South London cunts now, on their own fucking manor.

The rest of us couldn't see past the hordes of I.C.F. still jostling out of New Cross, but word soon came through that it was off with Millwall at the front. We all thought, 'Fuck this cool posing lark, lets get up there to get a blow in.' It was now a desperate fight to get up front, and our mob rushed forward, pushing through our own lot like maniacs, tripping some up.

The Millwall ran into The Rose, the first boozer down the road. We knew that once they were inside the pub, there would be no way of getting them out without smashing the pub up, and the Old Bill would be on the scene in no time. However, just as we went charging down on them, they started to come out of the pub again. At first it was just the same shitters that had run in, then more and more of them started to come out, many of whom we hadn't seen go into the pub. It wasn't curiosity that was drawing them out either, they were positively growling. Suddenly, these cocky South Londoners started swinging baseball bats around their heads. They were pulling up tools from everywhere, even getting them out of bins in the street. It was game on, pick your targets, said Millwall.

It was the moment that you expect it to go off toe to toe, where everybody just gets stuck in until pure violence sorts it all out. That moment never came. There were four or five lads around me who were game and we started going forward as our South London enemy came bearing down on us, baseball bats swinging. I saw that some of the West Ham around us were going backwards. They weren't just backing off either, they were on their toes. We'd all realised we'd fallen for one of our own moves and had been lured into a trap, but I thought that for all Millwall's manic bravado, we still had the numbers and the right bleeding faces. They must have been thinking, right, we've got you, you West Ham bastards, but I was close enough to them to see that they were still giving us some respect.

Suddenly, some fucking crazy bastard swung a baseball bat at my head. I ducked, looked around, and saw that it was all Millwall. Sensing that nobody was going to stand, I backed off with the others, but I deliberately remained in the retreating back line amidst scenes of chaos. I was still under the desperate illusion the I.C.F. were playing the old game of making out to run in order to lure your rivals in closer before all turning as one and steaming back into 'em. It never fucking happened.

The I.C.F. soon found themselves back on New Cross station platform, a darn sight quicker than their casual stroll out of the same station only moments earlier. This was one of those times when nobody seemed to mind too much that the Old Bill were now on the scene, giving it the heavy-handed push-around a bit. Nobody really said a word. What could they say? Most of the older ones were moaning at the youngsters for splitting the firm by chasing the first Millwall they came across before the rest of the firm were fully out of the station. Valid point, but still an excuse.

We later heard that Swallow had gone back out of New Cross station with part of the same firm and had offered out more or less the same Millwall firm that was in The Roses pub. They got as far as the one-way system and fronted Millwall up when they attempted to come across the Green, but it wasn't long before the Old Bill had had enough of it and rounded them up. It was good to hear some of us weren't leaving it, but it would take more than just fronting up Millwall to restore lost pride.

That New Cross humiliation would be the talk of all the London terraces. It was something every one of our rival clubs with a firm wanted to hear.

I lived across the road from the Brit and was in there more than usual that week, but nobody was talking about it. Nobody was keen to point the finger, because we were all there when it happened. This wasn't a situation the I.C.F. could live with. At times like this there had to be some sort of internal inquest to find out what had gone wrong and, more importantly, what needed to be done to put it right. Our entire past record with Millwall was at stake, along with our reputation as a firm.

The Palace game was an FA Cup match that resulted in a 1-1 draw. The replay was at ours that same week. We won the replay 2-0 but still nothing was said. You've never see so many West Ham lads walking around with the hump. By Friday, the first whispers began getting around Plaistow and Stratford. A lot of lads showed up at the Brit that night, but that was usual for a Friday. A few right faces were suggesting things were in hand, but I wondered, thinking that these were the same faces that should have had it all in hand last Saturday morning. We needed to know what the plans were. Kicking off with Millwall in some meaningless scrap wouldn't level last week's humiliation. It would just become forgotten among all the other skirmishes we had from time. We needed something special on Millwall to take away the feeling the rest of London was gloating about our retreat at New Cross.

I left the Brit and popped up at a few other places that night. The talk was the same. Something had to be done, but nobody seemed to want to take it on. When would the right faces speak? By pub closing time, everyone had found their way into Mooro's, the late-night disco/pub that was once owned by West Ham and England legend Bobby Moore. Things were beginning to perk up. Lads from both Canning Town and Stratford, who had entered probably the longest truce I can recall between them, were there. A few Essex boys, the Chads and the Hornchurch lads, and even some of the boys from the Ancient Brit in Poplar were up as well. All good West Ham lads. Word had spread to meet back at Mooro's in the morning and it was going to be serious. 'Don't turn up without a tool' was the message being passed around.

It was a good idea to use Mooro's Stratford as a place for us to meet. K Division, our local Old Bill, knew our usual routine – meet at the Brit in Plaistow, creep down to Plaistow station and hang out at Mile End station, inside and out. Changing the meeting place would keep the Old Bill guessing. More importantly, it would throw off the hangers-on, which every firm had.

Things were sounding interesting. Millwall had Sheffield United away. In Millwall's division, the old Canon League, there were only one or two games they would get excited about, ruck-wise. These were mainly games against Burnley, Hull and Sheffield United. This made our defeat last week look even worse, given the calibre of the firms we usually came up against most weeks. Still, Sheffield was a big away game for Millwall, so at least we knew there would be a full turn-out of their mob. We wanted to ensure they had no excuses when we set about doing the business.

* * * * *

Revenge is sweet: London Bridge – February 4, 1984

I arrived a little bit late. As I drove my van along Stratford Broadway, I saw all the boys hanging around the pavement, just outside Mooro's. It was a piss-poor turnout and mostly young 'uns. I reckon the meet was too early for a lot of the main boys, even though we knew Millwall were meeting 9 a.m. London Bridge.

As I pulled up, I was relieved to see Andy Swallow looking well up for it. We spoke about the previous week and he agreed that Millwall did have their day. He reckoned that it was lucky for Millwall that some of the West Ham lads had been at the back, not down near the pub fighting, because there was a big firm of us that day. He thought that if more of the lads had been at the front there would've been no way Millwall would have run us down New Cross Road. We couldn't get over how the firm had been so split, that there had been so many people that wanted to run down the road. In the end though, we all knew that Millwall's plan had been carried out well, and if we were to put it right we had to accept it and stop making excuses.

An Old Bill van decided to take a little look at us. They drove off, probably baffled at why so many young men were gathered at 8 o'clock in the morning when West Ham were at home with a 3 o'clock kick-off. The Old Bill didn't have a clue. We knew they would be back with more cozzers soon, so we couldn't hold on any longer waiting for the main faces to show. It would be too late, and we would be forced to take on Millwall at Euston, where the Old Bill would be in force.

It was decided that the Under Fives would go up on the Tube, using Stratford station, and that the older ones would go in a fleet of cars. This left the vans to take all the tools. In the queue to get in one of the vans, someone showed a little knife. 'Not a big enough blade' he was told, and turned away. 'What's your mate got? Right, get in.' We weren't for fucking posing that morning.

Andy was disappointed that a lot of the faces weren't there. He was also concerned about the younger ones going by train. As one of the oldest there, he decided he would much rather go by train to make sure they were all right. A few of us from the vans offered to go with him, but he just shrugged us off, insisting that he wasn't concerned for himself as he really didn't rate the Millwall lot.

We wondered whether the Old Bill, who would

inevitably come back to check out what we were up to, would look for us on the Tube. We hoped that Swallow's lot wouldn't get intercepted because we had split numbers of fifty to sixty and we knew there was no going back today. There would be too much loss of face.

This was it. With timing, and a bit of luck, we would all rejoin at London Bridge to sort matters out. This had become bigger than just the firm's reputation for all of us... it was now personal.

As we drove around the cobbled backstreets and archways to London Bridge station, we spotted some of the other lads that had driven up. They were hanging about a side entrance looking out for us and I made Animal and a few others get out to join them. It all kicked off as I was finding somewhere to park the van. Animal still remembers vividly what happened next:

The Millwall mob knew we were there. They had spotted us down the stairs leading into Tooley Street where we were kicking around a tomato while watching the Tube entrance for the arrival of the others. As we came around the corner, towards the slope that leads up into the station, we saw them coming down the slope at us. Luckily, at that very moment, Swallow and all of the young 'uns came out from the Tube exit to join us.

The whole Millwall away firm going to Sheffield that day were running for us. There must have been about 300-plus. They were led by that ginger fellow at the front. This geezer had such a grin on his face, as if he was going to have the day of his life. Then Swallow stepped forward, holding a machete case above his head with both arms. Then, with all the confidence in the world, he theatrically pulled the blade out. The blade edge just glistened in the sunlight and you could see the look of terror on the ginger leader's face. It went from glee to, 'Oh my God, I'm going to die!' It was a magical moment, and the cue for everyone else to pull out their tools.

Millwall must have known what was coming the instant Swallow put on his dramatic performance. Swallow's face was taut red with hate, he just charged at 'em.

Swallow recalls how good the timing had been that day:

Cor, if they'd come minutes earlier they would have got us, but everyone had arrived now, the lads from the Tube and those in the motors. We were all one firm again, all making a stand.

As we were walking up, I looked up to see the whole Millwall firm standing there, led by that big ginger fellow who looks like that snooker player, Steve Davis. Ginger was the Bushwhacker's top boy back then.

They were already coming at us. They couldn't believe we had come for them with such a small firm when they were out in force. They really thought it was their lucky day, especially after what happened the week before. But what they hadn't realised was we all had something under our coats. As they ran down at us, getting nearer and nearer, all the coats opened and everyone just pulled things out. I saw people with axes, machetes and lumps of wood with nails sticking out. We all just ran at them, and as we came up the slope they just ran back into London Bridge station.

Our clash with Millwall was so early in the morning that Animal recalls seeing the morning dew. He'd been up all night polishing and varnishing this pickaxe handle in preparation for the day we would take our revenge on Millwall:

I couldn't sleep, I just couldn't. This was going to be it. Then, in the morning dew, it was happening all over the shop. It went ballistic. We just ran at them, battering them. I'd given it to one so badly with the pickaxe [that] he had to lie down in a Portakabin to recover.

Swallow recalls that when they got into the station, the ticket man locked himself in the ticket booth as they ran Millwall over the ticket barrier:

There had obviously been a bar somewhere nearby, because a group of them came back at us throwing empty beer bottles from crates that they were carrying. There was so much glass flying through the air. I got hit on the head twice, which later resulted in three stitches on one side of my head and six on the other.

That's when we let them have it. As they tried to come back out of the station at us, one of our lot threw a Geordie petrol bomb at them. We were still steaming in. Millwall turned and ran.

I remember the sound... it was already going off without us. We ran into another lot of ours from out of the motors who were just as anxious to join the action. We made for the front entrances, but before we even got around to the front we caught some Millwall slipping out the side of the station into Tooley Street. They ran back up the steps as soon as they saw us.

All of a sudden, we heard a large bang. It went boom! like a bomb going off. It echoed throughout the station. We got around to the front entrance and it was like a scene from Ireland, the smoke and flames making it seem almost surreal. The lads were all looking smug and pleased with themselves, but we didn't have time to congratulate ourselves because it wouldn't be long before the Old Bill would arrive.

The first Old Bill on the scene got out, took one look, then got back in their car and drove off. That's when we knew it was on top, big-time. We needed to get out fast before the Old Bill came back, so we started slipping away, like we were never there. Many of the lads were thankful for the London Bridge black taxi service that day!

The Bushwhackers had been bushwhacked. We had needed to put an end to our London rivals' gloating and taunts about our show up at New Cross and to restore our reputation. London Bridge saw to that.

Only the week before, our rivals had been celebrating in pubs around South London. Now it was our turn. Everyone was full of it, 'Cheers. My round.' We were all reliving the events of the day with relish. Swallow:

I just jumped straight through the petrol bombs that landed in front of me. All Millwall could see was me coming through the flames. Looking back, they must have thought, 'Who the fuck is this? Superman?' Years later, on the rave scene and the England international scene, the ginger fellow and I would look back on that day and laugh. He told me, 'You were very close behind me that day. You very nearly caught me'. 'Yeah,' I replied, 'I know, you wear size 11 trainers.'

Chapter 19

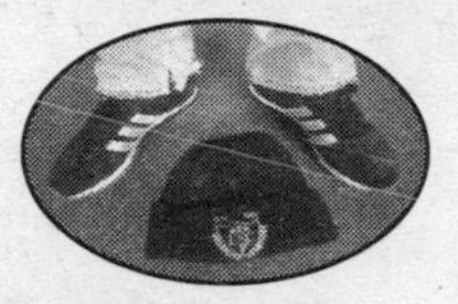

THE MAKING OF *HOOLIGAN*

I.C.F.

WE DIDN'T have sociologists running around with us, living our lives, so it never fails to amuse us listening to the crap they come out with about their research into football violence.

Contrary to popular belief, no police undercover operation truly penetrated our elite inner circle. That's why it came as no surprise that the I.C.F. show trials (Operation Own Goal) collapsed as they did.

The only outsider to ever get a close insight into what made us all tick was Ian Stuttard, or Butch as he became known to us, a film producer renowned for his television documentaries. At the time we met him, he was working with Thames Television. Here Butch talks about the making of his documentary on the I.C.F.:

My first experience of football violence occurred in 1965. Fulham were playing Liverpool in a Division One game at Craven Cottage and were leading 1-0. Some Fulham fans were cheerfully jeering the opposition when suddenly, from within their midst, a lone, middle-aged Scouser erupted. He was apoplectic with rage and turned to confront the Fulham supporters in a manner so ferocious that those around him were too shocked to rise to his challenge. The atmosphere remained tense until the end of the match. It was the first time I had seen anyone so agitated at a football match, and it is an episode which has stayed with me ever since.

Years later, when we had become all too familiar with football's troubles, I was talking to a friend (a Millwall supporter) in a pub in Paddington. It was 1984 and Millwall's hooligans were the equal of any in the land. He told me that the Millwall hooligans fought others like themselves because they liked it and wanted to be acknowledged as 'top boys'. This perspective was unlike anything I'd heard about football hooliganism before. He discussed organised violence, the structure of groups, tactics, leadership, communication, policing and fashion. Clearly, if some of those elements could be captured on camera, then a documentary film taking a closer look at what lay behind football violence might be possible. It could examine the motivation to fight, the form it took, and whether or not it was different from the way the media had always portrayed it. Was the violence really mindless? Would it be possible to get any of it on film as it happened?

That's what set me on my way.

A week or so later I mentioned my interest to John Taylor, a television colleague who used to present the London Programme for LWT. John had already looked at football hooliganism on his programme and had interviewed the man who was to become crucial to my project – Cass Pennant. I later learned that Cass was acknowledged as one of the leaders of the InterCity Firm – the I.C.F., the notorious gang which followed the fortunes of West Ham United.

I arranged to meet Cass and after a long discussion, during which I made clear my intention to approach the subject without prejudice, he agreed to help me. He stressed that he could introduce me and guide me, but that the measure of my success would depend on the relationships I made. My access would be based on trust and I would be excluded from certain activities. He warned me that I would achieve nothing by turning up and trying my luck with a camera. So began a period of six months in the company of the I.C.F.

In getting to know these people I was to discover that much of their world was very different from its depiction in the press. Among the unemployed thugs, who were typically associated with football hooliganism, were office managers, builders, soldiers, publicans, a solicitor's clerk and an assistant bank manager.

In the early weeks I also sought links with Millwall and Arsenal's hooligans, who enjoyed equally fearsome reputations. Millwall's thugs were the implacable enemies of the I.C.F. The two groups were dissimilar, the

West Ham people being thinkers and planners, while Millwall were less subtle. They appeared to have fewer strategists and tacticians and when duty called, everyone joined in. I was with Millwall during the infamous riot at Luton in 1985. They swarmed off the train, indiscriminately attacking Luton supporters on their way to the ground. Since Luton had no hardcore 'firm' to oppose them, Millwall's hooligans then turned on the police. The battle climaxed in the ground when the police were battered by a deluge of red plastic seats which had been ripped out by the hooligans.

All-out thuggery was not the I.C.F.'s way. For an away game they laid plans, which would vary according to circumstances. The challenge for them was to evade arrest by the police and to find the best way to combat the opposition. Should they surprise them by ambush or formally arrange to meet and fight? Should they employ deception? Should they divide their forces and strike in several places at once? There had to be structure which informed the way the I.C.F. operated and there had to be leaders to whom people could turn for guidance during their encounters.

Having looked at Millwall, I also wanted to compare Arsenal's hooligans. Cass Pennant had arranged to take me to meet some leaders of Arsenal's firm, the Gooners. The meeting was to take place at the Adelaide pub behind Highbury & Islington station. The Gooners would be assembling that morning to go to a league game away to Chelsea. It was a big risk to take me to them, as some of them were the very people who had been injured in an I.C.F. revenge raid on the Hackney cab the previous night. Using machetes and axes, five carloads of I.C.F. had left several Gooners in hospital. This had been a reprisal for the stabbing of two I.C.F. people the week before.

Cass had not been present at the raid, but I had.

The atmosphere in Islington on that Saturday morning was quite intense and I kept my camera in its bag. The Arsenal guys were outraged at Cass's effrontery in brazenly appearing and they seemed to be in two minds about what to do. They suggested that Cass was mad to even turn up and he was reminded that three of their number were still in hospital. Things were very delicate at that stage.

Cass stood his ground and argued that the meeting had been arranged before last night's events and he wasn't aware of what had happened – which was a complete lie, as he had had a call that morning advising him not to keep the appointment with the Gooners. As Cass put it to them that Arsenal shouldn't be left out and should consider co-operating with me, more Gooners were turning up to the rendezvous. They definitely weren't interested but they seemed undecided about what to do. Then Denton arrived. He was a leader, a top Gooner, and he knew nothing of why I was present. He simply knew Cass was a main West Ham man. Denton's mates, Scotty and Danny Miller, filled him in on the previous night's events.

It was a sunny morning but Denton's face looked like thunder. Cass and Denton spoke quietly to each other as all the Gooners gathered around, curious but not threatening. All the time Cass was in conversation I stood back across the road, mindful of Cass's instruction to make for the van he had arrived in if the meeting went wrong. The Transit had its engine running all the time and the driver's face wore an intense expression as he watched for anything untoward from Arsenal. The Gooners had all seen us get out of the van and they were unsure about what it contained.

The van was Cass' insurance policy. He would hardly have risked coming without back-up, would he? It was sobering to learn later that this meeting could have ended in gunfire.

Cass turned to me and said that it was all off with the Gooners, they would not co-operate because of the previous night's incident. There was too much tension and the Gooners were not of a mind to accommodate the I.C.F.. Now that there was no TV business to be done, Cass said that our hanging around any longer would remind them that 'I'm West Ham, and you know how popular that makes me'. It was all matter of fact, a bit like an unsuccessful sales meeting. No running, no panicking, just a signal from Cass to the van's driver, who hadn't taken an eye off him all the time. We were gone, leaving the Gooners staring balefully after us.

Sometimes the group seemed to operate without needing to communicate. This was vividly demonstrated one dark January night. West Ham were due to play a league match away to Wimbledon on the same night that Chelsea were at home to Sunderland in the second leg of the old League Cup. The police were expecting trouble at Chelsea, having made over 200 arrests during the first leg. I joined Cass, Andy Swallow, Danny Harrison and the others for the Underground journey to Wimbledon. The route took us past Fulham Broadway, which was the station nearest to Stamford Bridge, and the plan from the outset was to give Chelsea a nasty surprise by unexpectedly appearing when Sunderland were supposed to be their visitors.

We pulled into Fulham Broadway and I moved to get off. I assumed that the I.C.F. would be leaving the train, but I was told not to get off yet and stayed on. So the train went one station further along to Parsons Green. Here, nobody said, 'Let's get off now', and yet everybody knew to leave the train. I couldn't understand how this ghostly command system operated. Whether words were simply whispered or whether it was planned in transit, I don't know, but some 300 young men streamed out of Parsons Green station and on to the backstreets of Chelsea.

As planned, the I.C.F. stunned the Chelsea hooligans waiting around the pubs of Fulham Broadway by coming up behind them in a kind of flanking movement and catching them off-guard. The Chelsea Head-hunters were driven all around the backstreets of their own manor. Having triumphed on Chelsea's patch, everybody got back on the train to continue the fun at the Wimbledon versus West Ham match. No trouble there. Wimbledon had only a small core of supporters and lacked a firm capable of making a show against the I.C.F.

It was clear that there was more to this than I had first imagined, and I was gripped. Far from being mindless, this activity was organised in a rational manner, especially considering the odds against pulling off a successful 'away' encounter. It's like a raid on another town with its alien geography to negotiate, local police to outwit and avoid, and the constant threat of ambushes being laid by the opposition. Such challenges demand leadership, resourcefulness and communication skills, as well as good old macho bottle. I saw many examples of this at work over the months [I] *spent watching and filming.*

My approach differed from [the way I had tackled] *most of the documentary films I had made, where there is a period of research and preparation followed by the shoot, the edit, then transmission. Here, the research period began with just observing and meeting people. After a couple of months, I started using a stills camera a bit to get the I.C.F. used to being photographed and I watched how they reacted to my just being around and taking pictures. Reactions varied. There were some who wanted no photography and I respected their wishes, and in cases where some people were filmed inadvertently, I binned the footage.*

When I moved from a stills camera to a small video camera, I began to feel that I was building up a degree of trust with some people. The I.C.F. needed to know that my filming wasn't going to compromise them, that the risks of getting arrested were not going to be increased by my being around them with a camera. It was their world and they dictated what happened and the extent of my involvement in it.

When the film was finally edited and broadcast, only about ten per cent of what I had experienced and witnessed made it into the final cut. Some of the top people in the I.C.F., for reasons of self-preservation, mysteriously disappeared when the camera was around, especially on the occasions when I was not alone and used a film crew. Even though they were prepared to help with explanations and discussions to achieve a film that didn't sensationalise football violence, when it came to appearing in it themselves they were much less interested. They were wary and mostly avoided it, particularly the older ones who were wise in the ways of the media and the law. In spite of these limitations, I wasn't disappointed. I hadn't expected to shoot everything and I was pleased with what I got.

My initiation was a surprise. I was about to be tested out, though I didn't know it. I had spent weeks observing, attending matches, hanging out in pubs, but I had yet to film or record anything. Southampton were visiting Orient in an early round of the FA Cup and I was asked if I'd like to join Cass and some of the others in a small expedition. I went along, taking a camera in a holdall for the first time. Cass had with him a dozen or so serious-looking mates, mostly black, and he seemed to know them well.

Outside the ground we met twenty to thirty of the Under Fives, all wanting to join us... Cass didn't appear to want them to swell the I.C.F. ranks and sent them to a different part of the ground. It was later explained to me that the older group didn't want to draw any immediate attention to themselves. The name of the game here was infiltration and if they let the younger ones join them they would be sussed, and their cover blown. I followed the older guys into the Southampton end, by ones and twos. I had no idea what was going to occur, as West Ham were not even involved in the match.

As the I.C.F. regrouped at the back of the terrace behind the goal at the packed Southampton end, Cass said to me, 'Are you ready?' I said yes, thinking they were going to move off again to another part of the ground. I was wrong. Mayhem broke out. Using shock and surprise, Cass, Big Natley and the others, though vastly outnumbered, tore into the Southampton people surrounding us. The element of surprise was such that a number of the Southampton supporters froze. The ferocity of the attack had left several Southampton supporters injured and we were surrounded by enraged supporters. I had no time to use my camera and I was concerned that the second the opposition realised that there were just twelve of us we'd all be slaughtered. But what I hadn't allowed for, and what the experience of the I.C.F. told them, was that within a very short time, perhaps a minute, the police would be on the scene in numbers.

The melee was immediately broken up by the police and we were all ejected from the terrace on to the pitch and escorted round to the Orient end. Nobody was arrested, which I found staggering given the Southampton casualties littering that terrace, but as we walked around the pitch we were showered in snot and spit and vile invective from the Southampton fans. I had never experience the snot before. The Orient fans gave us a huge round of applause.

The reason for the exercise, I was told, was partly to teach the Southampton hooligans a lesson. It annoyed the I.C.F. that Southampton never came to Upton Park to confront them, yet a mile or so down the road they went mob-handed to little Orient who didn't have a firm, or a nucleus of hooligans. As Cass said, 'If you think you are going to turn up to bully our little sister we're going to put on a little show for yer.'

Cass explained, 'What we actually did was [seek] *out Southampton's toughest guys. That's why we moved to the back... the firm in the centre, behind the goal, were all tattoos and denim, laughing and joking and looking like the inhabitants of a bar somewhere in Southampton Docks. Instinct told us this was their firm. That's why we asked if you were ready.' I had a lot to learn.*

My camera often drew unwanted attention from the police. I recall an away match at Notts Forest. Both West Ham and Forest sat mid-table, and little was at stake in terms of the actual match, so there was a low turnout. I was with no more than fifteen to twenty I.C.F. guys, but they included the legendary Bill Gardner, Swallow and other experienced thugs. Cass wasn't there that day. The first half was tedious, and we adjourned to the bar and toilet area. With good timing, the Nottingham Forest hooligans made a show and fighting broke out. I used my small video camera and was arrested as the suspected ringleader, even though I was a good twenty years older than those doing the fighting. Although not charged, I was locked up for the whole second half of the match, but when I came out I managed to rejoin the small group of I.C.F. leaving the ground.

As we crossed the bridge over the River Trent I saw a large gathering of about 150 of the opposition lying in wait for us. We continued to walk, driven by about eight mounted police who were keen to get the Cockney bastards out of Nottingham. To our right was a huge advertising hoarding and as the foe advanced, the I.C.F. formed a closely packed triangle of bodies up against this hoarding so that nobody would get separated, picked off and devoured.

I will never forget what happened next. The Nottingham firm started to bombard us with rocks and bricks, and the mounted police seemed to evaporate. The small group of I.C.F., including myself, were backed up against the hoarding like coconuts in a shy. I could hear shouts of 'Stand! Stand!' from the leaders within the group, but all I could do was cover up to avoid being hit by the rocks. I got hit on my back and on one leg by bricks, but nothing hit my head and my camera stayed in its bag. I looked up from under my arms as I cowered against the hoarding. I saw Swallow, Billy Gardner and Big Ted not only stand but march forward, challenging the throwers. Ted was hit and the other two both took rocks in the face. Gardner was cut over the eye and

Swallow was cut on the head. It didn't stop them and they continued to march forward through the hail of rocks. The enemy all began to back off. That opened things up for the rest of us to escape sideways.

The police were no help. They got around us with their horses but not in a protective way, and harassed us all the way back to the station. My impression was that they were happy to see some Cockneys on the end of a few bricks.

The atmosphere on the train coming back was ecstatic. I wish I'd been able to film everything that day because it was such a good illustration of the tactics used and the obstacles faced. It had been a brave act to go forward against those odds and I imagined that was how the I.C.F. always responded to being outnumbered from their own experience. It was survival against the odds. The Nottingham firm knew their territory and where best to lay an ambush. Presumably they also knew they could rely on the Nottingham police for assistance.

Unfamiliar surroundings hold many surprises. This was clearly illustrated the day that hundreds of the I.C.F., together with thousands of regular West Ham supporters, made the trip to Manchester in March 1985 for a sixth-round FA Cup tie against the Reds. There were continuous skirmishes between the I.C.F., the Reds and the police, both before and after the match, that took place along the three miles separating Old Trafford from the station. The climax came when the I.C.F. were ambushed in the middle of a council estate. In fact, they had been caught in a pincer-like movement, with the Reds coming at them from both sides of the estate.

We stopped at a pub under a hail of bricks from the Manchester boys, smashing windows. We were trapped like sitting targets. There could be only one response, the I.C.F.'s best form of defence... attack. The I.C.F. burst out of all the doors of the pub, spreading themselves out to be less of a target. They steamed into the Manchester boys before the police got there and broke things up.

The atmosphere was one of war the whole day. The 4-2 win to Manchester seemed irrelevant to the score off the pitch. At one stage, the Manchester guys tried to grab my camera and three of them jumped me during the skirmishing. As I defended myself, the police arrived and tried to arrest me. This time the I.C.F. rescued me by surrounding the outnumbered officers, whom they intimidated into letting me go.

Although it was never my intention to fight, I would inevitably get caught up in the proceedings on occasions when fighting broke out. As a result, I was held and arrested by police no less than five times during the making of the film, although I was never charged.

Until now I had captured the moments using a small Hi8 video camera, but when I began filming with a documentary crew in the spring of 1985 I ran into problems. Filming became cumbersome and impracticable due to the speed and unpredictable nature of football violence, hampering my need to illustrate on film what I had experienced from the time spent with the I.C.F..

I wanted to show that this activity was not mindless, that there was a structure to it and that there was a reason why some young men wanted to pit themselves against each other. There are so many different aspects to it, the expressions of rivalry, the notion that their simple differences – such as being from a different place, having different accents or representing different teams – were enough to inspire young Englishmen to fight. They desired to be the best and just as their football teams aspired to become champions, so they aspired to be the top boys.

As with the teams who enjoy a strong tradition, there are numerous hooligan firms who have always had a good strong lineage or tradition. West Ham had its boys long before they were ever called the I.C.F. The tradition of having boys who will fight, particularly with boys who represent other areas of London, was established in Victorian times, before football gave it such an appropriate setting. There's a great deal of pride and status attached to these confrontations, and such is the intensity of the rivalry between the various groups that they would often face each other even when they were not playing each other in the match.

To explain all this, I included in the film a series of interviews with leading academics in the field of football violence from Leicester University – Professor John Williams and Eric Dunn. Their insights were extremely useful in providing me with the historical and sociological context of hooliganism. Later, these pioneers formed the nucleus of the government-funded

Sir Norman Chester Institute of Football Research.

The 1984–85 season had been a bad year for football. The Bradford fire disaster was closely followed by Millwall's anarchy at Luton and the nightmare of Heysel. Hooligan was transmitted in August 1985 and its timing gave rise to an interest from a government enquiry on football violence. The enquiry led to the Popplewell Inquiry (which subsequently became the Taylor Report). As a result of several TV and radio interviews I had undertaken, I was contacted by the Home Office and asked to speak to Lord Justice Popplewell about the phenomenon of football violence.

Among my suggestions was that they should meet the people involved and talk to them. I put forward the names of Cass Pennant and Andy Swallow, who had both been so articulate and helpful in explaining to me what I needed to know to make the film work. This was agreed, although it was stressed to me by the person representing Popplewell that the meeting should be discrete, almost secret. It struck me as odd that it would be deemed inappropriate for Justice Popplewell to be meeting self-confessed hooligans while conducting an official enquiry into football violence. Why was it necessary to be secretive about discussing these matters with those actually involved and who knew more about it than most?

I thought that it would be valuable for politicians and the judiciary to understand more about the people involved and talk less about 'mindless violence'. Cass and Andy thought it would do no harm to meet Justice

Popplewell, and they were curious. The meeting took place at Scotland Yard and lasted an hour. Soon after, I was thanked by the Home Office for arranging what Popplewell described as was one of the most valuable contributions to his enquiry. Nevertheless, Cass and Andy's contribution to the enquiry remained unofficial, presumably [it was] considered too politically delicate to reveal.

When the film was completed and eventually transmitted on ITV in August 1985, the viewing figures were very satisfactory, reaching an audience of some 7 million people. The coverage in the press was wide and varied. I took part in numerous radio and TV interviews, which always seemed to begin with 'Why, why do they do it?' I hope the film answered this.

Before the film's transmission, some of the press previews aligned themselves with certain Tory politicians and objected to it on the grounds that it glorified football violence. They wanted the film stopped, declaring it to be against the public interest. The film glorified nothing. It was an objective examination of football hooliganism as an entity and sought to explain why it took place and what the people involved in it got from it. What stood Hooligan apart from previous programmes made concerning football violence was that it was filmed from the perspective of the hooligans themselves. Although the academics from Leicester University were featured, the film avoided being judgmental. The I.C.F. was not condemned, and that is probably what some people objected to.

Hooligan made a big impact, which continues today and it is often referred to. Thames Television sold the film all over the world. The film also developed a little cult market amongst hooligan groups, with pirate copies passed up and down the country.

The popular stereotype at the time I started my research was that fighting at football resulted from a bunch of mainly unemployed, moronic youths and thugs who had nothing better to do than fight each other in a disorganised rabble. The film shattered that myth. These men were a highly organised group with a very varied mixture of people from different backgrounds and jobs, some quite successful. I was pleased that the film helped to lay a few ghosts on that score. I'd made films before and have made more since, Hooligan will always be one of the stand-out films for me.

Chapter 20

SAMMY THE ENGINE AND THE MANCS

I.C.F.

SAMMY THE ENGINE – yet another comical name for one of the Manc top faces. It made me think of Thomas the Tank Engine, but I presume the name was because he developed a reputation for always steaming in. He had a bit of an engine, this Manc. He was the last of the household Manc names that we had a decent run-in with.

At least the name Engine was a move forward from the Seventies. Back then, the Mancs boasted one lad that went by the name of Banana Bob; they also had a much-respected twosome known as Coco and Pancho.

Another Manc that we sought out was a chap called Snowy, a top face amongst their mob. However, when we did catch up with him, we'd either taken him by surprise or his Cockney Reds had run off and left him. The kill was on, but then came along Gardner with his law of

'We're West Ham and we don't take liberties.' We were all feeling gutted that Mr Snow hadn't been caught with a firm behind him, 'cause I would have liked to have seen how Gardner's law operated then.

There were times when the bloodlust gradually subsided to one of respect for your foe, but the respect of the likes of Gardner and co. had to be hard earned over many years. Snowy must have feared the worst, and by rights he should have got it, but he was shown the respect of West Ham's top boys. I'll give him his due, he never bottled and, by all accounts, he was a decent bloke.

It's a funny old game. Everyone was out looking to rip each other's heads off, but when the top men came together you'd get moments like this. Most of us all knew what Snowy looked like and, in the seasons following, there would occasionally be passing conversations with him as he was being led down Green Street by police escort with all the other Mancs. 'Alright Snowy. How yer doing?', always very polite and respectful. Snowy never forgot that it could have been his number up that day, and he would reply in kind. It was a show of genuine respect for someone who'd reached the top of his trade. In spite of that, we could never lose sight of the fact that he was still our foe, and we all knew that if the Old Bill hadn't been there, he would have been the first to have a go.

Our mate Animal, with his forty-two football convictions, wasn't going to miss a chance to add to that total when we found out that we'd drawn the Mancs for the quarter-finals of the FA Cup. Their entire firm would be going up for the game, without question. We were all convinced it was the Hammers' year for the Cup. Our luck seemed to come in five-year intervals and we all remembered walking down Wembley Way for the finals of '75 and '80. The five years were now up.

Animal recalls the day we all arrived at Euston to face Man United's mob:

We all met at Euston, crack of dawn, to catch the train. It was a really good mob, pure I.C.F. We had every fucking firm out that day and we packed that train to the rafters. I reckon the Old Bill at Euston would have phoned ahead to warn their counterparts at Manchester about the size of the mob coming up on the inter-city.

As we got in to Manchester Piccadilly, the Old Bill were already there, waiting for us. What they didn't know was that our mob had actually split when we got off the train. One mob, mainly Under Fives, had slipped out up the stairs and over the top of the station into an alleyway. This was an exit the Old Bill hadn't thought to protect, believing we'd all go through the main entrance doors.

I was in the mob that headed towards the Old Bill. They were trying to push us down into this little tube, but it was obvious that they hadn't realised just how many of us had actually come off the train. Our mob was so big that the few coppers there didn't have a hope in hell of pushing us anywhere. The Old Bill just got moved aside as we went out the main doors. As we walked from the station we saw another West Ham mob coming out from the back of the station and heading down the road. We left the commotion in our wake as we passed through Piccadilly; the shopping centre there was in total panic.

All the police activity must have alerted the Mancs' spotters to the fact that we had arrived. The Old Bill didn't do much to stop us. They just wanted us out the way, but we were already out on their streets in force. I could see the other West Ham mobs, the Under Fives, the Harrises and the Gardners. It was the old guard and the young West Ham all together.

We didn't have to wait long as the Man United mob suddenly came steaming around the corner. We just knew we could have them if we worked this one properly. So we had little tear-offs and began to back off, and kept backing off. Them Mancs thought they were having the result of their lives. What they didn't know was that by backing off we were bringing them level with the alleyway that our Under Fives had left the station through. The Under Fives would be coming out right behind them. Now we had them, and it went right off. The Mancs got battered, we mullared 'em.

Timmy Mac was another well-known and well-liked character at West Ham. He was a self-made man, having sold the family scaffolding business for a few quid. He says today that nothing beat the buzz of his football-going days, not even his first million. The rows we had with the Mancs came tops and the one Timmy best remembers was one that none of the rest of us will forget either. It was the sixth round of the FA cup, '85 season, when we had to go to Old Trafford:

The rows with the Mancs were the best. I always got into the most trouble whenever we played them.

It was a full on, everyone pitched in battle with the Mancs at the bottom of the slope outside Manchester's Piccadilly. The big mobs were going at it early morning to catch the police out. The Mancs had come out of every side street and West Ham ripped straight into 'em.

In the midst of it all this, a fellow known as Sammy the Engine burst out of the crowd and caught our Chrissy Harris a beauty, smashing his nose and breaking it. Now Chris was as game as they come and was always there, but he always had to keep half an eye out for his old man, Joe Harris, who always came to the games to watch his beloved West Ham. On this occasion though, the father and son double act worked the other way, with Joe looking out for his son. Chris wasn't half as bothered about his nose as his old man was. As far as his old man was concerned, the Mancs had taken a right liberty – it was his son, after all.

The Old Bill herded us all up and tried to put us all on buses, but there was no way we were gonna let that happen. We were gonna walk. Old Trafford was some distance, about one hour away, so we stopped off for a few beers at the pub first. Virtually unescorted, we led a trail of West Ham along duel carriageways, across greens and past red brick housing estates, kicking off with any Mancs we spotted along the route that looked half a firm.

When we reached Man U's ground, we regrouped up on the big forecourt outside. We thought we'd all have a walk round the ground to see who wants it. There were virtually no Manc firms around to give any scrap to, so we went round again in the hope that we would eventually find someone about. Then, close to the visiting supporters' entrance at the scoreboard end, who should reappear but Sammy the Engine. Old man Harris leapt straight on him and upped him, yelling, 'This is for my boy.' I have never seen Mr Harris so wild. He spanked him so hard that the Engine's glasses smashed and flew off his face. I couldn't stop laughing.

We all joined old man Harris and it went off again. The Old Bill came charging at us on horseback, batons flying, as they tried to split us up. We now found ourselves having to fight the police and Man United at once. A few City tried to get in with us at one stage, but we weren't gonna let that happen, so we had to teach them a lesson as well.

In the melee, we had been pushed around to the side, so we entered the ground through the turnstiles. Those without tickets simply jumped over. We sat in the seats on the side and as we looked around, we realised that we were in an area full of Mancs, with no Old Bill. We didn't need any encouragement. It was all off again, and that's how it continued all day. At half-time, the battle raged on below the stands.

Everyone wanted to know that day. No sooner had the Old Bill sorted out one incident, another one would start. It seemed like West Ham were everywhere that day. It was a far cry from the days when we would come up with just a single coach and a couple of hired vans.

With about ten minutes to go, we were down 4-2, so we thought, 'C'mon, we might as well go and make a show.' We headed towards the lower paddock beneath our stand. The idea was that we would split into two groups and enter through each side of the paddock, sandwiching the Mancs so that we could give them a good hiding. It was quite funny to hear the Mancs singing and taunting us with the usual chants of 'Goodbye, goodbye' and 'We... can... see... you... sneaking... out...', thinking that we were fucking off home. At that stage grounds still opened up the gates to all and sundry ten to fifteen minutes before the end of the game, so after leaving our section of the ground we walked straight back into the paddock area beneath our stand. We started splitting up in a couple of groups as we ran along the gangways and down the stairs, larruping every Manc we saw, lashing and punching 'em.

I remember all the West Ham at the scoreboard end roaring and cheering us on like it had made their day. Then the inevitable happened, the Old Bill showed up. They went absolutely mental. You have to remember that this wasn't long after the miners' strike and all that trouble, and they just hated us up there. They were grabbing hold of us, but instead of just throwing us out, they were giving us a good kicking first. I saw a few boys of ours get it big-style off these Manc Old Bill.

When were all outside again, still as a firm of about a hundred, the Mancs came roaring out, all wanting revenge for what we had just done. We were getting spread out and had to just hit anyone we didn't know or recognise, as there were thousands of Mancs all around us all tearing about the forecourt. We couldn't get any help from our boys at the scoreboard end, 'cause they were locked in.

During the fight, old Sammy made an appearance again, but this time he couldn't see, as he was minus his lenses. The word had spread that there were 'West Ham bastards running around' and the Engine was shouting, 'Come on, let's do West Ham.' He was unaware that Jono and Butler were next to him at the time and those two just steamed into him, giving him another serving.

I had promised to help Butch with his camera that day as he tried to get footage for the film he was making on us all. However, after the game had finished, I forgot my commitment to helping Butch and came out of the ground with only one thing on my mind... having it with the Mancs.

I came out of the scoreboard end with a little mob of fifty or so. We were the first ones out. We were told by a couple of West Ham that they'd been rowing with a firm of twenty City lads. They said it was still going on over at the little railway bridge. Firm-handed, we decide to rout the City lads and headed over to the bridge. Half of them were still lurking there but they ran on our first shout.

We turned back to see what was happening with the main mob of West Ham who were still in the ground when the road around us started to fill with supporters.

All of a sudden, all the lads from the Brit started to come through from fighting outside the ground, along with Mancs and the Old Bill trying to push their way through.

The whole street was in chaos, with all the little mobs trying to regroup. Everyone was headed in the direction of the little bridge again. Someone said, 'Come on, Cass. It's going to go with the Mancs on the other side', and sure enough, when we got to the bridge it went off.

The talking point amongst people after the row wasn't the fighting itself, but the mad old boy with a placard on a stick, marching around in the middle of the chaos as it kicked off all around him. 'Saints and sinners repent' he kept shouting, as we were steaming each other on both sides of the road. I'll never forget it. It was the craziest moment I'd ever witnessed in all my football-going years. We really felt like the world's biggest bastards with that nutter raving on and on. It had all been captured on the famous *Hooligan* documentary, along with our man Brian shouting out his famous rally call of, *'C'mon West Ham. We used to go through this lot, just forty of us. C'mon West Ham'.*

We wanted to shout at him, 'Brian, open your eyes and look behind you mate.' We were split on both sides of a bus, the road filled with a thousand Mancs. Behind them, the main mob of West Ham came out with Gardner and, by all accounts, they had the same number of Mancs again behind them. A road full of warring Mancs. You just couldn't ask for more. The Old Bill were around but they might as well not been there for all the difference they made.

There were about 200 to 300 of us left, plenty of good

guys. We were all split up but working together to keep the Mancs up in front of us and on their toes. Meanwhile, something like a thousand Mancs were still coming up behind us, keeping us on our toes as well. We were fronting, standing, giving slaps and taking them, all the time knowing that the other mob of West Ham were doing exactly the same even further back.

This was a pure classic. It had been going off between us since late morning and now, coming past 5 o'clock, it was like the big finale and everyone wanted it. Everyone was fighting, Mancs, Cockneys and Cockney Reds, all the way along what I believe must have been the Great Stone Road. Even Banana Bob was there, and he and a handful of older Mancs kept mouthing off in front of Old Bill. I remember the bulk of Man U were mainly on one side of the road while we were on the other, with the Old Bill in the middle of the road, trying to keep the firms apart. Every time it looked on for us the Old Bill jumped in, pushing one party or the other back on to one side of the road.

The Old Bill's control was only loose though, and there was a lot of serious stuff going on between the two sides. The scariest incident was when a group of us tried to lose the Old Bill by running down side streets of this industrial area, the Old Bill in close pursuit. The Manc police knew this area better than us and they kept using vans to block street exits. We eventually ended up in a deserted street of red brick houses, with all their windows boarded up. The Old Bill came up behind us and blocked us in. We looked to the top of the street and another Old Bill minibus appeared, full of the Filth.

It was like a scene straight out of an old war movie, when the Gestapo show up. We all just looked at each other. We were lost in some deserted street, blocked in by the Old Bill, and we all realised what we had to do. Go for it, now! We all charged for the lone minibus as the Old Bill were clambering out of it. It was every man for himself. It wasn't the reaction they were expecting and we must have startled them because we all got through and didn't stop running until we were clear of that ghost town.

We'd seen the Old Bill do some things that day that we had never seen or experienced before. They had no intentions of nicking anyone. It seemed like the only thought in their mind was to draw truncheons. I wondered if that was something else they'd practised with the miners.

Brett recalled how the day ended for us when we got back to the station:

All the way back to Manchester Piccadilly was rows. At one point, we reached a road where a little shunter train pulled in and stopped right above us at this little station. The train was packed full of West Ham and after they all got off they told us about the massive row they'd had with the Mancs at the last stop. It was Gardner and all of that mob, so we all joined up, swapping tales about all the rows we'd been having. I heard someone telling Gardner about one such row, saying, 'It's gone off in a little scuffle with that Sammy the Engine. The Harrises are right there again and Old Joe, Chrissy's dad, still had the Engine's glasses. He said something like, 'You'll be needing these' and threw them back to him.

When we finally made it to the station, it was full of West Ham. The Old Bill weren't letting anyone on the inter-city trains. They'd organised these Specials for us, which they herded us all on to. But while we were waiting in the train, we clocked our inter-city was right next to us. Someone opened a door and then leant out to unlock the door on the inter-city and we all jumped through. We were all trying to be respectable while sitting on this inter-city train, waiting for it to go.

The respectable behaviour didn't last long. As we were waiting, who should unexpectedly come walking along the platform with his cronies, but our mate the Engine. There were immediate shouts of 'It's him, it's him' and everyone started jumping off the train, screaming, 'Have him.' They just bashed the granny out of him and his mates 'til he ran off... minus his glasses.

It was one of those days when you just had to be there. To remind us of the crack we all had that game, someone hung Sammy the Engine's broken glasses up in the Brit pub.

Chapter 21

MANCS COME PLAISTOW

I.C.F.

ON THE way to the official one-off I.C.F. reunion at the Theatre of Dreams in 2001, we whiled away the time on Swallow's coaches by reminiscing about all the old Manc battles we'd had over the years. One in particular involved only a few of the boys and it interested me the most because there had been very few of our rivals willing to take it to us at West Ham. I also learned that this particular incident led to the bitterness that provoked the infamous ferry battle.

My good friend Terry Sherrin, now a thirty-nine-year-old interior refurbishment executive, recalled the incident when the Mancs got off at Plaistow station during the '85–'86 season.

We all met in the Raglan and the Vic because we had

been told by a Cockney Red a couple of weeks earlier that Man U were planning on getting off at Plaistow station to take the Brit. This was unthinkable to us. The Brit was well known as our pub, owned in partnership by West Ham's own Frank Lampard Senior and tucked away in the heart of the Plaistow/Stratford borders.

We hadn't been drinking there so much of late. Thanks to the outrage that the Hooligan *documentary stirred up, the Old Bill had been on us almost every time we'd meet there. We chose the Raglan and Vic as alternatives because they were located to the right of the station if you were coming out looking towards the direction of the ground. If the Mancs chose to go left towards the Brit, we were fucked, we would have missed 'em. We made a gamble, though, that if they did get off at Plaistow then they would come out and turn right.*

We had in our minds a little dry run they did a couple of seasons before. They got off at Plaistow station, turned right and walked down to the Green Gate. They turned left along the Barking Road, getting as far as the Boleyn pub unopposed. All the West Ham lads were up by the Queens pub at the top end of Green Street, waiting for the Mancs to come out of Upton Park station. About forty to fifty of us just happened to be at the Boleyn at the time and we had to hold them there. They were the biggest firm of Man U I'd seen for some time at West Ham. We couldn't believe that about 400-plus Mancs had actually made it to the fucking Boleyn on the corner of Green Street.

So we reasoned that if the Mancs got off at Plaistow, then they were likely to take the same route again.

Remembering back I was at the Boleyn with Tiddles, Bruce and Micky. There were a good twenty of us all together, with a few more dotted around. All the other West Ham were waiting at the wrong end of Green Street and we know we had to hold the Mancs. The cunts had come bouncing over the road chanting 'United'. That was all it took to get us going. In spite of the fact that we had so few lads, the twenty of us steamed in, straight in front of the escort. There weren't many of the Old Bill around and it really went off.

We thought this was it. They had a proper firm, Mancs, Cockney Reds, geezers, everything. It was the biggest Man United firm I'd seen at ours. We were still fucking holding our ground, though. The Old Bill knew there wasn't enough West Ham to worry about, so they concentrated on trying to contain the Mancs.

Then suddenly we heard that roar, the sweetest sound you'll ever hear when you're having a row and realise that you've bitten off more than you can chew. The roar came from the direction of the Queens. Bodies of West Ham filled the whole fucking road and all you could see was heads going up and down. The cavalry were coming! Our small firm were even more determined to hold the Mancs until the rest of West Ham arrived. Our reputation was at stake and there was no way we could let them round into Green Street, because that would mean the Mancs had done us and taken a liberty at ours. It was that thought that drove us and just a couple more minutes was all we needed.

The fucking roar went up again and the West Ham mob coming down the street steamed straight into the Old Bill and the Mancs. We started pushing them up the Barking Road, around into the street, and then we gave it to 'em.

Looking back, if we hadn't been there at the Boleyn they would have done us, taking the glory. The first team ever to come down the Barking Road and walk from Plaistow. Yeah, they had caught us out once by choosing to get off at Plaistow and nearly got away with it, but now we knew their likely route and we weren't going to give them a second chance.

So a year on we were at Plaistow, thirty to forty of us in all, looking at our watches. It was late and a few of the boys were getting concerned that it wasn't going to happen and worried about missing the match. In the end they slipped off to go on the train. My brother, Swallow and a few others jumped in the cars while BJ, Scully and I, along with several others, started walking up to the station. There were about six or seven of us in our little group.

All of a sudden there were twenty Mancs on the road in front of us and more coming up behind them. My immediate thought was, don't let 'em out of the station' We must have all been thinking the same thing because someone screamed out at that very moment, 'Don't let 'em out of the station doors or we're fucked.' Imagine our situation – we were the ones that had served the

Mancs up year-in year-out and now we were out on the streets, fully exposed, we weren't mob-handed, and their firm was nine feet away, bouncing along with a train full of 'em pouring out of the station.

We didn't have time to consider the odds and we knew what we had to do. We steamed straight into them. My mate and I immediately banged one each, and someone else in the group claimed another. I looked around to see Swallow, my brother, Hodges, Griffiths and the rest of them running out of their cars to steam in with us, not even bothering to shut the car doors. Our numbers had quickly swelled from six to thirty and we were all rowing. The Mancs couldn't all get out of the station and we were giving it to 'em. They had pulled out tools, the Mancs and were waving them about and we later heard that one of them apparently got stabbed. Tools or no tools though, we had them on the back foot.

Butler and the other lads who'd become pissed off waiting around started to make for the match and were, in fact, down on the platform when the Mancs' train pulled in. He later told us that a train load of them got off and ran up the stairs to the exits, bouncing and chanting 'War'. He then heard our lot roar, and the next thing he remembers is that they were slowly coming back down the stairs, cut, bashed and done in.

Meanwhile, we were still outside rowing with the whole Manc firm who were trying to get out the doors. All of a sudden a geezer pulled up in a van, a fucking builder armed with pickaxes and other tools, which he handed to us. Some Townies and local Plaistow geezers passing by on their way home also got out of their motors to have some of it. A lone copper on the inside of the station desperately tried to close up the entrance but the Mancs were determined to get out 'cause they weren't having any joy.

Up until now we had been stopping the Mancs from coming out of the entrance door to the right of the station. Unbeknown to us, some of the Mancs had earlier slipped out the door on the left, towards the Brit. As soon as those Mancs heard the ruck, they came back up the road and now we claimed them as well.

At one stage during the stand-off with the Mancs I nearly got taken out in our front line because one of ours decided to squirt 'em. He took it out, did the business, and the wind blew it right back at us. It left me and another lad bent up over a parked motor, gagging. What's more, I couldn't see 'cause I was covered in ammonia.

To think we weren't even sure if The Mancs would show, given that it was so late towards that evening's kick-off. But they had turned up and now we had what we wanted. With both fans tooled up, the stakes were even and there was virtually no Old Bill around. We knew the Mancs were up for it by the very fact that they had dared to get off at Plaistow. I reckon that if they had been able to get their entire firm out of the station, they would have done us. It really was a serious ruck that had lasted a long time. One of the Mancs received a really bad stab wound in all the fighting. He was the one that later received a get-well card [signed] *'I.C.F.'.*

It must have been twenty minutes before we heard the sirens and the Old Bill arrived in numbers. By that stage the Mancs were begging the Old Bill to close the doors to prevent us from attacking them with axes and shovels. By the end of the row our numbers had swelled to forty or fifty. There were lads just jumping off buses and getting out of cars to come to our aid. It was crazy and I still can't believe how long this row went on for without Old Bill arriving on the scene. It was almost unheard of in all my years of going to football.

It was a very close call for West Ham. In fact, it was the only time in all those years that they came that close to doing us. All of us had been caught by surprise as hundreds of them arrived, tooled up and wanting it. It was a fluke, a real fluke that we ended up head-to-head at the station, for if we'd all gone in the cars and fucked off, they would have been out on our streets, hitting all our pubs and claiming the stragglers. I remember Swallow, BJ, Scully, Hodges, my brother, Griffiths and the rest of us all looking at each other like it was Christmas. We were all thinking, they're here! They've got their top firm and we're standing just three feet away from them. We might have been a small group, but it was our firm, they'd come across the cream of all our top boys. They would've loved to have taken the credit for doing us with the names that were there that night. No, we'll never forget it.

I'll admit, the stunt pulled by the Mancs at Plaistow was something similar to the way we would have operated. We were initially surprised, but in the end the surprise was on them, as they hadn't planned on bumping into our cream. We hurt 'em to the point of despair, although it was never far from the back of our minds that it could have easily gone the other way. We all know how mouthy Man U are. When they came out that station, they were yelling, 'We'll do these West Ham bastards'. Five minutes later, their thoughts must have been more along the lines of, why aren't we doing them? Then, twenty minutes later, it was, 'Fucking close these doors. They're mad.'

In truth, we were forced to make the stand because we couldn't go anywhere. We couldn't back off because we were on the street and there were a whole trainload of Mancs in front of us wanting to get out. Timing and luck had been in our favour. If we'd been ten yards further down the road they would have been out on our turf, giving it to us with none of the Old Bill in sight. If we'd had just another half a lager, they would have been smashing us in the pubs.

The Mancs came out of the station that day like a marauding army looking to take a liberty. But there was no way we were going to let them on our turf for a second time.

Chapter 22

THE FERRY

I.C.F.

'COMPANY BOSS led bloody soccer riot' screamed the headline in the Daily Mirror. It was typical of the press coverage of the trial that followed the violent battle pitched between West Ham and Man Utd fans on board a cross-Channel ferry on August 7, 1986.

Eventually, fifty-year-old company director Joe Harris, dubbed 'the General' by the prosecution and media, was cleared of the allegations that he gave orders and led soccer hooligans into a violent battle and turned a hosepipe on rival fans. Eight others were convicted and sentenced to a total of fifty-one years in prison.

The full story of that incredible day in the middle of the English Channel has never before been told in detail. I want to put that right, to tell the story the way it actually happened, rather than the way it was told in the media and the courts.

The fighting had been so savage that the captain and his crew were unable to control it. At 1 a.m., as the battle raged in one of the busiest stretches of water in the world, Captain Joost Nargel desperately sent out a distress signal and turned his boat around to return to port. The stairways and ceilings were awash with blood and salt water as earlier tensions between our small but arrogant band of I.C.F. and the Mancs exploded into violence. The Mancs saw it as a golden opportunity to settle a few old scores, but it didn't quite turn out the way they had planned.

The magnitude of the incident was summed up later by Judge Watling, who said, 'It could have been a worse disaster than the Titanic.' In response, FIFA added an additional one-year ban to the five-year European exclusion already imposed on English clubs.

It was one of the most serious public disturbances in living memory, yet it had been sparked by a pre-season friendly that was deliberately not publicised by the clubs taking part. The clubs were hoping that it would pass off peacefully and pave the way to an early return to Europe. The local *Newham* Recorder later reported one West Ham fan as saying 'We were just going for a drink and a nice weekend.' No one could have begun to imagine that it would end with what one bloodstained United fan would later describe as 'the most horrific fight I've ever been in'.

A year later I was at Snaresbrook Crown Court, accompanied by four of the fourteen survivors of that infamous ferry boat battle, during the Operation Own Goal trials involving alleged ringleaders of the InterCity

Firm. Two of them had already begun six-year sentences for their part in it. The trial carried my thoughts back to that unforgettable I.C.F. day on the ferry and I thought to myself, 'Yeah, that one tops the lot.'

Big Ted recalls the event:

Details of pre-season friendly games had leaked out and, while sitting in the Brit pub one day, we decided to phone around and organise a trip to Holland. West Ham officials wanted it kept secret from their fans because they were afraid there would be violence and another round of bad publicity for the club. Ironically, we found out about the matches from one of the players!

After meeting up at Liverpool Street station, we planned to take the night boat to Holland to spend a week out there watching West Ham play in a tournament in Gronningen. Most of the West Ham fans had travelled on an earlier ferry from Harwich to the Hook of Holland. We knew we had a problem right from the start of our journey. When we arrived at Liverpool Street station the place was full of Mancs. There were hundreds of them. We found out they were heading for Amsterdam to watch Manchester United play Ajax and were getting the same train as us. There were only fourteen of us and we weren't sure what to do, but if we were going to go to Holland then we had to get on the train, so we did.

We decided to travel in the first carriage in case the Mancs played up. That way they could only come at us from one direction. As we bowled up to the front of the train, the Mancs already on board were hanging out of the windows giving us verbal, yelling out what they were going to do to us. As soon as we got in the carriage we prepared for a Manc attack. They kept coming up and having a look at us and we kept telling them to fuck off, but in the end the journey to Harwich was peaceful. They obviously thought there were more of us than the fourteen they could see. Unfortunately, we hadn't taken them seriously enough to see the gravity of the situation we had put ourselves in by boarding that train that day.

After a few beers we checked in to board the ferry Koningin Beatrix to take us to Holland. Us and the fucking Red Army. Aware of the situation we could possibly face, we informed the ferry company's booking staff that we were concerned about travelling with 400 to 500 Manchester United fans. Someone said to us, 'Don't worry about it. There's 300 to 400 Hell's Angels on board going for a motorbike weekend. They'll take care of them if there are any problems.' After hearing this we all decided to pay the extra to upgrade to first class to avoid any possible trouble.

Once the boat had set sail we made ourselves comfortable in the bar, choosing an area [that we would be able to defend] *in the event that the Mancs decided to join us. We were up on the eighth floor in a saloon ironically called the Inter-City Bar. There we were, with our own bar, and we thought it was meant to be. There were a few other West Ham fans in there but it was mostly ordinary travellers.*

While we were sitting in the bar we were told there

had been trouble between West Ham and Mancs on an earlier ferry, the St Nicholas, followed by many arrests. This alerted us to the danger. We also noticed that during the first hour of the journey one or two Mancs would occasionally stroll into our bar or walk round the outside, obviously trying to work out how many West Ham there were. Most of the Mancs at this stage were on the floor below getting drunk, singing and chanting about killing West Ham on the ferry.

About two hours into the journey, Taffy and little Danny went down to the duty free shop on the floor below. By this time there were about 150 Mancs fuelled up on booze and raring to have a go at us. Taffy and Danny were recognised while [they were] *in the duty free shop and some punches were thrown. Taffy was easily spotted because he was once a Manc, with a Manc tattoo, and was despised by them. We knew it was only a matter of time before they started on the rest of us.*

Taffy and a few others were standing outside the bar when some Mancs approached and started laying into them. Andy Swallow came rushing into the bar where the rest of us were sitting and told us we were in trouble.

Andy recalls that all the trouble began after he and three of the Harlow lads became curious about all the noise and increased activity occurring on the deck below us:

After having a few beers ourselves we thought a little winding up of the Mancs was in order. When we got down to the Mancs on the floor below we yelled at them,

'Who the fuck are you, then?' They started taunting us by yelling, 'Where were you at Manchester? Where were you then?' and I said to 'em, 'Where were you at Plaistow?', referring to the previous season when they had sneaked out at Plaistow station after the game had kicked off and we gave them a really big surprise and smashed them to fuck...

This reference to Plaistow didn't go down too well, as a lot of them had been there. The mood was getting uglier, but I was still holding court at the foot of the stairs. As some of them advanced towards me I said, 'Hold it! How many of you here come from Manchester? I'll fight any of you that actually come from there.' That shut them up for a while. I turned to one and said, 'You've got a lotta mouth. Where are you from?' He told me he was from Wolverhampton, so I said, 'Right, I'll fight you first.' Then I started pointing to about half a dozen other lads and offered them all out one by one, saying 'I'll fight you, then you...'

Now the Mancs were getting mad. They must have been thinking, who is this mouthy Cockney holding court, telling us what he's going to do? I knew I was pushing it, but I was in full swing and wasn't thinking about the danger ahead. The abuse was passing back and forth all the time, but they looked like they were circling around us by then. I'd noticed one holding an empty whisky bottle by the neck and sensed it was time to go.

I told the group I was arguing with in front of the stairs, 'I've gotta chip now' and with that we ran back up the stairs. As I looked back over my shoulder, I saw there were hordes of them, all tooled up and chasing me. I ran into the bar where the others were standing and yelled, 'They're here!' With that, our lot all ran out to the doors to confront them. There were two sets of stairs and Mr H. had the idea of defending himself by grabbing hold of a ship's fire hose and turning it on. He started hosing down the stairs to make them slippery, so it was difficult for the Mancs to climb back up at us.

Meanwhile, I was involved in a fight on the other stairs. To protect myself I put a life jacket on my head. Then I got a dustbin lid for a shield and armed myself with a heavy wooden bar I'd snapped off. I was using the bar to bang the lid as I stopped at the top of the stairs, chanting, 'More, more, more.'

We eventually forced the Mancs down the stairs to the seventh floor but they kept coming back up, massed in large numbers there. We regrouped over on the other flight of stairs being flooded with water. In the middle of all the fighting this big biker came up and put his hand up saying, 'Listen! Stop it! Like, peace, peace.' Someone rushed forward and punched him, sending him rolling back down the stairs. This biker was English but many of the others were from Europe and they were in small groups scattered all around the boat.

The only lulls in the fighting came when the Mancs regrouped to charge up the stairs again. In one of these attacks, two Mancs came up the stairs and one of them tried to reason with us by saying, 'Look, we're the Mancunians. We're the REAL Manchester. Let's stop this.' As he was saying this, someone threw a fire extinguisher and it hit him straight on the head. He slid down the stairs and his mate ran off.

Another Manc, obviously wanting to make a name for himself, thought he would show everyone just how brave and ingenious he was by putting a blanket over his head to keep off the water as he charged up the stairs. The idiot got drenched and the blanket got so heavy from the weight of the water that he couldn't get it off his head or see where he was going. Using our iron bars and sticks, we beat him all the way back down the stairs. Then we rolled him up in the soaking blanket, just like you roll up a carpet, and booted him to the bottom of the stairs. He struggled desperately but couldn't get out of the clinging blanket.

As I was running down the stairs someone threw a plant pot containing a big yucca plant and it hit me fair and square on the head, pot end first. I thought, yeah, I'll have some of this, and threw it straight back into the Mancs.

At some point in the middle of this big ruck we're having, I suddenly spotted two Dutch truckers standing right alongside us with a load of pint glasses, hurling them at any Mancs who charged up the stairs at us. They were shouting at the tops of their voices, 'We love the English and we love your football hooligans.' We looked at them in amazement and all thought the same thing… 'Fucking nutters!' but at least they were on our side.

One thing we didn't realise at the time was that the Mancs had been using their knives, trying to stab our feet and legs through the stairs from underneath every time we ran down. We didn't find out about this until I went to Manchester the following season and the Mancs kept taunting us about the way we got 'stabbed up'.

Big Ted recalls his own impressions of the fight:

How I survived, I'll never know. When Andy ran back into the bar with all the Mancs on his tail, the first thing I saw when we rushed out was Taffy getting smashed in the face with a bottle and about twenty Mancs piling in, throwing punches. We managed to rescue Taffy by steaming in and getting them back down the stairs, suffering only cuts and bruises. We were now on top of one set of internal stairs and we could hear the Mancs chanting, 'War, war, war!' down below.

All the drunken Mancs had obviously got together to attack us. Looking down the stairs to the next level there were more than a hundred Mancs waiting for their leaders. Meanwhile, someone tried to get a few other West Ham to help us, but they refused.

Mancs started coming up the stairs in large numbers, all armed with bottles, knives and lumps of wood they got after smashing up the duty free shop. They were also throwing bottles, but we'd armed ourselves and now it was hand-to-hand fighting at the top of the stairs. We were forcing them back down the stairs but we were in danger of being overwhelmed by the sheer numbers.

The turning point came when Mr H. had the

brainwave of operating the fire hose situated near the top of the stairs and then turned it on the bastards. The force of the saltwater jet kept the Mancs at bay long enough for us to get tables to make barricades at the top and to raid the bar for tools to defend ourselves. This quick thinking helped us survive the first wave of the attack, but this was only the start of an hour-long battle when we had to fight for our lives. With our very own 'fireman' Mr H. now in attendance, the Mancs came up the stairs with tables as their shields against the jets of water. They managed to get to the top of the stairs only to be smashed back with bottles, glasses and metal bars.

After about ten minutes the fighting subsided and some of the Mancs decided to use the internal stairs nearby. I took to covering these stairs with a couple of Under Fives, Sean Pearman and Bradley. We could see these Mancs coming up behind, led by a manic-looking Greek bloke carrying a stiletto-type knife and a half-caste geezer holding a carving knife. My only protection then was a bottle. It didn't look good, so I got the other hosepipe and tried to turn on the tap. Nothing! With the Mancs getting nearer by the second I was desperately operating the lever on the hose, but no water was coming out. I didn't know it then, but it was because there were kinks in the hose preventing the water from squirting out.

My salvation came when one of the boys cut the hose at about an eight-foot length. I now had a brilliant weapon that had a big brass head, which I could swing around my head like a lasso and give the Mancs a spanking as they ran back down the stairs.

We now had to cover both stairs and we asked one of our group, who seemed to have lost his bottle, to collect all the missiles up for us to throw. He was so shaken by what he'd seen as the battle progressed that he couldn't even do this. In the end, we managed to recruit a Joe Public to organise bottles, glasses and even the wall mirrors to use for our protection. We also tried to recruit a few Hell's Angels who had been watching with interest, but they said it was too violent for them and walked off.

It was at this stage, Swallow recalls, that a doctor walked into the middle of all the mayhem:

He came up in the lift, calmly strolled over, and introduced himself. He told us we should stop the fighting and then asked who had been hurt. One of us said to him, 'Fuck off! We're all right. You wanna go and see THEM!'

As the doctor left, the Mancs went into their next, and – as it turned out – final attack. This time, they attacked both sets of stairs to the bar. We were getting hit by all these crystal paperweights which they'd taken after another raid on the wrecked duty free shop. With Mr H. holding one set of stairs virtually on his own with that fire hose we could concentrate more on the other stairs, where we bombarded them with bottles, glasses and broken mirror shards.

We were now winning the battle. The Mancs were disheartened about charging the stairs and decided to turn it into a missile battle, but they had to throw up at us and we were pelting them from the top of the stairs. There was only ever going to be one winner.

In a further insult to the Mancs, our firm were constantly chanting 'I.C.F., I.C.F., I.C.F.' at them. With the stairs now covered in salt water and the Mancs' blood, Taffy and another guy were running down the stairs and cutting any Mancs who wanted to know.

Then, abruptly, the battle just ended, as Swallow recalls:

Suddenly everything just stopped. As we waited at the top of the stairs, it seemed to be very quite down there where the Mancs were milling around.

After a while, five of us went down to their level to find out what was happening. As we went down we were banging a dustbin lid with sticks and chanting, 'We want more! We want more!' but there was no reply. The Mancs had just vanished from their deck.

We were reporting this to the others back on our floor when a group of West Ham fans we didn't recognise suddenly came over. They hadn't been involved in the fight, but told us the boat had been turned around and was heading back to Harwich so that our English police could come on board. They said that the captain had sent out a distress signal.

It was at this point that the ship's crew appeared and locked us all in the bar.

We discussed the situation and were convinced that we weren't in any trouble because we didn't start the fight and were only defending ourselves to stop the Mancs from trying to kill us. Even so, some of us took the precaution of changing bits of clothing, shoes and anything which could identify us.

When the ferry arrived back in Harwich harbour we looked out of the window and saw lines of police cars and up to a hundred coppers waiting on the quay. There were also ambulances and we could see some Mancs being carried out to them on stretchers.

The police came into our bar expecting to find hundreds of West Ham fans. They were well prepared, with some in riot gear, but found only our small group. We were carted off to a large waiting area which was full of Mancs. They were totally gutted to see that our small group of fourteen had beaten them. The police then took statements and informed us we could not travel to Holland or go home.

We counted twenty-two stretchers going off with drips and some Mancs even leaving the boat in wheelchairs. We had only one injury, apart from my sore head where the flying plant pot hit me.

My dry clothes worked a treat, as the Old Bill were only interested in those with tell-tale wet gear from the flooded stairs. In the end just six or seven of our party were taken for questioning. The rest of us were split up and I made my way to the railway station for the train back to London. I found myself waiting on the platform with one of the other guys.

A train pulled in full of Man United and the Old Bill said to me, 'On you get.' The Mancs leaning out of the doors and windows were saying, 'Come on. He's with us.' I was telling 'em 'Fuck off. I'm West Ham', but they kept saying, 'No, no. You're Man United, same as us.' They were desperately trying to entice me on board their train and I knew they wanted to kill me. I just said, 'See ya. Gotta go!' and crossed over to the other platform.

I soon met the rest of our lot and it was only then that we realised that six or seven of us from the original fourteen had been nicked.

When the train pulled back into Liverpool Street station there was a complete media circus waiting for us. There were BBC and ITV news cameras, the News of the World and the Evening Standard. They bombarded us with questions and we felt like we had just come from a war. We all felt a huge sense of relief that it was all over and were happy to oblige the British media.

We were still buzzing from what we had just been through and we told them what had happened: 'There were fourteen of us and about 150 of them. We smashed them all over the place. And don't forget... put in the paper that it was the I.C.F.' we boasted, proudly.

In all the years I had been going to West Ham there had never been a more intense or life-threatening ruck than the one on the ferry that day, in the middle of the Channel. I will never forget it.

Ironically, one month before the ferry battle, Prime Minister Margaret Thatcher had congratulated football chiefs on the 50 per cent cut in soccer violence since England had been banned from European competitions, following the Heysel Stadium disaster in Brussels in which thirty-eight fans died.

The ferry battle brought a further ban on English clubs, preventing them playing in Europe. This now extended to friendlies, ending the hopes of FA head Ted Croker and Sports Minister Dick Tracey of having the existing ban lifted.

The incident resulted in fourteen arrests and four stabbings. On March 13, 1987, eleven of those arrested, including five from West Ham, were prosecuted on offences ranging from affray, assault and theft to criminal damage. Investigations by the British Transport Police had taken six months to complete, due to the complexity of dealing with offences that took place on a Dutch vessel in international waters.

On November 9, 1987, five West Ham and five Mancs stood trial at Chelmsford Crown Court, in Essex. Judge Brian Watling found that the captain's attention had been diverted from the safe navigation of his ship, thereby placing the lives of 2,000 passengers at risk. He stated that the acts of those involved were 'tantamount to an act of piracy on the high seas'.

Those convicted were to face severe sentences, as an example to all football hooligans. HC, MS and SP, all of West Ham, each got six years.

Two defendants, JH and DH, were acquitted. One of these defendants admitted to being a West Ham supporter but stated that he was only looking out for his son, as any father would in the same situation.

The outrage and emotion that followed the ferry battle was splashed across front-page headlines. We knew what the papers thought of the incident; later we were to find out what the court made of it all. But what about the two sets of fans involved? Terry Sherrin recalls a conversation at Old Trafford:

That season, after the ferry, it was Man U away. A Manc with a mark on his face spotted Swallow and I and several others as we walked up the stairs. He turned to Swallow with a glaring look and said, 'You gave me this', pointing at his scarred face. He said that we had been out of order that day. Andy asked him how we could have been out of order when there had been only thirteen of us and 200 Mancs. The Manc said, 'I'll never forget that day. You lot were out of order because you were tooled up.'

There was a pause of disbelief at what the Manc had just come out with. Andy said, 'What a mug. You got bashed by thirteen West Ham. We only used the tools that were there, so why didn't you lot use the same tools?'

At that point another Manc chipped in with, 'Is this your I.C.F.?', obviously unimpressed with our low numbers. No sooner had he said that, about 300 West Ham turned up. Andy said to him 'This is the I.C.F. and it was lucky they weren't all on the ferry, wasn't it boys, or you would never have gotten off that boat.'

You could feel their hatred towards us and there were

plenty of verbals that day, but it didn't go much further because they knew from personal experience which of the two firms could back it up.

Chapter 23

BLACK HAMMERS

I.C.F.

EVERYONE I INTERVIEWED felt uncomfortable even talking about the question of being black and supporting West Ham. Clearly, black is not part of the club colours. Personally I've always been there throughout and never had a major problem within West Ham's support, even when the British Movement had targeted the club's supporters in a recruitment drive.

We had a problem with racists and a period of far-right politics – it crept into youth culture when we had another skinhead revival in the punk era of '78–'79. I think quite a few clubs had the same problem around the country.

I remember arriving in Sheffield – we were against Wednesday, and their hated rivals Sheffield United introduced themselves to us and offered to fight alongside us against Wednesday. Anything to have a pop at your hated rivals. Quite a few clubs entertained this joining-up bollocks, but it's not something we would suffer any more. Our motto was 'West Ham go with no one', and, as we've already seen, that stretched to the England games as well.

When these United lads appeared you could see what everyone was thinking, especially as they were all dressed in full skinhead regalia. We were all I.C.F. and our clobber was totally designer casual wear. We certainly had no skins amongst us and we all wore trainers. You had more chance of spotting a black chap among us than a skinhead.

At that time there was a skinhead movement over West Ham. They all gathered and postured in a section of the West Side the Old Bill chose to ignore.

The West Ham West Side skins with their far-right leanings appeared to be loathed by the majority of the I.C.F. – not because of their beliefs, more for the fact they never appeared to have the bottle to travel away. 'Away' for them was a London derby game!

The Sheffield lads in black combat gear and cropped hair sensed they weren't welcome and started to slip off before some liberties occurred. Beforehand, I got talking with one of them, who said he was surprised we didn't have any skins among us.

I told him simply that we didn't like politics being imposed on the firm. The London skin with his dress code meant only one thing to us – you're declaring your interest in the far right.

This Sheffield skin realised instantly where we thought

he was coming from and looked shocked – he was vehemently opposed to far-right views. Walking towards the group, he told me how the Sheffield scene was fought out by skinheads based on rival political views as much out of any football loyalties.

In the early Seventies I don't remember seeing many black supporters period, not just black fans at West Ham. Those who did go to West Ham were known faces. In fact, at many of the away matches I would be the only black supporter. Back then, most of the black lads I knew were never interested in going to football. In a way it was understandable, because there were no black players at the time.

We were one of the rarer clubs with a really popular black striker, Big Clyde Best. There was also Ade Coker – whatever happened to him? I remember how fondly the older fans talked of the popular John Charles, who played for us in the Sixties.

When the skinhead revival returned to the terraces in the late Seventies, with its sinister far-right connections, the new racists immediately targeted the emergence of the professional black football player. This was seen to best effect in the Ron Atkinson West Bromwich Albion team of the time, which featured Cyril Regis, Remi Moses, Brendon Batson and Laurie Cunningham.

The black supporter was definitely taking a new interest in the football scene, but not over at West Ham. The East End was tainted forever by a media that never forgot how Moseley's black shirts rose and marched in London's East End. The sight of National Front and

British Movement members standing outside the ground handing out their filth-peddling newspapers, like Bulldog, gave the press all the ammunition they needed. The interior of the ground, particularly the Lower West Side, was the focal point for 'Sieg Heil!' chanting. This was also the area from which bananas, aimed at black players on rival teams, were chucked.

It all had an effect on those both outside and inside of West Ham, but it wasn't the true picture. You had the I.C.F. with its unwritten rules, codes, honours. What was 'in' and what was 'out' came from them. The message was clear – personal politics and rivalries had to be kept aside. The only thing that mattered was your loyalty to West Ham; the only colours that mattered were claret and blue; the only rule that mattered was you don't fucking run.

Animal, now known as Olajide Ikoli, was a black skinhead at the time. He admits there was a real buzz knowing you were being accepted by another culture and that this culture hated you: 'Everything at West Ham in those days was pure racism, but they accepted you and stuck by you even when the skinheads were singing "Ain't no black in the Union Jack."'

If we had a problem at West Ham, it was nothing to the trouble I experienced travelling around the country on away trips. Some of the big northern clubs stank on the question of colour. It didn't stop just at the supporters. Ron Atkinson was out on his own, and it took a long time for clubs to bring black players into their first teams – it took Everton longer than most. Some of the most racist fans I ever encountered were from Liverpool.

I put Leeds right up there too. And at Newcastle in 1980, was it just a coincidence that before they threw that petrol bomb – which came whizzing over my head, landing and exploding directly behind me in our away section – the adjoining Geordies had been chanting, quite loudly, 'Chicken George!' and pointing their fingers at me, (remember the TV series *Roots?*). The support behind me that day from the West Ham I.C.F. lads never wavered.

I.C.F.'s Nat reminded me it wasn't always like that. Some of his black mates took issue with West Ham's NF connection. Others who came from the East End went as far as going to Arsenal instead, because they feared West Ham's firm were extremists. They couldn't be convinced otherwise.

Then it went the other way. By the mid-Eighties, we had more black support than any other London club, though we were still stuck with this racist tag. Chelsea fans had it too. I clearly remember a big off with Chelsea in and around the streets along the Fulham Broadway. Quite a few of their boys were showing out big-time, but what got me was that the more prominent ones showing out were all black. Yet at the time, the press and media were making out that Chelsea had the most racist supporters in Britain.

A time came when I had to test what the I.C.F.'s real position was on the question of race. It was during the '78–'79 season, back in the dark days when we knew the NF were there at Upton Park. They weren't running the show, but that didn't stop the far-right groups winning a few new recruits. Some of the main boys switched over to them from us. It caused a few splits. One season, I'd be so welcome I was dossing down at their houses the night before travelling to an away game. Then the following season, after all that NF propaganda, I'd walk into a pub and they'd suddenly look away; they didn't want to talk no more. For me, it wasn't a case of tolerating racial problems on the terraces, more a case of living with it within a football culture the ethics and morals of which were based on a rather different outlook to that of the rest of the world. It really was the Alf Garnet mentality. Providing you could take a joke, it was part and parcel of going to football. The only time you'd take real offence was when racial abuse was dished out by rival supporters.

During the season in question, however, something inside told me I no longer felt quite right with it all. I had a conscience and suddenly it hit me: I wanted to know where I really stood with those I was prepared to risk a kicking for, week-in and week-out.

I walked into the side where the NF lot used to give the old Nazi salute every match. There would be a firm of about 200 of them, all chanting 'Sieg Heil!' The untouchables section of the Lower West Stand enclosure was the home of West Ham's far-right fanatics. They were predominantly skinheads from the sprawling council estates of Essex. I walked into the middle of them and all the 'Sieg Heiling!' hands went down. They weren't sure who I was, but the word went round – who would have the front to walk into the middle of all of us? The hands kept going down row by row as I worked my way down the terrace. I could hear them asking each other, 'What's going on with the coon?' 'I think he's something to do with the I.C.F.' came the reply.

I thought I was going to get turned over, but I didn't care. They could only win the battle and not the war. I was convinced that if they did me, the I.C.F. would be waiting for them outside and they'd get annihilated. In fact, the I.C.F. over in the corner of the South Bank had spotted me and attempted to get on the pitch in order to give me a hand. But I had it under control. These day trippers weren't the real West Ham hardcore – they didn't want to know. The Old Bill stood at the back, watching me, expecting the inevitable. When it didn't happen they came down and said they were going to nick me to prevent trouble. So I shifted. But I felt I made my point that day.

Not everyone made a point over it. Some did, but most just felt that it shouldn't be part of going to West Ham. And it wasn't just a problem for us black Hammers – it affected us all. Fortunately, the far-right tendencies were never strong enough to take a permanent hold and by the summer between the '81-'82 season it had completely passed over.

It's interesting to hear other lads' reflections, looking back to that time of racial turmoil. Jimmy Smith says he realised the changes going on over West Ham when he came home after being away:

I came out of nick in the summer of '81 and got a call from my mate Boozy, who alarmed me with the concern in the tone of his voice. He said, 'I'll tell you what, West

Ham's really changing. Those fucking two brothers there are doing everyone's head in.'

I took a few more calls like that as I tried to catch up after being away. The morning of my first home match, on the out I walked into the Prince and I tell you what, I thought I was in Germany in the late 1930s.

You had the two brothers with one of their cronies walking about in a full Hitler Youth uniform. As they held court in one bar you had all the normal I.C.F. lads in the other. The atmosphere wasn't healthy and there was a lot of stirring going on. It had the makings of a civil war.

Lol Prior recalls a classic story about just one moment that sums up the atmosphere at that time: 'I was in the Imperial when somebody played "Ghost Town" on the jukebox. One of the brothers walked up, saying, "What is this nigger shit?" and kicked the box, knocking the record off. All the I.C.F. faces were there and they ordered out to the brother, "Fucking put the record back on... mate!" The record went back on.

Bill Gardner asked if I remembered the black West Ham supporter who often came with us: 'The fellow was from Wolverhampton, but the NF had it right in for him. We played Coventry one time and they spanked him because of his accent, but he was West Ham through and through. He took so much stick that he was forced to pack it in. At that time with the National Front thing going on, to be a black supporter was a joke.'

Nat summed up that whole dark period for me, when

he said as a kid you didn't think much about it then, but as you get older and look back you think 'bloody hell'.

* * * * *

The popularity of the I.C.F., and those of its black members who stuck it out throughout the Seventies, had a major impact and influence on the upsurge of black supporters following West Ham in the mid-Eighties.

Press and media reports of the club's racial problems during the late Seventies, together with the lack of worthwhile action from the football club, actually isolated its ethnic community further.

Today the situation at Upton Park has totally changed. The FA's 'Kick Out Racism' campaign has stopped racial abuse of players. The reason for this, I would argue, is that there's a very different supporter in the stands now to the kind of fan that once stood on the terraces.

Although the 'Kick Out Racism' campaign has succeeded, it has failed to attract greater numbers of the ethnic minorities to the game. The number of black Hammers fans is less now than it was during the lowest levels of the early Seventies. The reason for this can be traced back to the financial costs involved – ticket prices increased and fans could now only buy tickets in advance. Plus, for all your political correctness, if people are not interested they won't come. The black community I know would still rather play the game or watch soccer on TV than enter a football ground, which as we all know, has a culture of its own.

Chapter 24

IT'S OVER

I.C.F.

AFTER SEEING what we got up to, any right-thinking person would conclude we were all crazy, mad bastards intent on only one thing – killing the beautiful game, the game we loved above all. I guess we created our own world and culture. A world where we cared little about the dangers involved. It was a world that, once you were in, it was difficult to get out of. In fact, most of the lads contributing to this book have said that they were the best days ever.

I spent more than a year interviewing a cross-section of the I.C.F. and analysing my own experiences for this book. In carrying out this research, I started to think about how the whole thing came to an end for all of us. Everyone knows the I.C.F. as it was is no longer active. It is now just a terrace legend and has been that way since the battle on the North Sea ferry. The only exception was, naturally, the game against the old enemy, Millwall.

Watching the tragic events at the Heysel Stadium in Belgium in 1986 unfold on the TV screen had an effect on me personally, one very similar to the emotions aroused when the world witnessed the tragic events of September 11. My first thoughts as I watched the massed Liverpool fans build up for one big charge on the Juventus supporters were that the Scousers would have to be really together. At that time the Italians had been fighting back and forth with the Liverpool fans. In an earlier round, the Scousers had been badly knifed up when Liverpool had played another Italian team, Roma. I thought, if these Scousers aren't together they could be in for some of the same again. Your face edges closer to the screen, eyes following the TV cameras. You've been there yourself, so you can easily follow what's going to happen next. Panic sets in among the crowd and you realise something horrible is happening. You see those wretched faces appealing to you from out of the TV screen. You're in another country, too far away to be able to do anything, yet you can see everything that's happening. They're being crushed at the fence. Yet in their blind panic, those causing the crush can't seem to see who they're treading on. The Scousers causing it can't see either, as more Liverpool fans come through the gate, steaming in from over the top of the Italians.

The images I see, I know all too well. I'm ashamed to say I was there once and just like the Scouse we too were charging about when West Ham lost 4-2 to Anderlecht in the Cup Winners' Cup Final of '76.

As the Heysel Stadium tragedy unfolded and we learned that thirty-eight fans had lost their lives I felt the same shock and was just as horrified as any member of the public. Since when did any of us become Joe Public? You know damn well if that had been your own team playing that final and not Liverpool, that could have been you steaming in, hell-bent on doing your bit.

I wasn't alone in what I felt. It was like a huge wake-up call for us all. As a former football hooligan, I've long thought the events at the Heysel brought us out of that dangerous world we'd been part of for so long. I said as much in my autobiography. But as Swallow and Gardner reminded me, we'd all but retired before then.

So what did do it for the I.C.F.?

There were a collection of reasons for the end of the firm. Football violence still takes place, even today, though nothing like on the scale of our day and our time. Did we feel we'd taken it as far as it could go? Were we all really insane savages out to ravage our national game?

Looking back to when we were kids in the Seventies, I'd say it was all an adventure. Being adolescents gave us a new-found freedom, a new excitement. There was a thrill, a buzz in going to football; there was also a sense of belonging. Football violence was an addiction that was a way of life for us. Every club had its firm or mob and it appeared everyone was up for it, at least in the First and Second divisions. If you ever tried travelling the London

Underground Tube wearing your team's colours at the time, you'll know what I mean.

In the Seventies, you fought your rivals on the strength of the colours they wore. It was all fists and boots; now and again someone would call out, 'Look out, he's got a blade!'

Then came the Eighties, the decade of designer violence. Hooliganism was taken to another level. Every firm had a name and it was the names and the faces you sought out, not the colours. Nobody wore team scarves any more. These were the really dangerous years. In the Seventies you got a slap or a right kicking, but you would still be back for more the following week. In the Eighties, I saw some lads who decided to drop out altogether. Police crackdowns meant the violence inflicted had to be quick and swift, therefore weapons were used more frequently. You fought as if every battle was the last one you'd see for a while. It was as if we were on a roller coaster that no one wanted to get off.

It was easy to see how it all became the norm, if you were into going to football. You would just come into it and carry it on where another had left off. A few generations were sucked in and that's why I would argue that to break the hold football violence had on the game, it would take a complete decade of football being virtually trouble free. The violence and thuggery was never mindless – it had a culture, it was the fashion, it had an addictiveness not easily shaken. It becomes a trendy thing to do when it's seen to be happening all around our football grounds.

To search out the source of the demise of football

violence, look to the last decade – the Nineties – and you will discover what I would refer as to a relatively trouble-free period. The football violence of the Nineties became isolated, it was on a far smaller scale, and the worst of it was lost in the lower league divisions. But here's the significance: look now at the age group. The lads involved would be in their late thirties and forties, the same group that grew up with it all through the Seventies and Eighties. Now you've got a complete generation missing. The lads who go football now that are, say, fifteen to twenty-five years old and would have been the age group to follow on, haven't a clue as to what it was all about for us. They would have only heard about what went on. And that means the generation following them won't just not have a clue, they wouldn't even be interested. This is what has happened at most of the major hooligan clubs referred to in this book, particularly the Premiership clubs.

I probably sound like another sociologist, but I'm not. I know what I did, what I enjoyed doing, what I chose to take part in. I also know about that bond we shared, that buzz we all experienced. I also know that, for the most part, there is no explanation for what we were after. That's why I say authority could never beat us alone.

There was definitely a collection of reasons for the end of that era. In my opinion, four points in particular are very significant:

i) Loss of the terraces, all-seating and new stadia.
ii) CCTV, new police powers and a crackdown by the authorities.

iii) Cost, commitment to attend and the inability to just turn up on the day of the match and get in.
iv) The alternative interests of the fans themselves – brought about, for example, by the rise of rave – and the failure of the next generation of potential hooligans to follow its predecessors.

I'm not alone in thinking it can never go back to the way it was and that our time was as bad as it could ever get. Listen to what the others contributing to this book have said and you will see why the only I.C.F. chant heard on the terraces today, is the taunt by our old rivals of *'Where's your famous, where's your famous I.C.F.?'*

We had some good times over there, football became irrelevant for a time because the team was so bad, everyone went because everyone knew that on Saturday you'd be with your mates, with your comrades. Nine times out of ten nobody knew each other's names, but you knew on that Saturday... you'd all be together. Now you don't know any of the faces sitting around; those you do are split up all over the shop.

I had just found what I wanted to do in life when I had yet another court appearance, another football nick going back so far I had forgotten all about it. Luckily, I got a good probation officer and this time I just woke up to it all. He said I could go one way or another after the case, the choice was mine.

That business with Arsenal after the smoke bomb went off that year played a part, with the Old Bill mounting pressure. They never let up on us from then.

We all thought it was too hot for us. No one was really going, Bill went on his own; none of the Brit were going. We just decided it was no fun, no fights and we'd done everything. We'd all got other things to do – after all, we had been at it since thirteen, fourteen most of us.

The Icky lot, Chelsea's firm, all got big bird, didn't they.

We came out of that court case and it just became from what we were used to, to [a thing of the past]. *Wasn't worth it for us; in fact, it just wasn't us any more – we weren't even chasing people now. It was over.*

I went to a forty-eight-hour rave in a field, I think they called it Woodstock. They had all these security hired, all in black. It was all South London and East London, I couldn't believe it: there's Millwall there and West Ham and no trouble. Swallow got on stage, said East and South are now together. That's what did it for me. Also, seeing all you lot in Scrubs looking at ten years while I was serving a year for the same offence I used to get a fine for. It made me think a bit.

The experience of rave music did have some effect on the lads who went to football. If the end was due to a natural progression of events, the rave link was an interesting one for me. I had long since been in the nightclub security business – it was sort of my own way out. I remember those first early rave days; it all took off during the summer of '88. The summer after our Operation Own Goal and I.C.F. trials had collapsed – in our favour – I agreed to help the security on one of these raves, organised by Swallow. I saw a few Chelsea and Arsenal dudes floating about, but by far the biggest firm were Millwall and West Ham. This was an 'East' do, as it was somewhere in Essex, and I knew some of the West Ham had been going over to raves in Downham, which was 'South'. Football lads don't change just like that. I tensed up, ready for a confrontation, when I saw lads arriving as a firm. I remember Danny Harrison coming up to me in front of all these Millwall and advising me to relax a little, as they now got on with that ginger one whom we likened to Steve Davis. As this was Danny and Swallow's scene, and with West Ham and Millwall getting on fine together, I could only think there was some business going on I didn't know about. So I thought I'd just sit back watch the night's proceedings, as I was being well paid to. Just me and a pal on the door with around 200 top football faces behind us inside. I certainly didn't need to use the metal detector to know all parties were well tooled up. I waited for the inevitable, thinking my promoter mates were rather new to the club game.

But come the end of the evening, which is always the next morning with these events, it was me who had been educated. Nothing happened. Nothing was going to happen, nothing looked likely to happen. This was the start of the rave scene the outside world was just finding out about. I kept wondering what would become of all the hostile rivalry over football if the scene I witnessed that night caught on.

Throughout the Nineties the rave scene was a nice niche for some of the lads who had always been ahead of everyone anyway. After not doing badly out of it, they moved on, as the scene became mainstream and moved back to licensed clubland. That said, now and again you get a moment when you think it might all still be there, you sense someone could be up for it. I remember only a few seasons ago standing with West Ham's away support at Leicester, the chant of *'We hate Millwall!'* echoed out around us. It was coming from unfamiliar faces at the back of us. I looked across and caught Gardner's eye then got sight of Swallow positioned a few rows along. We all smiled that wry kind of smile; privately I was chuckling to myself. At half-time I asked them if they were thinking what I was thinking when we all looked around to see who was actually doing all the chanting. Have any of these ever, ever, fucking met Millwall?

To understand how it all came to a head you have to remember how it was for us. The risks and dangers aside, we really did have a lot going for us. We could usually stay ahead of the police and authorities; we were the more organised on that score. When they did get to grips with us, the laws never gave them the clout they wanted. We were also consistent in exposing the police's inconsistencies. Tactics used successfully by them in one town would not be used in another, and if the personnel in charge changed the following season, there was no guarantee that the same methods would be deployed again. Each force we encountered seemed to regard the others as rivals, for the forces never thought of co-ordinating any of their successes. To us, there would always be another game, another opportunity. Such were our own successes, we were always grabbing the headline news and when we brought our style, pose and culture to people's living rooms via the Hooligan documentary, it was as if a romantic light had been shone on us – like Robin Hood, we were bandits who had done good. We imagined Maggie Thatcher's law-and-order disciples pacing up and down the corridors of Downing Street.

With all the other things going on during the same period, however, we found ourselves waiting for the inevitable crackdown. Soon Maggie had us within her sights and somewhere between the start of the Taylor Report and the end of the Popplewell Inquiry, the lid began to close.

The crackdown wasn't going to deter everyone. Most of the clubs with firms had given up taking their rivals' ends well before this time. They still had the money to travel any way and anywhere they wanted. They were organised enough to be able to out-manoeuvre police by engaging their rivals in areas the police were unprepared for. The Old Bill just couldn't be everywhere. We had the grounds, city centres, the pubs the stations. If they could cover all of that, then we would change the times for them. So, if the police were expecting us to arrive at midday, we would arrive far earlier, purely to catch them out. Such was the I.C.F.'s reputation, opposing fans just knew we would show and at least be half prepared.

Then the police scored a real equalizer when they bloody well introduced closed circuit television to combat us. Together with better radio communication and briefed-up spotters, they were able to cover lost ground. What happened now if we pulled that early morning stunt? They had some bloody hooli-van with a spy camera inside tailing us as we walked the streets. They'd put another tail on the other mob and we'd be walking, walking, walking miles around some poxy northern town looking for the opposition – looking for them in the wrong direction. A complete waste of a day out. The police co-ordination that had clearly been lacking previously, arrived dramatically now with the forming of a national criminal intelligence unit. The forerunner to this had already proved successful, when one or two officers had been appointed to travel away games with us. The police would use the same officers all season and didn't mind us knowing that their brief was to get to know the faces in order to assist the 'home police' in identifying the right trouble-makers.

Proper searches were carried out at every ground we went to, from the moment we left the station until we reached the turnstiles. Long-due widening powers of arrest and newly classified offences meant the days you had half a chance of merely getting chucked out of the ground were no more. The tide had turned. There even appeared to be a news and media blackout. Our antics were now reduced to small column inches and complete riots that went on away from the grounds didn't get mentioned at all. I never got to the bottom of that one, but I can still recall most of the lads would be up early to get the Sunday papers, then ringing up their mates. A typical conversation would go, 'Nothing in my paper, anything in yours?' 'Nope, nothing.' 'How can that be, you was there, it kicked right off, got to be damn near a riot!'

The police now had it sussed over football; they didn't need the farce of those show trials. They had been all about getting the country's image right in order to ensure the return of the clubs back into the lucrative European football competitions. The police had got on top with crowd control and the mass change to all-seater stadia had a massive effect too. In fact, I would go as far to say it ripped the culture out of us. We seasoned campaigners, set in ways that had long been the norm, were lost in a new era and succeeded by a new type of fan.

Seating and segregation inside the grounds was really the start of the end. The appeal of the terraces was in part its anonymity. There was an excitement in being anonymous – the excitement of the unexpected. 'Who are they?' 'Look, they're not us.' It's going to go off any minute and then it does go off, but it ends just as anonymously when everyone slips back into the uniform ranks of supporters. But there's no anonymity when you're sitting in a marked, allocated seat with a camera trained on you. You could miss the rest of the season to turn up the next season, but your number would still be up. Gotcha boy.

The casual supporters who picked and chose their games, often swelling our number whenever what we called a big game was on, further hit us hard when they stopped taking cash from those wishing to turn up and pay on the day at the turnstiles. This all-ticket and season-ticket entry narrowed things down to the really committed supporter.

Seated stands took away the ability to meet and remain in large numbers. Having no say or control of your seat allocation also destroyed that communication link we needed.

The bonding and comradeship we all shared, giving us a strength and unity, couldn't be achieved when you were trying to find all your mates across rows of plastic seating. We would never hear, 'Knees Up Mother Brown' sung on the North Bank again, that's for sure.

Potential trouble spots could now be more quickly recognised by police and identification made that much more easier. To us, trouble at football was never about unemployment. That was sociologist talk brought about by outsiders trying too hard to understand it all. But the era of new stadia in the Nineties brought affordability into play. It was no longer a laugh going to football – it had become a costly commitment. Even those in work now found themselves left on the outside.

Building new grounds often meant a relocation and a complete shift of territory, away from local inhabitants to docks, industrial estates and retail parks. I found this did much damage to whatever noble cause we hid behind, even though it ensured the clubs' survival and progress. A strong bond to the territory and location of your club was an important part of football culture. It gave us our cause.

It allowed us to feel a sense of justice when we defended our territory, the very heart of any club's support base.

The trend for all-seaters made it far more expensive to follow your team. No matter how much certain clubs tried to dress the package price-wise to attract supporters, they were never going back to the old standing-only prices. It allowed the suits and anoraks to populate our beautiful game. Sitting up amidst dizzy heights in some swank new stand discussing the merits of whether to fly up to Newcastle for next week's away match. Everything about going to football looked and sounded 'nice'; rowdy banter and rowdy songs gave way to polite moans and applause. Going to football was never about being nice; going to football was to go to Derby. If you ever went to that old Baseball Ground, you'll know that it was like invading someone's front room. Dense rows of terrace houses with their front doors bang next to the turnstiles. Even the houses across the road stood virtually an arm's length from the ground. This is what you call a football community, this is why your mere presence will evoke a response of 'Who the fuck are you?' from the local inhabitants, to which you would reply in kind.

Changes in the wealth and the location of clubs and supporters alike has removed the value and purpose to the cause of defending one's territory. Going to Derby as an away fan nowadays means being confronted by the staff of retail park businesses who inform you that you can't park here.

All credit to my own club for choosing to rebuild the ground rather than move away from the community of its roots. As I write, building work continues at Upton Park and the end result will be a stadium no long-suffering Hammers fan could have ever imagined. Supporters of a club and stadium like that deserve success in the future. But the club itself, and football in general, is always a reminder of the past for me, and it is with regret that I stand outside the club's main entrance in Green Street, looking up to marvel at the exterior of the new West Stand that wouldn't look out of place in smart Docklands. Then I look at the club's postcode and see this magnificent stand filled with fans from the postcodes of Essex and beyond. I find myself wondering if new West Ham fans are attracted to the club by the pull of its territory and East London memories, or whether the bond to the club would mean more if the club moved its location to, say, Romford. Lost in my past, I realise people move on and now I'm happy to take my seat, because this place is the only reminder of days long gone.

I guess this is the place where we could say we all grew up, the place of best-ever days, so for just a tiny piece of that past I will always be a Hammer, as I cheer them on in that fantastic stadium where the fans can no longer remember any songs – even 'Bubbles' is never completed. Oh, they might have been bad old days to some, but fortress Upton Park wasn't always dependent on the team's results. What are they singing on my old North Bank now? Did I hear *'Shall we sing a song for you, West Ham?'* It's not something I've seen anyone pick up on, but it's a major point to my claim that football violence will never return to the scale that it was once at.

The major example of football violence during this past decade occurred when England fans went to the World Cup '98 and Euro 2000. That's if you could call it violence – to me, much was made of what I would only describe as rowdyism. Why do I play down those scenes of disorder watched across our screens? Because the real violence to me is not in the numbers of arrests, which is always going to involve the English. Fast-tracking, targeting, dress it up anyway you want, we are always going to pay for past reputations.

Remembering those scenes, take a closer look at the age group involved. It's no longer the majority of the fifteen to twenty-five age group that made up the football gangs during the Seventies and Eighties. Those involved today appear to be in their late thirties and forties, which puts the dinosaurs at the forefront of today's football violence. Who are these guys? They must be the same lads we all knew, lads who would have had a lower profile back then, who now feel they can come forward and take on the risks of going football for a row, even though there's never going to be enough of them to keep it going.

The important factor now is that the generation who would have taken over from their predecessors, those young males of the Nineties, are not in evidence on the hooligan front. Which goes to prove that you can use strong methods and tougher restrictions, but at the end of the day it comes down to the fans themselves. They will decide.

For a long time now, and certainly the last five years, football violence has not really been a part of the

Premiership, the league my club play in. I would even go as far as to say it's not looking likely to happen. So, do the clubs – and you, the taxpayer – continue to pay for police numbers and operations that no longer have to accommodate the level of violence and disorder that occurred in the Seventies and Eighties? From time to time, the National Criminal Intelligence Service, and the media will come up with stats and figures, especially before a World Cup, to tell us that football violence is on the increase again. But when you study these figures closely, their annual totals couldn't match the arrest figures that sometimes occurred in a single match back in our time. As Bill Gardner notes earlier in this book 'It's different times now. People have moved on, and if you ain't you're a dinosaur. It's as simple as that. The people who go now wouldn't know what that experience was like.'

Chapter 25

SHALL WE SING A SONG FOR YOU?

I.C.F.

IT SADDENS ME to be at Upton Park nowadays, to listen to the opposing fans' taunt of *'Shall we sing a song for you, West Ham?'* and to hear West Ham struggle to complete a rendering of our own anthem 'I'm Forever Blowing Bubbles'. Add to that the groaning, moaning effort of trying to sound hard when chanting *'C'mon you Irons!'*. The day is only saved when the lads that follow West Ham away rescue us with the enthusiastic *'Claret and Blue Army'* chant. We are a club with just three songs.

I'm not saying West Ham supporters have ever been big on singing football songs, and certainly not to the extent of Chelsea, who have made an art out of it. But for many years we did have songs. We made our own – songs that bonded and united all Hammers together. Singing was all part of the theatre of going football. It played a similar role to that of a drummer boy leading troops into battle.

You can take in the match-day atmosphere by drinking in the pubs along Green Street, the fans kitted out in their replica shirts and hats. However, take a walk around the backstreets, away from Green Street, and you'll take a step back in time. You won't see any bright display of team colours in these pubs, but you know they are totally West Ham, because from the landlord to the DJ and the masses crowded in the bars, everyone is sporting tattoos of crossed hammers and club crests. The pub vibrates from the noise of its regulars belting out old West Ham favourites, songs remembered by the older lads and passed on to the young and the new. Fans from Carlisle to Belgium, from South Africa to Australia and New Zealand all travel back here. Exiled Hammers, all united with the local in the heart of Newham borough. United in song and cheer, the soul of West Ham is in here.

On one occasion at this pub I saw Bubbles, all dressed in black under a leather trench mac. He had made up one of the songs, the words of which will never leave me. It was written in celebration of the rout of the Red Army back in '75, when we gave the Mancs their biggest ever hiding as a mob. Bubbles was known as our song-maker king, the man who brought our past alive and who recalled our memories for us. Those were the days when the terraces had their own original songwriters, the Bunters, the Scoebys, and Bubbles.

Our favourite drinking song was Bubbles's ode to the Man United slaughter:

Some speak of Man City and Bury as well,
Of Oldham Athletic I've often heard tell,
But the team to remember, the team to recall,
Is the great Man United,
The best of them all.
We went down to Wembley on a fine day in May,
With a bunch of supporters so loyal and so gay,
And when it was over and when it was done,
We defeated Benfica by four goals to one.

The first goal by Bobby, who out-jumped the rest.
The second was scored by the wee George Best.
The fans they were singing, 'Well I never did',
And the third goal was netted by the young Brian Kidd.
The Stretford were singing and asking for more,
So Bobby obliged by making it four.
The team to remember, the team to recall
Is the great Man United, the best of them all.

We went down to West Ham in '75,
We'll take the North Bank, the South Bank and side,
United would win and stay top of the league,
The Stretford End would have a fine time indeed.
Our team was invincible, so was our mob,
With Pancho and Prentice and Banana Bob
But when we saw the Cockneys, we went in the side,
Though some thought the South Bank the best
place to hide.

West Ham won the game and went top of the league,

The great Man United were beaten indeed.
And as for our fierce mighty Stretford End yobs,
We were beaten to fuck by the East London mobs.
We were ran in the street, we were ran in the side,
At the front of the South Bank we put up a fight,
But the Cockneys were many and ready to ruck,
And the great Man United were beaten to fuck.

The earliest songs I can remember were very simple, usually based on pop songs. This one was based on a song called *Tweedle Dee, Tweedle Dum* by Middle of the Road:

Tweedle-Dee, oh Tweedle-Dum,
We are the West Ham and we never run
We took the Wolves, the Stretford End and Shed.
We'll fight the Man United until they're fucking dead.
Oh Tweedle-Dee, oh Tweedle-Dum
We are the West Ham and we never run.

In those days there wasn't a firm as such, so everyone gathered on the North Bank. I can recall singing, *'We're the North Bank, we're the North Bank, we're the North Bank Upton Park'*. By the time we had turned Upton Park into a fortress, that same song was adapted to *'We're the North Bank, we're the South Bank, we're the West Side Upton Park'*.

Back on the North Bank, pop tunes reigned supreme:

(To the tune of 'Wandr'in' Star')

I was born under the North Bank stand,
I was born under the North Bank stand,
Do we know the Arsenal, yes we know them well,
Do we know the Chelsea Shed, well they can go to hell,
I was born under the North Bank stand.
I was born under the North Bank stand,
Boots are made for kicking, guns are made to shoot,
If you come in the North Bank end we'll all stick in the boot.
I was born under the North Bank stand.

(In celebration of any win by the team)
Merrily we roll along, roll along, roll along,
Merrily we roll along, up the football league.
As we go we sing our song, sing our song, sing our song,
As we go we sing our song, up the football league.
UNITED!

If there were any other fans about we would always sing a song to the tune of 'Distant Drums':

I hear the sound of distant bums, over there, over there,
And do they smell, like fucking 'ell, over there, over there,
And if they come, they will be done.

When your team scored, just about everyone in the crowd started singing 'Da... da... da... da... da... da' to an American military song, jumping up and down all the time. Another popular song for most of the teams was 'You'll never walk alone', when they scored, and 'We'l support you ever more', when they let in a goal.

London teams also sang 'Maybe it's because I'm a Londoner' and 'Knees up Mother Brown', which usually incited the crowd to the point at which a train carriage would be wrecked or everyone would fall down the terraces.

Other North Bank favourites were:

(To the tune of 'The Bow-legged Chicken')
Bertie Mee said to Bill Shankly, 'Have you heard
Of the North Bank Highbury?'
Shanks said, 'No, I don't think so, but I've heard
Of the North Bank West Ham.'

Oh we hate Bill Shankly and we hate the Kop,
We'll fight Man United until we drop,
We don't give a willy and we don't give a wank,
We are the West Ham boot boys.

(To the tune of 'The Ugly Duckling')
There once was a team called West Ham
Who played in claret and blue,
And all the other teams in all the other leagues
Said ,'Oo, we can't beat you,
Oo we can't beat, oo-oo we can't beat,
Oo-oo we can't beat you.'
And they came and they played and they won
all their games
And they're shit or Division Two.

The following song was a Tube journey favourite on the way to an away game:

My old man said, 'Follow West Ham
And don't go to Arsenal on the way.'
We'll take the North Bank in half a minute,
We'll take the Shed, with all the North stand in it,
We take the Scousers, Man United northerners,
We give them a kicking every year.
'Cos we are the boys with the Cockney accents
'Cos the West Ham boys are here.

There was also one for the Chelsea lot back then that gave no mention of sticking their blue flag up their arses. It went to the tune of 'The Ballad of Bonnie and Clyde':

Chelsea F.C.
They had a reputation for smashing up the station
On the Southern Region.
Two thousand West Ham, they laid a deadly ambush
The only Chelsea fan that stayed was Greenaway.
Greenaway, he tried to take us alone,
We left him lying in a pool of blood
And laughed about it all the way home.

If there was a fight, you would all shout the following, to the tune of 'Run Rabbit':

Oo altogether… Oo altogether

As you steamed in and when we won, like we always did;

You'll never take the North Bank,
You'll never take the North Bank,
And run Tottenham, run Tottenham, run, run, run.

The first song I remember about a firm was sung to the tune of 'Chirpy Chirpy Cheep Cheep':

Last night I heard the Arsenal singing a song,
Oo-wee, Teddy, Teddy Bunter,
Woke up next morning and the Arsenal were gone,
Oo-wee, Teddy, Teddy Bunter, Teddy, Teddy Bunter Firm.
Where's the Arsenal gone, where's the Arsenal gone,
Where's the Arsenal gone, where's the Arsenal gone,
Far, far away.

Mile End had their own simple chant, to the tune of the Seven Dwarfs' 'Hi-Ho' – '*Mile End, Mile End, Mile End-Mile End-Mile End*.' They would all jump up and down, sort of bunny hopping, as they sang. It sounds pretty pathetic, but when they jumped they were able to edge nearer to the other mob each time, and no mob could touch them.

When the mood turned ugly, there were songs to vent your anger and frustration, which were usually directed towards the Old Bill. There was only one such song for the ref, which everybody used, sung to the tune of 'Oh, My Darling Clementine':

Where's your father, Where's your father,
Where's your father, referee?
You ain't got one, 'cause you're bastard,
You're a bastard referee.

The following was one of the songs used to wind up the Old Bill:

He ain't done nuffink
He ain't done nuffink,

When any of the lads got chucked out:

FU, FUC, FUC me walking down the street, say hello.

(To the tune of 'London Bridge is Falling Down')
Harry Roberts is our friend, is our friend, is our friend,
Harry Roberts is our friend. He kills coppers.
Let him out to kill some more,
Kill some more, kill some more,
Let him out to kill some more, good old Harry.

(To the tune of 'The Laughing Policeman')
There was a Cockney copper. His name was PC Jim.
He wandered through the South Bank
To get his head kicked in.
We nicked his brand new helmet and much to his surprise,
A dirty little skinhead come and kicked him in the eyes.
Oh, ha ha ha ha ha ha ha ha, hee, hee, hee, hee, hee…

These songs were sung from the back of the crowd, and they never failed to wind people up. If you think the words to these songs are bad, there were a couple reserved for two separate sets of supporters that were well below the belt. One was sung by numerous other teams to Man United, regarding a certain fatal plane crash. The other song, reserved for Millwall fans and just as unsavoury, involved a train incident. Thankfully, both these songs appear to have died out and aren't sung in the ground any more, maybe because they were more like drinking songs than football songs.

One song that has stood the test of time, first sung in the early Seventies, goes to the tune of 'Me And My Girl':

The bells are ringing for the claret and blue,
The South Bank's singing for the claret and blue,
When the Hammers are scoring,
And the South Bank are roaring,
And the money is pouring,
For the claret and blue, claret and blue!
No relegation for the claret and blue,
And some day we're gonna win a cup or two,
Or three, or four, or more
For West Ham and the claret and blue.

A real favourite is 'The Bells are Ringing', 'cause when you hear it, you know everyone is happy and contented. Other great favourites were the little songs for players and managers. If a player got his own song, it meant he'd finally won a place in the East Enders' hearts. One such song was to Geoff Hurst, sung to the tune of 'The First Noël':

Geoff Hurst, Geoff Hurst,
Geoff Hurst, Geoff Hurst,
Born is the King of Upton Park.

Another was to the tune of 'Michael Row the Boat Ashore', with the words 'Send our Jimmy to Mexico, Alleluya', which referred to Jimmy Greaves going to the World Cup in Mexico at the time he was playing for West Ham in the 70s, and a song to Ron Greenwood to the tune of 'Grocer Jack':

Ron Greenwood, Ron Greenwood,
Is it true what people say,
We're gonna win the football league?

There were plenty of ingenious and witty songs of the time. In fact, there seemed to be one for every occasion:

(To the tune of 'D.I.V.O.R.C.E.')
Peter Taylor is thirty years old,
Got the mind of a six-year-old,
You'll find him at the synagogue,
He's a dirty Tottenham Yid.
And when he comes to Upton Park,
He always has a shit game,
The man who kicks him silly,
Super Billy is his name.

Oh Billy Bonds is our man,
He's sometimes as fucking hard as any Tottenham fan,
And when he goes to White Hart Lane,
He always gets a big cheer,
There's Irons all around the ground, we take it every year.

(To the tune of 'Chick-Chick, Chick-Chick Chicken')
Pop, Pop, Pop, Pop Robson, score a little goal for me,
Pop, Pop, Pop, Pop Robson, I've seen you on TV,
You ain't scored a goal since Easter
And now it's half-past three,
Pop, Pop, Pop, Pop Robson, score a little goal for me.

(To the tune of 'Ging Gang Gooly')
We've got 'Arry, 'Arry, 'Arry, 'Arry Redknapp
On the wing, on the wing,

(This led to 'Albert Tatlock in defence', 'Ena Sharples in the air', etc., etc.)

Another classic was reviewed when the son of a former West Ham star turned out in a claret and blue shirt. Sung to the tune of 'White Christmas':

I'm dreaming of a Frank Lampard header,
Just like the one at Elland Road,
When the ball came over,
And Frank fell over,
And scored the fucking winning goal, winning goal!

CASS PENNANT

It was the heart and soul of our supporters that came out in these witty songs. But the most famous of all the West Ham songs was our anthem, of which we would only ever sing the chorus:

(Verse)
I'm dreaming dreams, I'm scheming schemes,
I'm building castles high.
There born anew, these days are few,
Just like the sweet butterfly.
Then when the day is dawning,
They'll come again in the mornings,
Where shadows creep, when I'm asleep,
To lands of hope I stray.
Then at daybreak, when I awake,
My bluebird flutters away,
Happiness, you seem so near me,
Happiness, come forth and cheer me.

(Chorus)
I'm forever blowing bubbles,
Pretty bubbles in the air.
They fly so high, they reach the sky,
And like my dreams, they fade and die.
Fortune's always hiding, I've looked everywhere.
I'm forever blowing bubbles, pretty bubbles in the air.

ALSO AVAILABLE BY CASS PENNANT:

CASS
By Cass Pennant
£5.99

ROLLING WITH THE 657 CREW
By Cass with Rob Sylvester
£16.99

WANT SOME AGGRO?
By Cass and Mickey Smith
£15.99

To order your copy, please phone 0207 3810666. Alternatively, you can post your credit card details, a cheque, or a postal order to:

John Blake Publishing
3 Bramber Court
2 Bramber Road
London
W14 9PB

Postage is free within the UK. Please allow 28 Days for delivery.